Smart Leading and Parenting of Teenage Kids in the Digital Era

A Neuro-Managed Strategy

Books Published by Allied Publishers for Dr. Siddhartha Ganguli

1.	Live Happily, Work Happily	-	2009 3rd Impression 2014
2.	SUCCESS Can be Planned and Earned	-	2010 Reprint 2013
3.	Greying Gracefully: Planning for Retirement and Old Age Happiness	-	2011
4.	Conscious Management	-	2011 Reprint 2014
5.	The Making of a Winning Child	-	2012

Smart Leading and Parenting of Teenage Kids in the Digital Era

A Neuro-Managed Strategy

Siddhartha Ganguli, *PhD*

ALLIED PUBLISHERS PVT. LTD.

New Delhi • Mumbai • Kolkata • Chennai • Bangalore • Hyderabad

ALLIED PUBLISHERS PRIVATE LIMITED

Regd. Off.: 1/13-14 Asaf Ali Road, **New Delhi**–110002
Ph.: 011-23239001 • E-mail: delhi.books@alliedpublishers.com

17 Chittaranjan Avenue, **Kolkata**–700072
Ph.: 033-22129618 • E-mail: cal.books@alliedpublishers.com

15 J.N. Heredia Marg, Ballard Estate, **Mumbai**–400001
Ph.: 022-42126969 • E-mail: mumbai.books@alliedpublishers.com

No. 25/10 Commander-in-Chief Road, Ethiraj Lane (Next to Post Office)
Egmore, **Chennai**–600008
Ph.: 044-28223938 • E-mail: chennai.books@alliedpublishers.com

P.B. 9932, 1st Floor, Sunkada Chickkana Complex, Loop Lane Off Race Course Road, Next to Hotel Maurya, Gandhi Nagar, **Bangalore**–560009
Ph.: 080-22262081 • E-mail: bngl.books@alliedpublishers.com

Sri Jayalakshmi Nilayam, No. 3-4-510, 3rd Floor (Above More Super Market)
Barkatpura, **Hyderabad**–500027
Ph.: 040-27551811, 040-27551812 • E-mail: hyd.books@alliedpublishers.com

Website: www.alliedpublishers.com

ISBN: 978-93-89934-28-1

Published by Sunil Sachdev and printed by Ravi Sachdev at
Allied Publishers Pvt. Ltd., 1/13-14 Asaf Ali Road, New Delhi–110002

Acknowledgements

I am deeply indebted to the teens—Arka, Sauvatra, Tryambak, Samya, Sanchayan, Utsab, Prarthana, Dipayan, Aditya and Trisha who have participated most actively in my 'Teen Mentoring Project (TMP)' from time to time providing me with the opportunity to gather practical knowledge about the working of the teenage brain in our society. I also owe a great deal to their parents who have acted as 'Facilitating Supervisors' and allowed me to interact absolutely freely with their kids. I had great opportunity to study their natural parenting and mentoring styles to ensure balanced upbringing of their kids.

Continuous encouragement was available from my wife Utpala and our three kids—Abhishek, Abhirup and Ishita. Technical assistance flowed in readily from Pervez Alam who has been under my tutelage from 2006 without any break.

Molecules of appreciation came from my students, scholars and followers: Ranjan, Goutam, Alok, Asis, Jhimli, Priyanka, Shubhrajit, Mohan, Bhabani, Indranil, Anjani, Ashok, Biswajit, Ashim, Sarnendu, Ranajit, Debasish, Nikhil, Maqsood Alam, Iqubal, Junaid, Dipankar, Jatinder and others—when they read the script in phases.

I have always been welcomed by my publishers, the big brand Allied Publishers of Delhi, particularly Sharad Gupta who has held my hand this time also when the entire world is facing uncertainties under the pandemic circumstances. Jagdish Singh of Allied's editorial department has provided unstinted editorial support all through.

Dedication

My mother Asha and father Monoj,
wherever you are today.

I know you'll be reading whatever I have shared here regarding Teenage Leading and Parenting!! I must admit that the core of my ideas are not mine—I had learnt them from you as you had selflessly led, parented and mentored me when I was passing through the most vulnerable period of my life—the teenage. I've only provided a coat of polish to make the tips suitable for today's digital era.

Preface

> "The real danger is not that computers will begin to think like men, but that men will begin to think like computers."
>
> —***Sydney J. Harris***, *American Journalist (1917–86)*

I had gone deeply into the study of the human body—postures, gestures and gait—the style of walking. As a professional manager, I had ample opportunity to study people's non-verbal expressions—their body language. At my biomedical research unit at the University College of Medicine (Goenka Hospital) (UCMGH), University of Calcutta where I used to spend my weekends, me and my research colleagues developed a gait study set-up for studying the pattern of walking of amputees after they were fitted with artificial legs and trained to use the prosthesis for walking without any crutches or other walking aids. This was a very successful project that gained international attention. I had to travel and lecture abroad on the gait study and published, along with my co-researchers, around 40 scientific papers—all in peer-reviewed journals like Biomedical Engineering and Ergonomics, on gait and energy expenditure studies. Top researchers from the West came, visited and spent some time with us at the UCMGH Bioengineering Unit.

Having a reasonably good understanding of the body, I got interested in the dynamic functions of the human brain. However, I could find the complexities of the teenage brain perplexing. I had to travel so much for my work that I could not study my own three kids much during their teenage. I took the plunge to mentor teenage orphan boys in the 'gurukul' style which gave me the opportunity to study them from close proximity as some of them would travel with me when I started conducting body-brain-mind-soul workshops all over India and neighbouring countries.

Based on my experiences of grooming my own and those 'gurukul' kids as well as cases studied through 'The Winning Child' clinic that I used to run, I started writing about 'Parenting'. Several books that appeared in Bengali became very popular; then I published, through Allied Publishers, *The Making of A Winning Child.*

Meanwhile, the digital technology came upon every aspect of our social and economic life with the introduction of mobile phones, bank ATMs and internet banking. While the systems and procedures were getting digitalised, the adventurous teenage brain got attracted towards digital gadgets like smartphones, desktops and laptops even for entertainment like watching videos and movies, listening to music, playing games and engagement in social sites like Facebook, Instagram and Twitter.

Suddenly, we had the most unexpected invasion by the Covid-19 virus. The whole educational system was compelled to undergo a drastic change. Work-and-study-from-home culture had to be introduced; school, college, university students had to attend on-line classes, tutorials and professional coaching, take exams on-line.

Under such circumstances, what happens to the teenage brain? How they should be led and mentored? This and related questions prompted me to delve deeper and I took up a pilot project called 'Teen Mentoring Project (TMP)' where I had to interact regularly with teenage children and their supervisory parents (just one parent per child) to make practical observations.

In that process, I have developed 15 (fifteen) Brain Tools which are very handy techniques for teenage application and 3 (three) Brain Tools for Smart Leading and Parenting.

The book is divided into two parts. After Part 1, Part 2 talks about all the Brain Tools. In Appendix I, I talk, In some detail, about the 'Gut Brain' which has now been recognised as the 'Second Brain' no less important than the 'First Brain' inside the cranium. In Appendix II, I have shared a standard diet chart for a teenage kid.

New year, 2021

Contents

Part-1

Digital Destiny

I, 1940-born, was brought to this marvellous planet with an 'Analogue Destiny'. At school, college and university levels, and also at home, I was accustomed to use 'Analogue Tools' like plain and simple foot rulers, measuring tapes, slide rules, thermometers, watches and clocks, gauges and weighing scales. My children were also born in the 'Analogue Era' but got the taste of digital tools with the popularity of digital watches for teenagers. My grandchildren are all born with a 'Digital Destiny'. By 'Digital Destiny', I mean use of *Digital Devices* is built into their 'Birth Plan'.

Some of them have reached their teens. So, it is my children and their contemporaries who have teenage kids must roll up their sleeves and try to follow what I mean by 'Smart Leading and Parenting of Teenage Kids in the Digital Era'. I wish such readers happy reading, happy smart leading and happy smart parenting!!!

The sentences below carry some information which are meant only for the brains which are cluttered with questions—in other words, curiosity. If you do not belong to such a rare category of readers, just skip it.

Incidentally, the human brain is neither analogue nor digital, but works using a signal processing paradigm that has some properties common with both. Unlike a digital computer, the brain does not use binary logic or binary addressable memory, and it does not perform binary arithmetic.

Information in the brain is represented in terms of statistical approximations and estimations rather than exact values. The brain is also non-deterministic and cannot replay instruction sequences with error-free precision. So, in all these ways, the brain is definitely not digital.

Introduction

Key Points: *The Dawn of the Computer Era; The Digital Era; The 1950s Scenario; My Digital Hassle; You: The Owner of a Living Brain; A Peep into Your Brain; Why Teenage Kids; Positive Neuro-chemicals; Positive Neuro-electricity; Brain Hijacking; ROI (Return on Investment); Mentoring; SMART Parenting.*

[*Note:* I have no gender bias. For brevity's sake, I've used only male gender to signify both.]

The Dawn of the Computer Era

The Calcutta of the mid-1970s. IBM India had installed its mainframe computer in its Regional Directorate at the crossing of Park Street and Camac Street in the heart of Central Calcutta. Union Carbide India had also gone for an IBM mainframe machine in its Regional Headquarters at Jeevan Deep, Chowringhee. Calcutta-headquartered British multinationals like Indian Oxygen, Metal Box India, Dunlop India, Shaw Wallace, Imperial Chemical Industries (ICI), British Paints, Williamson Magor, Goodricke Tea had all gone for mainframes of British make—the International Computers Limited. The foreign banks were also abuzz with mainframe installation programmes and projects. There were signs of India getting computerised—all over the corporate sector with which I was involved. I had just joined as the Secretary and CEO of the Calcutta Management Association and all these companies were very actively involved with our activities. The computer manufacturers IBM and ICL were also active with us.

I was a big zero as far as computer and its applications were concerned although I was quite close and friendly with those skilled technologists who used to be the keepers and care-givers of the giant machines. I would have nostalgic thoughts about my University of Glasgow days where I was engaged as a research student and scholar in the early 60's. We used to have computer classes in the University's Main Computer Centre. There was a giant machine and facing it was a big lecture gallery—where students and scholars from different departments would assemble all together. From time to time, our computer instructor Professor Gillespie disappeared—he was not to be seen anywhere around. Once we gave him a call: "Hello, Professor! Where are you?", he would give an immediate response: "I am here—trying to tame and fix the misbehaving dinosaur." Then he would suddenly appear just the way he had disappeared and say with a beaming smile on his oval-shaped face: "I've tamed it! You're challenging me rascal" (he would swear as he was so happy after taming the mainframe giant). That was the 'Jurassic Age' of computers!!

Back to mid-1970's! Moving with the computer honchos in corporate corridors, I could only pick up a few technical jargons, one of which still vivid in my memory is: 'GIGO'—'Garbage In Garbage Out'. Now that I happen to deal with the more-than-several-billion-dollars' worth computer squeezed into our skull–the human brain, GIGO rings a bell every now and then as it fits in with one very busy circuit of the most precious tissue structure placed between our ears—the 'Default Mode Network (DMN)'. It features daily when I get engrossed deeply in my neuro-scientific research on the impact of digital era on our brain functions. When our brain is not engaged in any specific 'Task' (Brain in 'Task Mode Network' or 'TMN'), all kinds of useless rubbish thoughts pop out from inside the thinking machine; this is the function of the brain's 'DMN'. 'DMN' is the brain's autopilot.

The Digital Era

From mid-1970s, I travel fast to the penultimate week of 2019.

'Digital India gets a boost': The 'Business' page of *The Telegraph*, Kolkata of 29 December 2019 carried this headline. To promote digital payments, the finance minister had just announced some special incentives. The banking system in India started getting digitalised quite some years ago with the introduction of debit and credit cards, ATMs, auto-updating of passbooks, mobile messages, transactional e-mails and internet banking. Banks' customers, riding on the digital rollercoaster, are in the process of getting habituated to the challenges it offers but, at times, suffer from frustrations as the system develops faults and does not co-operate promptly resulting in time wastage. This is just one main scenario—banking, in the digital era which me, my three children and their teenage children are witnessing today. We, all three generations together, must digitalise ourselves to get updated and adapted to today's systems.

The 1950s Scenario

The scenario was absolutely different when I was a teenager. I remember accompanying my father to the Imperial Bank [which became the State Bank of India (SBI) after nationalisation], Bhowanipore Branch in South Calcutta. He, a leading barrister practising at the Calcutta High Court, had to wait in a long queue with a brass token in hand to withdraw a cash of a paltry sum of ₹ 1,000.00 only which could run a family of four for a fortnight most comfortably in those days. He would get, from the teller, a bag full of coins, a combination of notes of one, two, five- and ten-rupee denomination. He was not lucky enough to become a digitalised customer of SBI as he breathed his last before the dawn of the digital era.

My Digital Hassle

I, my father's elder son, born in 1940, have been exposed to both the worlds—the non-digital and the digital. Nevertheless, having spent the springtime of my life in the non-digital world, I fumbled and faltered in using the digital system in the autumn and winter of my lifespan and my young team members became my saviours. [I ran a body-brain-mind-soul management and development boutique *Learning Club* for 35 long years, from 1983 to 2018 and had a team to support my work.]

For marketing of our services, we used the e-mail and for all financial transactions including tax payments we banked on internet banking from 2006–07 onwards.

You: The Owner of a Living Brain

You, having been launched on this planet in the 1960's and later, are smarter than me having begun your career with PCs and mobile phones in the booming phase of the digital era. You would have got adjusted to the digital giant wheel without an inkling of vertigo. Nevertheless, you do not own a digital brain with fixed circuits. On the contrary, you own a living one with flexible, plastic circuitry.

However, your brain, a product of 2.5 million years of evolution, still has neural networks which are old-fashioned, habituated to the non-automated styles of Decision Making (DM) and Problem Solving (PS). The circuits have not been remodelled to cope with the challenges of digitalisation. Digital technology, of its own, has not taken into account the capabilities and limitations of the human user either.

Besides, when AI (Artificial) takes over the burden of work activities in the govt., business and industry systems, what would be left for the human brain to work on is anybody's guess. To what extent your such Decision Making (DM) and Problem Solving (PS) skills would be called for in the AI dominated world of work? How would you manage your entire Neuro-system with its inherent design to avoid tissue obsolescence?

You not only have to 'Lead' yourself but also 'Parent' and 'Mentor' your teenage kids to 'Lead' themselves in a totally new and novel 'NEURO-MANAGED (NM)' way!!

These and other related topics would be discussed in this handy volume for which I have selected the title *Smart Leading and Parenting of Teenage Kids in the Digital Era: A Neuro-managed Way.*

A Peep into Your Brain

Your brain is a work-in-progress throughout your life. Have you ever thought what happens to the trillions of circuits in your brain with everyday new experiences and exposures? People, in general, are preoccupied with thoughts about their body; brain hardly features in their thought process. With me, I hope, while reading this book, you will take a 180-degree turn from that mind-set, and get to know a few basic facts about your brain—its structure and functions. With new experiences and exposures, old brain circuits which are of little use get pruned and new circuits replace them. Brain has the power of 'plasticity'—which is the power of rewiring to replace those that do not help you any longer to cope with the demands of your changing environment. And the more expert your brain is in such change management, the more developed and advanced it is compared to other backward brains.

Your brain is a three-storeyed structure. You have your spine—inside which runs the spinal cord. The top end of your spinal cord extends into the brain stem, a pair of cerebellum and other adjoining structures. These together constitute your *hindbrain* which you have inherited from your amphibian and reptilian past (this ground floor of your brain is also described as the 'reptilian complex'). The *hindbrain* is responsible for our 'survival'—for keeping us alive; therefore, it is the first brain part to develop in a foetus in its embryonic stage.

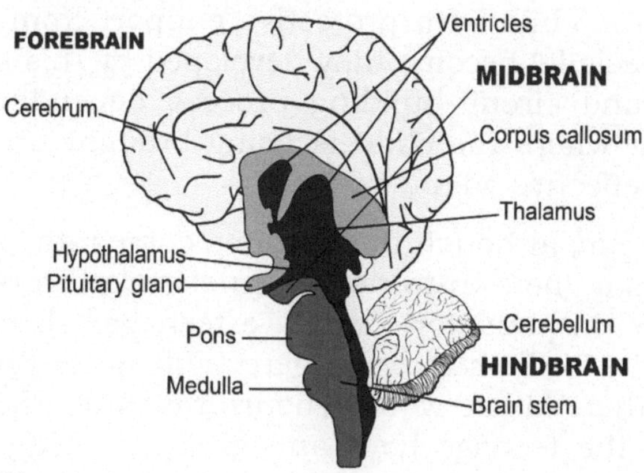

Fig. 1: A Cross-section of the Human Brain

On top of the *hindbrain* is the *midbrain* which all mammals have. You have inherited it from your *paleo-mammalian* past ('Paleo' meaning the Old Stone Age—a period in human pre-history). In the *midbrain*, you have your emotional centre which is responsible for joy, anger, fear, surprise, sadness and disgust. Strongest amongst your negative emotions are anger and fear. Whenever you are under stress, the root cause may be anything, the 'fight (anger)' -or- 'flight (fear)' switch inside your *midbrain* is triggered on. So, the first floor of your brain carries out a very important function for you—your safety and security—it protects you from any danger, which is an essential requirement for your survival.

The uppermost floor of your brain or *forebrain* is the latest addition, known as the *neo-mammalian complex* or the *neo-cortex*. It is present in the relatively new species of mammals like primates and monkeys, the most modern of them being chimpanzees, bonobos (pygmy chimpanzees) and gorillas. The *neo-cortex* is a 6-layer structure, thickest in humans.

Why Teenage Kids

The brain tissue with its 8,500 to 10,000 million neurons or brain cells (there still is a little controversy regarding the exact number as it is indeed difficult to measure accurately) get fully formed by the time a child reaches its pre-teens—10 to 12 years of age. The *hindbrain* and the *midbrain* which are essential for survival of the child with protective support from the parents (mother especially) become fully developed by this age following a pruning and circuit-building process depending upon the environment where the child is being brought up to fulfil the objective of effective adaptation.

In the *forebrain*, although the neurons come into existence, the inter-neuronal (neuron-to-neuron) networks start developing randomly as, in prehistoric times, a teenager—boy or girl, had to get ready to lead a hunter-gatherer's life at the onset of adolescence. Mother Nature would ensure that with the attainment of puberty, the teenage boys and girls get ready to fulfil the Biological ('survival and replication') and Social ('effective bonding with others') Imperatives (BSI) which happen to be the materialistic goal of our existence (or, purpose of our life) since the dawn of life on this planet.

The neurons in the teenage brain are thus desperate to create circuits and get inter-connected through those to materialise the said purpose of life. For survival and replication, the primary hunger is for food as is too obvious. What you do not know that the teenage brain is acutely hungry for positive neuro-chemicals and positive neuro-electricity for the consolidation of cell-to-cell ('synaptic') connections.

Positive Neuro-Chemicals

Let me explain. There are four positive neuro-chemicals which all of us desire to have, more so the teenagers in order to facilitate the brain reorganisation process in them. These are: Endorphin—'E' (nature's own internally generated stress-manager); Dopamine—'D' (the positive chemical that is released inside the brain in anticipation of a reward and again on achievement of a task or reaching the goal); Serotonin—'S' (the 'feel good' neurochemical or mood balancer); and, Oxytocin—'O' (the love and trust-building chemical which is responsible for getting into and sustaining a healthy relationship). I have added Melatonin—'M' which is the sleep-inducing relaxation and rest-providing chemical. Together, they are a happy bunch—EDSOM!!

Since the prehistoric teenager was getting ready for a hunting-gathering role, his DRIVE for such occupational activities would come from the hunger for EDSOM. And let us ride the time machine and travel back to those pre-historic days when humans were living a pure jungle life without any well-developed language for communication and without any organised social unit like a well-bonded family. A typical teenager, when not engaged in any hunting or gathering mission—standing, sitting, reclining or lying idle, would have a very active 'Default Mode Network' (DMN) of his brain tinkering with thoughts of past successes and failures in respect of mobilisation of resources for survival. During such DMN engagement, the brain will scan through the past experiences of hunting and gathering in detail to formulate strategies for future actions—availing the emerging opportunities and averting the potential threats.

Teenage was the threshold when a boy or a girl had to take on new roles and responsibilities of mobilising resources for living. Dr. Stephen Porges (1945–) who became famous by proposing a new domain which he called 'Affective Neuroscience' had indicated that in pre-historic teenagers, driven by their appetitive motivation, the teen brain's 'Seeking System Circuit (SSC)' would get activated leading to the implementation of the EEL (Explore, Experiment, Learn) strategy. So, the pre-historic teenage brain was adequately utilised for personal and social gains. And utilisation of the EEL strategy would produce, as rewards, the happiness chemicals EDSOM.

Today the environmental scenario is totally different. In our country, our culture is such that a typical teenager is still under the protective umbrella of his (no gender bias) parents [I am thus taking the liberty of redefining teenage in our Indian context for boys: 13 to 28–15 years and for girls: 13 to 23–10 years]. Although today's scenario is different from that of the prehistoric era, the brain—its structure, its design, its architecture, its functions still remain more than a million years' old. The DMN in the teens are thus without any meaningful engagement. It is very easy for the jobless DMN to get engaged in digital time-wasting and time-passing activities which are meaningless and without any gainful purpose. So, today's teenage kids have got to be 'Mentored' (I define 'Mentor' as a friend-philosopher-and-guide). It is the basic responsibility of a parent to take up this 'Mentoring' role and one who takes it up with love and care and executes it most sincerely, I call him a 'SMART Leading parent' or 'SMART Parent'.

A SMART Parent will help the teenage kid to select a proper career goal (today there are thousands of career goals available compared to the twin hunting-gathering and personal and group security of prehistoric times) according to the teenager's DREAM. Depending on his DRIVE (that is, motivational charge or 'Passion'), the DOMAIN (field of operation) will also need to be chosen so that eventually he gets all his positive neuro-chemicals produced 80 percent of the time (90 should be the 'ideal').

Positive Neuro-Electricity

Neurochemicals done! Now I need to tell you about neuro-electricity. Our every cell is an oscillating mechanism. It is an electro-chemical device with continuous ups-and-downs—fluctuations in the level of the chemicals as well as electricity. You now know a little about the brain chemicals. Now let me tell you about brain electricity. When you have deep sleep—gone into an unconscious state, your brain cells display 'delta' wave which is 0+ to 4 hertz or cycles per second. A newly born infant's brain remains most of the time in delta up to the age of 2 years. It is necessary for rapid growth and development of the brain and body functions for survival and healthy growth. From 2 to 6 years, the child maintains a brain wave pattern of 'theta' which is light sleep: 4 to 7 hertz. From 6 to 12 years, the growing child must maintain, in its brain, 'alpha' which is 7 to 14 hertz. 'Alpha' is a half-awake, half-asleep 'reverie'-type creative state of the brain and the growing brain's productive urges are expressed most during this period. Haven't you seen how a 6 to 12-year-old child spoils pages after pages by sketching, drawing and painting; how he starts painting on the walls also?

Fully awake brain state is represented by 'beta' wave—14 to 32 hertz. With the onset of teenage, the brain should remain in beta positive (14 to 25 hertz) to gain advantage from its power of concentration and focus thus reducing the proportion of beta negative (25 to 32 hertz) which is brought about by negative emotions—mainly anger, fear and sadness. Teenage is a period, when kids tend to have frequent bouts of irritation (on the way to anger and annoyance), anxiety (on the way to fear and phobia), or sadness (on the way to depression).

They have to be guided as to how to practice Neuro-management (NM) which according to my definition is: positive brain-state: 80 (90 ideal) and negative brain-state 20 (10 ideal) [Easy to remember the 80–20 Pareto's Law. Pareto was an Italian mathematician who had determined that 80 per cent of problems have only 20 percent root causes.]

Brain Hijacking

Now what is so special about the Digital Era? Use of digital gadgets like smartphones, tablets, laptops and desktops provide ample opportunity for the release of positive neuro-chemicals and generating positive neuro-electrical waves when the teenage brain gets engaged in playing computer and video games, watching pop movies or porn clips, listening to pop songs, and spending time chatting and text messaging on social sites. The teenage brain tends to be easily HIJACKED by the rewards that digital devices offer at the touch of your fingertips.

Soumen Roy, a 16-year-old boy, studying in Class XI of a reputed South Kolkata English medium school is a striking case in point. He has just joined the 'Teen Mentoring Project (TMP)' that I have started 4 months ago with a few teenage boys and girls for research purposes. Ever since he has joined, I have asked his mother to keep a time log of his daily digitalised hours and in one month's study, the finding is: on-line classes from his school: 2 hours; on-line classes from his tutors: 2 hours; on-line coaching for engineering entrance: 2 hours; playing video games and chatting with friends: 4 hours; watching movies and videos in smartphone: 2 hours; personal chores (brushing the teeth, going for toilet, having bath, dressing up, having his meals and snacks): 4 hours; sleep (in phases): 8 hours. Wouldn't you describe Soumen's case as one of 'Digital Hijacking'? The two smartphones that he uses (one for the on-line classes and another for chatting and other entertainment purposes) have been his life partners ever since the Covid-19 pandemic has taken the control of our lives.

What is his ROI—the return on the time, energy and effort that he invests on his digital entertainment? He earns his positive brain chemicals and positive brain electricity all right, but at what cost! Neither he earns any money, nor does he gain any knowledge or meaningful experience. On the contrary, there is a chance of his getting digitally addicted which he has already become. So, his time, energy and effort—all have to be properly channelized meaningfully and purposefully.

What is SMART Leading and Parenting

I have already shared with you my idea of 'SMART Leading and Parenting'. It will, nevertheless, be discussed by me in detail in a subsequent chapter. For the purpose of introduction, let me tell you that it is a 'Mentoring' function which a parent has to essentially perform; and whosoever does it, I call him the 'SMART Leading Parent' or 'SMART Parent'. Those parents who would integrate 'Mentoring' into their 'Parenting' role would qualify to be 'SMART Leading Parents' or 'SMART Parents'!

Are you OK now? With me 100 percent?

CHAPTER 1

Digitalisation Everywhere: A Tool-Dependent Society

'Key' Points: *Digitalised People; Zone of Comfort and Convenience (ZCC); More on Decision-Making and Problem-Solving; Tools: Extensions of Bio-power; Language—a Tool for Expression; Tools That Restore Lost Human Capabilities; Tools That Extend Human Capabilities; Tools That Steal Your Capabilities.*

Digitalised People

My father Monoj had witnessed two world wars. As an infant, I had a little indoor experience of the 2nd World War, during the air raid signals, being held tight to my mother's breasts so much so that I could hear her pounding heartbeats clearly. And, as a kid, I had the mixed fortune of experiencing the tribulations of partition and rising of the new nation—independent India. As an adult, in the 1970's, I got the hack of how our country broke the shackles of manual work and got overtaken by computers. In my mid-old and old-old days, I have got and am still getting the taste of how our growing economy is getting digitalised in this millennium.

I will share a totally novel example here. About a decade ago, I was visiting the Regional Directorate of a top industries confederation on the invitation of the CEO. Talking about the impact of rapid digitalisation, he cited the instance of his personal secretary sitting just outside as you enter into his spacious office. He shared that the young lady was glued to her digitalised work station and would not budge an inch from her allocated space for a face-to-face interaction with the boss. Even for trivial things, she would stick to her gadgets to send mails and messages expecting the boss to reciprocate in the same manner.

"What would be the impact of her attitude and behaviour?", the CEO asked me. Prompt was my answer: "First of all, being totally sedentary at her workplace, her muscular-skeletal system would get affected in course of time as the body and brain cells follow one prime biological law—'use me or lose me'. Secondly, having lost the personal touch of and with people, her 'Social and Emotional Well-Being (SEWB)' (*which is of crucial importance when you live and work with and amidst people)* will get affected and the body and brain parts dealing with inter-personal and social interactions would suffer due to lack of total activation. She would become like a robot which she cannot be after all as she is designed to possess and utilise her personal resources—body powers, brain powers, mind powers and soul powers. Thirdly, her relationships with internal and external suppliers and customers will deteriorate thus eventually affecting the organisation's performance and operating results. This is certainly not what the digitalisation experts had visualised."

[*Note:* In modern management, each employee in the organisation's operating system is called a 'Work Processing Unit (WPU)'. He is getting the supply of 'inputs' for his processing from other employees within the organisation who are his 'Internal Suppliers' and also from external sources of supply—'External Suppliers'. Once he completes his processing part, he gives his 'outputs' to his 'Internal Customers' for whom those 'outputs' become 'inputs' and they start their processing work. Eventually, at the end of the chain, the final 'output'—a product or a service is kept ready for dispatch to the 'External Customers'.]

That was a decade ago. The same thing happened in 2018, when a young outstation scholar carrying an iMac visiting my boutique sitting in my living room started communicating with me through Facebook. I was busy working on my digital device just a room away. And, funniest of all, he was reclining on the sofa. The event was repeated a few days later when another visiting scholar from North Bengal, sitting on the same sofa, started chatting with me using his Jio mobile.

Old practices and habits were changing and nu-Gen folks were picking it faster than us the old-Gen people widening the existing generation gap further. [Amazingly, this habit has now become widespread with the Covid19 pandemic forcing employees to adapt to the 'Work from Home' culture.]

These two 2018 incidents have got imprinted so deeply in my mid-brain's *hippocampus*, the long-term memory centre (regarding our brain's structure and functions, I have already given you a gist exposure in 'Introduction'), that when my life-partner Utpala (who, at the time of writing, was convalescing from a surgical intervention to fix her broken right shoulder joint with rush nails), asked me to get a fresh towel from the clothes cabinet while I was performing my daily rote aerobics, I suggested her to send me a text message.

These are just a few handy instances of the social impacts of fast digitalisation. Every day, we come across so many of them in our life's Big Revolving Stage where we are all playing different family, social and work roles.

These are all outcomes of the technological evolution taking place now at a very fast pace. And the hidden purpose of technological evolution is to devise tools and techniques for helping us to have increased comfort and convenience. I shall elaborate my concept of 'Zone of Comfort and Convenience (ZCC)' now.

Zone of Comfort and Convenience (ZCC)

Those of you who are familiar with the discipline of business management would certainly have come across the concept of 'Management by Objectives (MbO)'. This management 'mantra' which used to be the daily chants for managers in MNCs in the late-60s, 70s and 80s, was proposed by the father of modern management and my management guru Prof. Peter Drucker (with whom I spent a few days at the World Management Congress where he was the Keynote Speaker and I was the Rapporteur; besides sharing the same publisher, Allied Publishers of New Delhi). Every manager must set some specific objectives (preferably quantifiable) and then go on meeting them by action planning and action implementation.

Our creator, Mother Nature, is undoubtedly the manager of managers. We, humans, are launched on this beautiful planet by her with twin objectives: 'Survival' and 'Replication'. First of all, we have to ensure our own survival at minimum energy cost and, then, ensure reproduction of next-gen humans who are not only healthy and fit but also can lead their lives happily. For replication also, we belonging to both genders must conserve energy otherwise how can we pass adequate energy to act as creators of humans. This is a very interesting situation. On the one hand, we have to spend energy for survival; and, on the other hand, save energy for creation of biological zygotes. Our entire body and brain systems are thus designed for following the 'Minimum Energy Expenditure and Maximum Energy Saving' principles. Based on this, I have developed my ZCC concept which has turned out to be quite popular.

Simple examples exist in our sensory organs which are receptors of external stimuli. Eyes, which are receptor organs for visual signals, have their own tolerance limits which constitute their 'Zone of Tolerance (ZT)'. In darkness, nothing is visible to our eyes; these biological masterpieces are not capable to see anything if light does not exist. So, there is a lower limit that the eyes have. At the other end of the spectrum, if the light is too glaring, the eyes shut themselves automatically as there is an upper limit for the eyes. The proportionately wide space between the lower and the upper limits is the ZT. However, within the ZT, there is a 'Zone of Comfort and Convenience (ZCC)'—a range which does not cause any strain to our eyes, rather we see things comfortably and conveniently.

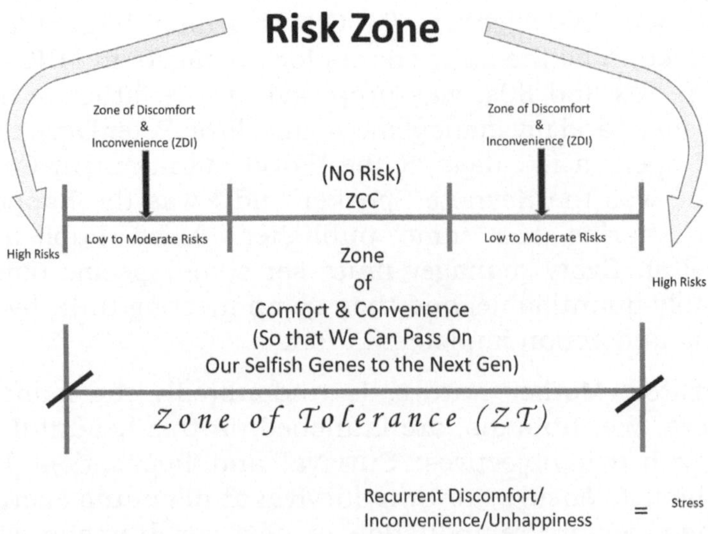

Fig. 2: Zone of Comfort and Convenience (ZCC)

The same principle is applicable to our ears for auditory stimulus, our nose for olfactory stimulus, our tongue for gustatory stimulus and our skin for tactile stimulus. If the stimulus happens to be beyond the ZCC either on the lower or the upper side, then we start feeling 'Discomfort (D)' and 'Inconvenience (I)'—which, if repeated, we tend to suffer from 'Stress (S)'. To remain within the ZCC means 'Minimum Energy Expenditure and Maximum Energy Saving'. As far as the nervous system is concerned, the observation is most interesting. If your 'Decision Making (DM)' and 'Problem Solving (PS)' endeavours remain within the spectrum of the old, primitive structures—starting from the abdominal end moving towards to head end: the 'Gut Brain', the 'Heart Brain', the 'Reptilian' and the 'Paleo-mammalian' Brains, the energy cost is lower and the time taken is lesser for the activity than if you move on to take the help of the 'Neo-mammalian Brain' or the 'Neo-cortex' because then you're crossing the ZCC boundaries and entering into the relatively new cortical structure which is still ZDI for most of us.

[***Notes:***

1. Modern brain research studies have revealed that there are trillions of 'neurons' or 'brain cells' in our digestive system and there is a most active 'Gut-Brain Axis'. So, we have the 'Gut Brain' or the 'Enteric Nervous System (ENS)' at the gut level. Some neuroscientists have described the ENS as the 'Second Brain'. Our heart is also not just a simple blood circulating pump—it has several thousand 'neurons' and a most sensitive and active 'Heart-Brain Axis'.
2. To get details about the fast and slow processes of decision-making and problem-solving, read 2002 Economics Nobel Laureate Princeton University psychologist Daniel Kahneman's book *Thinking Fast and Slow*, New York: Farrar, Straus and Giroux: 2013.]

More on Decision-Making and Problem-Solving

Under such ZDI circumstances we generally consult another person which I call: Decision-Making-Pair (DM-P) or Problem-Solving—Pair (PS-P). One very common DM-P example is: whom to call at your little child's birthday party; should the parents be also invited; whether it will be breakfast party, or lunch, tea, high tea or dinner; what would be the menu; where the venue would be; how to invite people—call them up, or just WhatsApp message or mail; whether the food will be cooked at home or ordered from outside or a combination; etc. etc. Such a DM exercise would be fruitful as a DM-P if you and your spouse put your heads together. The 'Neo-mammalian Brain/Neo-cortex' works faster with a little provocation from another person. If you involve your teenage kid in such decision-making exercises then it will help in stimulating his developing forebrain.

When the problem is more critical like getting rid of the rodents who peep into our ground floor kitchen, eat away papad from the top of the storage cabinet, biscuits from the container kept on top of the fridge, then not only me and my wife had to put our heads together, we consulted several people including a student of mine who runs a pest control service agency. It is 'Problem Solving—Team (PS-T)'. The 'Pair' in the previous example and the 'Team' in the present example represent the ZCC concept. Encouraging your teenage kid to use 'DM-T' or 'PS-T' with his peer would indeed be a smart step on your part as a parent. Many parents carry a belief that children, even when they are in their teens, are no-brainers as regards decision-making and problem-solving. Should you be one of them, let it be a thing of the past and you start your teen parenting journey with a clean slate mind.

Why don't you steal a little time from your busy schedule and make a short list where you have applied the ZCC concept by way of DM and PS—that is, you have used DM-P or DM-T or PS-P or PS-T? (If you relate what you pick up from my lines to your real-life experience and activities this way, you will get 'neuro-managed' faster, as your brain's concerned circuits would function in a well-coordinated fashion.)

TOOLs—Extensions of Bio-Power

Our closest large primate ancestor chimpanzees have been observed to insert twigs into holes of large tree trunks to take out ants and termites. Although, primarily veggies, amongst their most favourite non-veg stuff, are tiny insects. The twigs served as TOOLs as the chimps could not access the insect nests with their fingers much though they had tried. The twigs became extensions of their 'physical abilities', which I describe as 'Bio-power'. That is what a TOOL is. The British primatologist and anthropologist Dame Jane Goodall had most meticulously studied such habits of tree-dwelling chimpanzees in the forests of Africa for almost half a century.

How relevant are the chimpanzees' tool-making and tool-using habits in the case of humans? According to a recent research report from the University of Witwatersrand (Wits) in South Africa, Middle Stone Age humans, who lived around 2,80,000 years ago, used TOOLs in the form of wooden digging sticks, as an extension to their 'Bio-power' to extract starchy roots from the ground to be consumed as staple diet in those days. ["Early humans, tucked into carbs too, shows study", *Times of India*, Kolkata edition, 4th January 2020, p. 13].

The broad career of the human tribe probably ('probably' because all these speculations are based on fossil records) started millions of years ago (2.5 to 5.3 million). The development of TOOL-based and symbolically structured modern human culture developed only tens of thousands of years ago, during the geologically recent Pleistocene Epoch (about 2.6 million to 11,700 years ago). [*Encyclopedia Britannica*: Britannica.com/science/humanevolution.]

Language: A Tool for Expression

Since the dawn of civilisation, man has taken the help of cultural and technological evolution to devise TOOLs and develop techniques to expand our 'Zones of Comfort and Convenience (ZCC)'. Examples are galore—widely spread all over and around us. A very interesting example is: 'Language' which is nothing but a TOOL for expression, for inter-personal communication. Going back into pre-historic times, man used to express himself entirely non-verbally using postures, gestures and voice modulations. Albert Mehrabian (1939–), Professor Emeritus of Psychology, University of California, Los Angeles, conducted pioneering research in the 1970's and his finding was that the three elements that constitute our liking for a person who speaks and puts forward a message, account differently: 55% facial expression, 38% tonality of voice, and only 7% word-based language; so, non-verbal—93% and verbal—only 7%. Therefore, isn't it apparent that the 'non-verbal' mode was good enough up to the point when communication was limited to mere social exchange; and, language had to be developed to widen the expanse of the ZCC when 'Decision Making (DM)' and 'Problem Solving (PS) had become a necessity in the 'Paired' and 'Team' Interaction situation as I have explained a little while ago? Most interestingly, the non-verbal expressions originate from the hind (Reptilian) and mid (Paleo-mammalian) brains whereas the word-based language function(s) are carried out from the Neo-mammalian brain/Neo-cortex involving the Supplemental Motor Cortex in the Left Brain, the Broca's Area in the Left Frontal Lobe and the Wernicke's area in the Left Temporal and Parietal Lobes in right-handed persons.

Tools that Restore Lost Human Capabilities

From the 'Expression, Communication, Inter-personal Transactions' function which is social, let us come to a humdrum physical example. I was weak in eyesight from my early boyhood, so I was recommended to use spectacles, and I got hooked to a pair ever since. A decade ago, I got cataract removed from both my eyes, and during a quick-fix phaco surgery, I was fitted with artificially powered lenses in both to replace my 'bio-power'. These have provided me with a visual 'Zone of Comfort and Convenience (ZCC)'. If those are removed, I will be thrown into a 'Zone of Discomfort and Inconvenience (ZDI)' and, if not remedied quickly, shall undergo visual as well as emotional stress. My wife had a right shoulder joint fracture about a year and a half ago—she had the fragmented bones fixed with stainless steel wires and rush nails to get her back to the muscular-skeletal ZCC.

Two interesting examples as to how technology is helping us to maintain or expand our ZCC!! These are instances from the health care field where technology is giving you an appliance to restore some lost function or repair something and redefining your existence as 'Post-human' (it is the term used, now-a-days, when you use some appliance to restore some lost human capabilities, physical deficiency or impaired function). I worked in this field for twenty-five years when, as a part of my honorary bioengineering assignment at the University College of Medicine (Goenka Hospital), University of Calcutta, I conducted extensive research on internal surgical implants, orthoses and prostheses like artificial legs.

Tools that Extend Human Capabilities

Going back to where I started, technology has also given us TOOLs and tackles to extend the capabilities of our body parts. All engineering hand tools like screw drivers, spanners, pliers, drills, hammers, chisels, scissors, spatulas and saws—their old and most modern versions have enriched our capabilities. I have no quarrel with them. In fact, earlier in my career, I used to admire Dr. Rudolf Drillis, of New York University School of Engineering, who had done lifelong studies on such tools that extend our physical capabilities.

Tools that Steal Your Capabilities

My quarrel is with those tools and techniques which steal your capabilities and increase, in the process, your limitations so much that you become dependent on them—a slave of technology, as is happening with the advent of digitalisation. Starting with simple digital calculators to android phones—gadgets have become indispensable role players on our life's revolving stage. Our body and brain—whose bio-powers took millions of years to evolve are being put to lack of use—forcibly pushing the organs and other body parts into obsolescence.

Do you realise that all your digital devices which use only word-based language as their medium of transaction reflect only 7% of the total message content while taking the help of pictorial symbols to express the subtle emotions?

CHAPTER 2

Happiness: A Windfall Gift of the Digital Era

'Key' Points: *The 3-dimensional Model of Happiness; The World as well as Happiness in Your Grip; Digital Destiny: A Happy One; Digital Shocks; Digital Impact on Human Biology; Neuro-electricity: Brain Waves; Digital Devices and Brain Wave Patterns; The Economics of Digital Devices; A Smart Leadership Strategy Application; Self-discovery and Self-knowledge; Smart Management of Threefold Realities.*

The 3-Dimensional Model of Happiness

I have researched deeply into the body and brain states representing *Happiness* ever since the beginning of this millennium and, in the process, have come up with a 3-dimensional model of *Happiness* which I am sharing with my readers for the first time.

The first dimension is: momentary spontaneous release of the happiness molecules in the brain on a specific experience of sight, sound, smell, taste, touch, or anything else, like someone's behaviour. It is just a transitory phenomenon and I call it *Smart Happiness*, because it's a crisp and smart event. Coping with a stressful situation and feeling happy by getting a sudden rush of happiness chemicals is also an example of *Smart Happiness*.

The second dimension is: a little longer-lasting happiness, which stays on for a few hours, a few days, or even a few weeks as it happens on a special achievement like getting a rank in the exam, or on a special event like getting married, or the arrival of a cute-looking healthy child. I call it *Short* (for 'Short-lived') *Happiness*.

The third dimension is a permanent happy state (which 'Neuro-managed Lifestyle' produces by way of 80–90% positivity and 10–20% negativity) which I call *Sustained Happiness*.

We all have ready access to the first and second happiness dimensions; for the third we have to adopt a 'Neuro-managed (NM)' lifestyle, glimpses of which you will get in this volume, from time to time.

The World as well as Happiness in Your Grip

Payal Arora is a researcher, author and lecturer at Erasmus University, Rotterdam, Netherlands. Her new book—*The Next Billion Users* (Cambridge, Mass.: Harvard University Press, 2019) "examines the online lives of millions of people in China, India, Brazil, and across the Middle East—home to most of the world's Internet users—and discovers that what they are doing is not what we imagine". Digital media consumption has become a critical way to keep their sanity, deal with their stress, and get out from the tedium of a job that does not tap into their capability; and not allow their brains' 'Default Mode Network (DMN)' to get engaged and, in that process, switch on the mind's emotional whirlpool. [Being a 'Neuro-Management (NM)' scholar, I am fully aware of the part that DMN plays in most people's lives, which Payal Arora has not mentioned in her commendable volume.] Digital exposure has thus become a common means for earning *Happiness* of the first two dimensions—*Smart* and *Short.* Digitalised life is no better than a mechanism for escape from the unpalatable realities of existence.

Digital Destiny: A Happy One

Nevertheless, what I want to stress upon is that while the digital age is full of such trivial blessings, it interferes with the natural powers and capabilities of humans who are on the highest step of the evolutionary ladder. '***Digital Destiny***' has converted the two-legged standing and walking animal into a seated (and, sometimes, a reclining or lying) animal, glued to the screen of the TV or PC monitor or the smart phone. Finger-aided writing in long hand has been replaced by typing on the computer keyboard or android touch screen thus interfering with the parameters of our fingers adapted to writing.

This is the opportune moment for sharing a real anecdote with you. I was spearheading the reputed professional management body, Calcutta Management Association (CMA) during a golden era of my life: 1974–80. Many foreign companies and multinational corporations (which have since been taken over by Indian business houses or the Govt. of India) were our most active members. Their Chairmen and MDs used to adorn our governing body and many of our committees, sub-committees and panels used to be headed by their senior managers. Mr. R. (who is a renowned Bengali novelist and writer) was the PR manager of XYZ Ltd., a British company, whose Deputy MD was on our board. I was friendly with R. because of my literary streak.

One day R. rang me up at noon time and invited me over for a business lunch at a small Chinese joint just across the road from his corporate office. The season was winter. Enjoying some hot mushroom soup and chicken chop suey together, I suddenly asked him a personal question: "I know that you had a writing talent from your high school days and now you write prolifically and there is hardly any novel of yours which is not a best-seller. How do you manage your time being placed at a high managerial level of such a top-class company like XYZ Ltd.?" Prompt came the answer: "Doctor, writing is not merely a passion, for me it is a mission. I will explain to you." Mr. R. continued: "When I started writing regularly, I thought what should I write and for whom. Then I suddenly got an insight. I thought Bengali middle class housewives, in the afternoon when they have finished all their household duties and are ready to take rest with their husbands away to their workplaces and the kids to their schools and colleges, would have most disturbing thoughts which made them unhappy and spoiled their mood. I wanted to enter into that mental space with my stuff and make them happily engaged. My entire writing strategy revolves around this objective and I've been successful. Most of my Bengali readers are such women."

What R had done (without knowing the science of it) is: he had helped those middle-class women to have their brains' 'Default Mode Network (DMN)' (which is our brain's 'autopilot' described by some neuroscientists as the 'monkey brain') deactivated and vacated to be occupied at the 'present moment (here and now)' by his interesting stories. DMN plays a very crucial role in our lives; which certainly has a 'plus' side as it is the source of all our inner thoughts related to 'Self' (that is, 'I' and 'me') but it could be disturbing at times when negative trains of thoughts become predominant. How does the DMN function? Whenever, we are not engaged in any specific task (which activates our brain's 'Task Mode Network or TMN'), the DMN gets switched on and it brings all kinds thoughts related to 'Self' and 'Others'—the timing being past and the future. For many of us, such thoughts would just be time-wasters. Digital devices are replacing the brain's in-built DMN circuits and providing some *Smart* as well as *Short* spells of joy in the case of poor people in rural societies and also for those who are jobless or having insecure jobs in unorganised and semi-organised sectors. Digital devices, do you realise, are bringing not only the whole world but also *Happiness* within the grip of these unhappy people leading a stressful life.

They are getting their supplies of EDSO (4 main happiness chemicals) without putting in any manual, intellectual or creative effort. E (Endorphin: endogenous stress-reliever) is being generated due to participation in chats and gossips. D (Dopamine: anticipatory reward chemical) is being released on 'feeling good' after watching a movie or winning in a video game or somebody clicking the 'like' or 'love' sign after looking at your post in Facebook. S (Serotonin: endogenous mood balancing chemical) is being produced on being exposed to digital entertainment including music that you like. O (Oxytocin: endogenous love, bonding and trust molecule) is obtained on being in touch, at the flick of your finger, with near and dear ones via voice or video calls. There is also an opportunity for you to earn M (Melatonin: endogenous relaxation and sleep-inducing chemical which generates restful alpha and theta brain waves) by listening to soulful music, especially flute.

Dear Reader, do you realise that without any effort, today, you are getting *happiness* in your grip? Do you realise that it is the digital era's GIFT to you—a windfall of your ***Digital Destiny***?

Unfortunately, the fact remains that our body and brain have been equipped and conditioned, through millions of years of trial-and-error effort with systems and circuits to EARN *Sustained Happiness*. *Sustained Happiness* has to be EARNED through effort and that is what is GOOD for you; that helps you to maintain your physical and mental health. Digitalised life is not pro-health.

Digital Shocks

I got a frightening digital shock the other day! As I opened the page of my friend DK in my smart phone messenger, smartly flashed a message from The State Bank of India (SBI) – ₹ 12,500/- credited to your Savings Account No............ My credited amount, my Savings Account No. all became visible and thus known to my professional acquaintance DK with whom I exchange greetings every morning and night. How risky! And, this happened when SBI itself sends, off and on, cautionary messages such as this one: don't share any of your banking information—account no., ATM/debit card no., internet banking password with anyone even to a bank representative.

What a farce! My privacy and data security have been encroached in the digital device. I immediately rang up a student of mine who claims to have earned some expertise in digital technology and told him about it. He took it most casually and said to me—"Sir! The honeymooning phase of digitalisation is still not over; so, such lapses are bound to happen and one must not take it seriously." On my side of the phone, I was suffering from anxiety as the event had struck a chord in the limbic system of my emotional paleo-mammalian brain which houses the 'Fight-or-Flight' centre wired up with the adrenal glands adjacent to the kidneys and I could feel a rush of the anxiety molecule 'Cortisol (C)' inside my brain. From the other end of the phone, I could hear my student's voice say: "It will take some more time Sir, may be months or even a year or two, to have things sorted out and settled down. Meanwhile, Sir, be SMART enough to withstand such occasional digital shocks striking you totally unawares."

I took what he said as words of wisdom and got back to the normal state of mind through a few cycles of deep breathing (breathing in: 1, 2, 3, 4,; hold: 1; breathing out: 1, 2, 3, 4, 5, 6.....a little longer to allow the gases sedimented in the lower part of my breathing apparatus to come out instead of being held back.)

Within a day or two, I got another shock as on the screen of the page belonging to RC—a lady student of mine, another SBI message flashed out: "TDS of ₹ 205/- deducted from your FD Account No...........on date." This time I was SMART enough to handle it. I sent a message to RC just to ignore the SBI message as it had nothing to do with her. My SMARTness helped me to avoid the otherwise expected rush of 'Adrenaline (anger molecule A)' or 'Cortisol (anxiety molecule C)' inside my brain and ensure that the EDSO—happiness chemicals' balance was maintained. My 'Central Nervous System (CNS)' could manage to follow the biological law: "Repeat Happiness, Avoid Unhappiness". Unhappiness chemicals, Adrenalin and Cortisol, are both released from the Adrenal Glands which are also connected with the 'Root Chakra (Muladhar)'—the network of nerves located near coccyx, the tailbone stump that still exists to prove that once upon a time we were tailed animals. This Chakra is responsible for making us feel stable, secure and grounded.

Every morsel of food and every drop of water that passes through our food pipe and reaches our stomach positively stimulates our 'Gut Brain (GB)' and two happiness chemicals—S (Serotonin) and D (Dopamine) are released. Believe it or not, the GB has a lot to do with the happiness of people who 'eat to live' rather than 'live to eat'. We, humans are, as a matter of fact, hungry and thirsty for these and the two other happiness chemicals and also for the sleep-inducing neuro-molecule M (Melatonin) which is essential for our well-being. [So, henceforth, I will include M amongst happiness chemicals and refer to them as EDSOM].

However, the craving for happiness and thus for EDSOM is understood to vary from person to person and there is a 'Happiness Set Point Theory' which governs it. Having researched on 'happiness' for nearly two decades (search Google for my best-selling books dealing with 'happiness'), I got tempted to delve deeper but then restrained myself because the objective here is altogether different.

However, even without a stomach full of your favourite food and a wet throat with no inkling of thirst, an individual can earn happiness by other natural means. The potential does exist in the marvellous design of our body and brain. Today's population is happiness-starved due to the unnatural, uneven pressure of family, social and work roles, so they have no knowledge, time, or interest in earning happiness naturally through their lifestyle. Organised people have no other choice than to bank upon digital devices—at their workplaces as most of today's industrial work is digitalised; in the social context, the motivation being to keep up with the peers; and, digital destiny is chasing them at home also in their family roles. People, at the bottom of the socio-economic pyramid for whom such multi-skilled modern digital devices are unaffordable, are also begging-borrowing-and-manipulating money to acquire and own gadgets and get digitalised and, in due course, falling prey to health problems—some trivial, some critical.

Like me, have you ever been subjected to digital shocks, totally unawares? If 'yes', then could you handle the situation SMARTLY?

Digital Impact on Human Biology

I will mention a few examples how digital devices are going against the natural laws of human biology.

Our brain, as I have mentioned earlier, is not of recent origin. Its circuits are a couple of million years old. Our optical circuits, barring occasional exceptions, have been accustomed to witness slow movements: slow-moving monsoon and autumn clouds, slow-flying birds, butterflies and insects, easy-going ripples in ponds, regular-rhythmic riverine and sea waves, slow wind moving branches of trees and fallen leaves on the terrain. Fast-moving visuals like TV ads are too jarring for the eyes. The TV era was tolerable as perhaps a small percentage of the eyes of the whole world's population would remain glued to TV for most of the waking hours. The post-TV digital era has brought new visual turbulence. "People are growing weary of the constant stream of ALERTS on their phones and struggling to make it through a meal without checking screen", says a *New York Times* report by Tiffany Hsu.

When the info-environment is switching to fast-moving inputs, the receiver (info-customer) must check whether his brain has the capacity for such reception and knowledge integration, info-storage and retrieval.

This is the right place to bring in the topic of 'Neuro-electricity' which I have not talked about much while concentrating on 'Neuro-chemistry' so far apart from a mere introductory reference in the 'Introduction' part of the book.

Neuro-Electricity: Brain Waves

Our body and brain have all kinds of energy distributed and circulating throughout. These personal resources of ours have: chemical energy (body and brain chemicals—blood is a chemical and brain has 20 percent of the whole body's blood in circulation); light energy (bioluminescence—the human aura around our body visible only to clairvoyants and photographed only by Kirlian cameras); magnetism (heart radiates electro-magnetic waves); and wind energy ('Vayu'—there are 5 main types of 'Vayu' helping us to maintain body and brain health and fitness being responsible for functions like movement and flow).

Now, electrical energy is also, being present everywhere in our living system. Every cell has electricity which follows an oscillating wave form. Heart's electrical activities are recorded by ECG. Similarly, brain's electrical wave patterns are captured by EEG. Brain waves are basically of 5 types. Beta waves (14 to 30/32 cycles/sec or hertz) are present during wakefulness. Beta positive prevails when we are in a positive state of mind and its range is 14 to 25 hertz; while beta negative appears when the mind is in any of the freeze-fight-or-flight modes and the range is 25 to 30/32 hertz. Alpha waves are present when we have just woken up from sleep and are still in a daze. This is the time when the brain, being in a *reverie*, is ready for creative output and the range is 7 to 14 hertz. In my 'Creativity' workshops, I used to teach the participants how to do Alpha meditation to generate Alpha brain waves. Theta represents light sleep and the range is 4 to 7 hertz whereas Delta is deep, sound, dreamless sleep and the range is 0+ to 4 hertz. Delta is also attainable during 'Yogic Samadhi'. Gamma is a rare kind of brain wave which comes only when you experience a sudden insight or inspiration and the wave pattern exceeds the beta range; that is, more than 30/32 hertz and it can go up to 50/60 hertz or even beyond.

Our brain and brain waves follow a natural development pattern. A new born child remains virtually in Delta wave up to 2 years of age. From 2 to 6/7 years, it follows Theta. From 6/7 to 12 years, the child's brain remains largely in Alpha and this is the most creative phase during the child's growing years. From 12+, the child starts generating Beta positive during wakeful consciousness. Only when the child is under 'stress' due to some stimulus, its brain waves follow Beta negative and burns more energy than when it is cool.

Digital Devices and Brain Wave Patterns

Digital devices are generally fast-moving, so they are likely to bring Beta negative brain waves in the user's brain. They are not good for a growing child to get exposed to. When we read books, newspapers, magazines or printed documents, we cannot read very fast as we handle the reading activity with Beta positive waves in our brain. The moment we try reading faster, Beta negative will appear and take away our concentration. Digital devices are more harmful for those who suffer from ADD (Attention Deficit Disorder), ADHD (Attention Deficit Hyperactivity Disorder), ASD (Autism Spectrum Disorder), OCD (Obsessive Compulsive Disorder), Bipolar Disorder, Schizophrenia and Depression; because under normal circumstances, the brain wave range for all those who suffer from any such disorder is Beta negative. Digital devices should not be companions of those who suffer from brain disorders like Parkinson's or Alzheimer's. And, digital devices must not be kept under or by the side of your head pillow as its waves will interfere with your own natural brain waves.

The Economics of Digital Devices

Digital devices have not only social but also economic implications. Less time spent with mobile devices means fewer chances to reach consumers on these devices, increasing the cost of mobile advertising in the short-term. In advanced as well as developing economies, companies now spend more on smaller screen ads than on television and print combined as digital engagement time has eaten up a big chunk of TV watching and print media reading time.

A retired school teacher I know has given up altogether his earlier regular habit of reading newspapers and magazines as he gets all the latest news stuff and promotional ads at the flick of his fingers. Newspapers and magazines take up space and there has to be a special planned action to dispose of the old copies. The same habit has been adopted by a 2nd year BA (Hons.) student who is glued to his android and makes it a point to go for the latest phone models and apps. by urging money from his dad who is employed as a supervisor in a municipal market. The school teacher, who is in his 74th year, suffered a cerebral stroke only the other day with haemorrhage in the basal ganglia of the left side of his hind brain. Currently, under hospital care, he has lost, though temporarily, the power of limb movements on the right side of his body. The 18-year-old college student prepares for his semester exams by searching the net in his smartphone until very late at night or rather early in the morning and gets up at 10 O'clock in the morning every day lacking appetite. After a quick wash, he rushes for his college, frequently skipping his breakfast. He does not have appetite for breakfast as he had adequate Dopamine (D) generated from his Smartphone use before he retired from activity late at night or early in the morning. If enough D is generated from Head Brain activity, you do not have requirement of D to be generated in the 'Gut Brain (GB)'. Haven't you noticed that when you are engaged in a brain activity you immensely enjoy, you lose your appetite. Hunger pangs disturb you when your brain is not engaged in an absorbing 'Task Positive Mode Network (TPMN)'.

With all the exposure I have just given you, can you identify the root cause(s) of a health problem that you or anybody that you know closely have been facing in the digital era?

An Example of SMART Leadership Strategy Application

The last few pages were devoted to project the prevailing digital scenario. Most of us are in the process of getting grooved into a narrower or short-spread 'Zone of Comfort and Convenience (ZCC)' compared to the yesteryears' post-TV era. We do welcome, unconsciously, more automation and more advanced digital technology as that would take away from us the burden of work and leisure activities that we do not enjoy, instead find boring and most irritating. There could perhaps not be any better short-cut way of generating the happiness chemicals EDSOM inside the 21st century brain.

The demonic invasion by most advanced technology into our living and working does not dishearten or depress me because I am a cent per cent positive thinker and optimist. My optimism is not just a windfall or just a stroke of good luck. Our brain, which used to be like a dark continent until a few decades ago, has unimaginable qualities which had helped man not only to survive but also to evolve over millions of years, against all kinds of odds and adverse environmental circumstances. Those powers, that remained unknown and unexplored to human scientists of modern era, are now getting exposed with the advent of latest available brain-investigation and imaging technology.

For the last few years, I have dedicated myself totally to study the capabilities and limitations of the human brain. Most interestingly, what would have been regarded as a 'strength' or a 'capability' for our prehistoric ancestors has now come to be considered as a 'weakness' or a 'limitation'. The most striking examples that immediately come to the mind are the 'freeze-fight-flight' mechanisms which used to constitute major self-defence strategies for coping with 'stressors' (primarily, ferocious predators). These mechanisms are located in the reptilian ('freeze') and paleo-mammalian ('fight-or-fight') portions of our 'Head Brain'. If digital devices generate 'stress' for you, you just cannot cope with such stress by getting frozen or being angry or afraid which are auto-responses built into your neuronal circuits. You have to use your fertile brain to improvise some new relief strategy such as working on your PC or laptop with slow, soft, background instrumental music to absorb your irritations, if any, and continue working with almost zero-stress. It has worked out to be a SMART decision or problem-solution. This is exactly what prompted me to develop the concept of 'biorhythmic music' to be used when I teach at my workshops. Like in any lecture or seminar, my participants' brains undergo biorhythmically phased fluctuations: a phase of 'Attention' on the teacher, followed by a phase of 'Lack of Attention'. A trained team member of mine, who is sitting facing the participants with computerised music, can make out the on and off of these two phases from the body language (posture-gesture) changes of the participants, and he quickly changes the tune, rhythm, volume and so on to maintain an 'Even Attention' situation.

Even with the sparse knowledge gathered so far, I have gained so much faith on our brain powers that I now look out for such challenging environmental circumstances. I treat them as opportunities for devising suitable strategies to come out unfazed and unhurt. That is the background of my SMART Leadership concept where 'leadership' refers to 'Self-Leading': leading yourself and 'Leading Others'—especially your teenage kids, if you have any, in the right direction. So, it boils down to SMART parenting!!

Why I emphasize 'Teenage Kids' as a target group for SMART leading—or, let us be more direct, SMART parenting? As I have already mentioned a little while ago that until the age of 12/13 years, a child's brain does not have a steady oscillation of Beta brain waves (14 to 32 cycles per second) because of the fact that the hind and the middle portions of the juvenile brain—the reptilian and the paleo-mammalian complexes, were growing and getting consolidated. Once that stage is over, now it is the turn of the forebrain or the neo-mammalian neo-cortical portion to get properly organised to respond to the external dynamic environment. Teenage is the age of adolescence when the body is undergoing rapid changes both in boys and girls. In the pre-historic times, the brain used to get ready with the 'Seeking System Circuit (SSC)' installed as the teenagers had to adapt themselves to the hunter-gatherer roles. They had to transcend from dependence to independence for becoming responsible for the survival of their own and of other dependent members of their tribe. They also had to get ready for reproduction of the next generation. The brain circuits do undergo a stormy change during teenage to cope up with such new responsibilities. The social environment is totally different today from what it used to be like in pre-historic times. We have created today our own specific 'Zones of Comfort and Convenience (ZCC)' suitable for the modern era. So, the brain circuits have got to be properly installed and channelized to earn EDSOM in a healthy manner otherwise the teenagers would become digital addicts. There lies the importance of SMART leading and SMART parenting!!

'Self-Discovery' and 'Self-Knowledge'

SMART leadership starts with 'Self-Discovery (SD)' which provides you with 'Self-Knowledge (SK)'. Having SK means you are aware of your 'Strengths' or 'Plus Points' (particularly 'Capabilities' of your brain and the central nervous system) that will help you to attain 'Well-Being (WB)' in the environment where you are placed and operating presently, by availing of the 'Opportunities' that exist and averting the 'Threats' that stand in the way.

SK also means knowledge about your 'Weaknesses'—your relevant 'Deficiencies' (particularly 'limitations' of your brain and the central nervous system) which ought to be overcome to earn 'WB'. You must not waste time bothering about those 'Weaknesses' which are not easily surmountable. If you are SMART, you will set as your goal: not only overcoming some critical weaknesses deterring your progress, but also turning some of them into 'Strengths'.

I wonder if you have already devised some SMART coping strategies for absorbing (or rather, withstanding) digital shocks. (One of them, of course, is—as one of my readers mentioned, just ignore and let it pass.)

A SMART parent sets as his goal: 'Self-Discovery (SD)' and acquisition of 'Self-knowledge (SK)' not only for himself but also for his teenage kid with the ultimate aim being 'Well-Being (WB)' of both by being environment-sensitive.

SMART Management of Threefold Realities

We have been living in three realities. On the one hand, there is the 'Objective Reality' of the sky, the sunshine, the breeze, the plants, trees, flowers and fruits. On the other hand, we have 'Artificial Reality' of the digital devices. The third reality is 'Imagined Reality' which we can visualise, we can create within our mind. The first two are REAL, which we can see, hear, touch as both are within the reach of our sensory and motor powers.

Our prehistoric ancestors were getting their supplies of happiness chemicals (EDSOM) and happiness electricity (alpha, beta, theta, delta and gamma) from the world of 'Objective Reality' whereas the techno-modern ones amongst us have shifted ourselves from that world to the world of 'Artificial Reality'. The third reality is 'Imagined Reality' where the world is entirely made up by you.

An indispensable part of the world of 'Artificial Reality' is the world of 'money'—the 'Economic Reality'. Nevertheless, it has now been a proven fact that money cannot bring sustained happiness. You may be happy with X amount of money today. It gives you some purchasing power. Tomorrow, X may not satisfy for more than one reason; you may desire X+. The day after tomorrow, your economic hunger may be X++ and, like this, it goes on. The same principle applies to digital devices which have strikingly short lives because of extra-fast changes on the technological front. More versatile gadgets are introduced driving the old ones into obsolescence. As you want to keep up the pace, not so much with the technology, but with the Jones's, that if you are unable to acquire the latest, you lose your happiness, get depressed and tend to suffer from 'Dopamine (D)' deficiency which you may probably make up by eating more—leading to obesity or, otherwise, a transitory diabetes or gastroenterological problem. So, one cannot earn SUSTAINED HAPPINESS by owning and using digital devices.

This is a case where SMART leadership and SMART parenting could be helpful. There are two basic neurotransmitters which are amongst those responsible for our brain's day-to-day working. 'Glutamate' is the main excitatory and GABA the main inhibitory neurotransmitter in the mammalian cortex. How do they work? You love sweets; and, I keep a plate full of delicious sweets on the table in front of you. The 'Glutamate' released inside your brain prompts you to extend your right hand to pick up a sweet, but then suddenly good sense dawns on you that you have a tendency to have your blood sugar go up easily and since already your stomach is full as you just had lunch a little while ago, consuming another sweet will not be a wise action for you. You exercise your self-control—GABA is secreted which inhibits your desire to take action.

Apply the GABA technique whenever you desire to change the model of your smartphone, kindle, laptop or desktop. Use the logic area of your left frontal lobe to frame a self-message that the device you are using at the moment is functionally adequate for your requirement; therefore, you need not go for the latest model unless you have substantial tax benefit (consult your tax consultant). Your brain's logic centre will switch on your free will and help you to restrain yourself. Lack of control and restraint is a character weakness which does not make you SMART for the digital age. Being SMART means, you are neuro-managed.

The third reality is the 'Imagined Reality'. If you have difficulty in taking the GABA route, use this strategy. You imagine that you own the latest model of the gadget that you wanted to go for and also imagine the you are using it. Involve all your senses and movements. 'Dopamine (D)' will be secreted inside your brain as it would have otherwise happened should you have really owned and used the latest model. Our brain is not rigid; it has a lot of flexibility. This characteristic is known as 'neuroplasticity'. You only have to know that it exists and also how it could be brought to the surface and utilised to your advantage.

CHAPTER 3

Self-Discovery: A 'Must' for Smart Leading and Parenting of Teenage Kids

'Key' Points: *Self-Discovery; Human Resource; The Pancha Kosha Model (PK); Domain Gift; Self-Acceptance and Self-Love; Self-Leading; Three Case Studies; What More About the Pancha Kosha Model One Must Know; Pancha Kosha Exercises for Digital Age Kosha Fitness.*

Self-Discovery

For SMART leading and parenting your teenage kid, you must DISCOVER yourself and also the kid. You must KNOW who you are, what are your and your kid's personal resources and natural propensities; and, to what extent these will help or hinder healthy progress in this digital era, especially to ensure that you and your kid make wise use of digital devices and do not enter into the 'danger zone' to get digitally addicted.

Why is it important that you as the parent must not get digitally addicted? Because, if your teenage kid finds you being glued to digital gadgets most of your waking time, the most active and impatient mirror neurons of his brain (which is a natural tendency during the pre-teens and teens) would tend to copy you literally to consolidate his operating base. And, in the currently prevailing 'work-from-home (wfh)' culture when you and your spouse are likely to be digitally engaged during and, may be, beyond working hours, you must *smartly* explain to your teenage kid the 'why' of your digital engagement, so that his mirror neurons get the provocation to mimic you for any purposeful use of his smartphone, laptop or desktop like attending to on-line classes or appearing in tests, tutorials or net surfing for reference materials.

To begin with, make a 'Self-Discovery (SD)' for acquiring 'Self-Knowledge (SK)' as to what kind of 'Human Resource (HR)' you are (apply the same approach for KNOWING your teenage kid also)—what are your inborn potentials by way of your body, brain and mind powers. Unless you know, what you are good at and what you are not so good at, how can you have 'Self-Confidence (SC)'. 'Self-discovery (SD)' and 'Self-knowledge (SK)' are thus essential for building a solid 'Self-Confidence (SC)' base. This approach of mine needs a little elaboration.

Human Resource

'Human Resource (HR)' is just like any other natural resource. Our mother planet is extremely rich in natural resources, Take for example, one natural resource—the fossil fuel, coal. The Bengal coal of the Jharia-Ranigunj belt in West Bengal, is of a different quality than Jharkhand's Dhanbad-Bokaro coal. Bihar, MP, UP, Maharashtra and Odisha coals, all are different from each other. They are, however, 'coal' all the same. Although they all qualify as 'coal', because of their different inherent properties and qualities, all of them are not equally suitable for the same or similar applications. They are classified into different grades and categories. Same is the case with crude petroleum, iron, manganese, copper and other ores. In the same note, every human tribe or 'kula' is different from another. Every individual inherits the genome from his (no gender bias) parents who had owned the genome of their respective parents.

The Pancha Kosha Model (PK)

'Self-Discovery (SD)' entails discovering what kind of human resource you are: what kind of applications the resources that you are born with, are meant for? Let me bring the 'Pancha Kosha (PK)' model here as I find PK, which was conceptualised by the creators of the Taittiriya Upanishad, embedded as the last three chapters of Yajurveda—likely composed in 6th century B.C., is a most appropriate one in this context even in modern times.

According to 'Pancha Kosha (PK)', the 'True Self' or the 'Real Soul' of a being (that is, your 'spirit') which is a part of the 'Universal Pure Cosmic Energy' is enveloped by five energy-rich or energy-containing layers, expressed as 'Sheaths'or 'Koshas' in the order

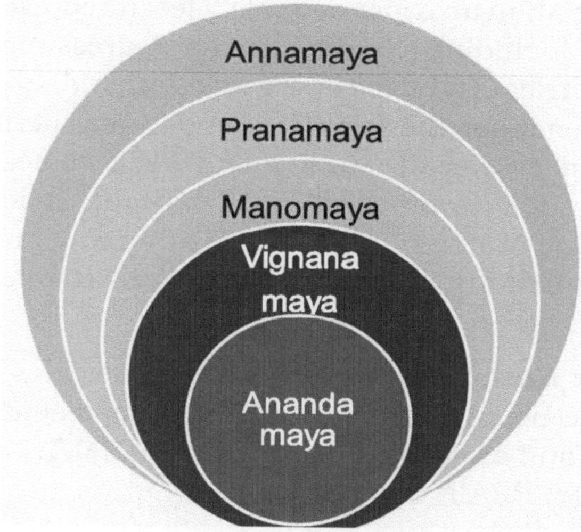

Fig. 3: The Pancha Kosha Model

given below, along with the brief description of what each of those represents:

Annamaya Kosha (AK): (It is the 1st sheath closest to the body and it represents the 'Gross Body'—visible and made of the five elements—earth, air, ether, water and fire. It contains the energy that we collect from the food and other inputs into our biological system.) AK represents everything materialistic that fulfils our BODILY desires for food, drinks, beverages and all articles and items for a comfortable and convenient lifestyle. I symbolise the whole gamut of AK by the 'Dietary Energy (ED).

In order to know to what extent, you and your teenage kid are governed or influenced by AK, ask the following questions:

What is your nature? Do you like food and beverages? Are you DRIVEN by materialistic desires for a comfortable and convenient living? Do your natural propensities provide you with the potential to be a dietary energy (ED) provider in the broad materialistic sense? A farmer, a farm owner, an agriculturist, a farm products stockist, a grocer, a vegetable or fruit vendor, a fishery-poultry-piggery-goatery farm owner or vendor, a dairy man, a chef, a baker, a confectioner (Indian/western), a brewer, a hotelier, a hospitality specialist, a dietician and nutritionist, a food technologist or even a broad-based chemical engineer.

I do interpret AK in an expanded role. I feel it represents anything materialistic including clothes, garments, dress materials, wrist watches, electrical and electronic gadgets including smartphones and fancy items (for the feminine gender, jewelleries and other fittings and accessories). So, if your DRIVE comes from any of these and such items and you may be involved in the manufacturing or marketing of those or supply material inputs for their manufacture, then you belong to the very broad AK group.

Pranamaya Kosha (PK): (It is the 2nd layer which forms a part of the 'Subtle Body' as it is not visible). It represents the 'Breath Energy (EB)'and anything to do with the HEALTH and FITNESS of your BODY, BRAIN and MIND.

The questions to be asked are:

Are you or your teenage kid get DRIVEN by feelings and desires related to health and fitness?

Do you have the inborn potential to be a breath energy (EB) provider: a therapist (physical, psycho, neuro), a chiropractor, a yoga teacher, a gym instructor, a meditation instructor, a physical educator, a sports or games coach, a healer, a doctor (of any stream), a nurse, a paramedic, a biomedical engineer, an medical electronics or instrumentation technologist, an insurance expert (life, health, medical), or one who is in the safety and security profession like in the defence, police and allied forces, or in the manufacture and supply of defence and security items including fire extinguishers and fire engines; and, of course, an automobile designer or an automobile engineer or one who is engaged in automobile manufacturing, marketing, repairing and servicing (my term 'automobile' covers any vehicle like a bicycle a 2-wheeler, a wagon or a truck); or, for that matter, in mechanical, production, aircraft design, aeronautical, marine engineering and, naval architecture, or electrical, electronic, communication, or computer engineering?

Manomaya Kosha (MK) (It is the 3rd layer which is also a part of the invisible 'Subtle Body'). It represents the entire gamut of your EMOTIONS and FEELINGS related to others and thus, the 'Emotional Energy (EE)'.

The questions to be asked are:

Are you or your teenage kid get DRIVEN by people-related emotions and feelings?

Do you feel that you or your teenage kid have the inborn potential to be an emotional energy (EE) provider: an emotional entertainer—a musician, an actor, a dancer, a choreographer, a mime artist, a comedian, a joker, a circus man, a theatre personality, or a film maker, an athlete or a sports person; an emotional input-provider like a journalist, a print or audio-visual media person, a novelist, a story teller, a poet, a painter, an architect, a builder, an interior designer, a furniture designer/maker, a fashion designer; or an emotional guide like a psychologist, a psycho-therapist, counsellor, or a priest, or a preacher?

Vijnanamaya Kosha (VK): (It is the 4th and the penultimate layer—the terminal part of the invisible 'Subtle Body'). It represents the INTELLECTUAL ENERGY (EI) that helps you to go deep into anything with your brain's power of logical and analytical thinking:

The questions to be asked are:

Are you or your teenage kid DRIVEN by intelligence and intellect?

Do you feel that you or your teenage kid have the inborn potential to be an intellectual energy (EI) provider—a serious and keen student seeking deep knowledge, a highly knowledgeable teacher-tutor-professor, or a trainer, a coach, a mentor, a researcher in any field, a philosopher, a theologist, a critic, a reviewer, or a content writer?

Anandamaya Kosha (AnK): (It is the 5th and the last layer—the 'Causal Body'.) It represents the CREATIVE or COSMIC ENERGY (EC) that helps you to create, innovate, discover, intuit or have an inspiration or insight.

The questions to be asked are:

Are you or your teenage kid DRIVEN by an inherent and spontaneous urge to create?

Do you feel that you or your teenage kid have the inborn potential to be a cosmic or creative energy (EC) provider—an inventor, a discoverer, an innovator, a creator, a philosopher, a spiritual guide (guru) or a life coach in modern times?

[*Note:* Are you an economic energy (EEco) provider? An economist, a banker, a tax consultant, an accountant, a wealth management specialist. Since 'Annamaya Kosha (AK)', in my perception, represents all things materialistic and thus, hedonism, 'EEco' can be included to be a part of 'AK' and, therefore, ED.]

Domain Gift

What is your and your teenage kid's DOMAIN gift from Mother Nature—your 'Dharma'—your natural properties and propensities? What is your 'CALL'—your 'True Passion'?

The questions that you ought to ask would include:

What kind of arena is most suitable for my own and my teenage kid's ***peak performance*** leading to 'Total Personal Well-Being (TPWB)' symbolising *happiness*? Shall we get the support of our Strengths and Rectified Deficiencies to ensure our TPWB? If the environmental scenario changes, will the same 'Strengths' and 'Rectified/Corrected Deficiencies' support us equally well to grab the 'Opportunities' and avert the 'Threats' or do we have to identify some hidden 'Strengths' and apply them in practice to tide over the situation?

Self-Acceptance and Self-Love

Once the 'Self-Knowledge (SK)' base is strong, it will lead to 'Self-Acceptance' which is the opposite of 'Self-Rejection' which generally takes place when you start comparing yourself or your teenage kid with others and find out that you are lagging behind. This happens when your SK base is weak—you do not know enough about yourself. If you accept yourself with grace and confidence, you will have the mental state to practice SMART leading and parenting; otherwise not. 'Self-Acceptance (SA)' will automatically lead to 'Self-Love (SL)'. SL is a high 'Self-Esteem' situation. You will know what your 'Self-Worth' is and you will be proud of yourself. This is an essential prerequisite for SMART leading and parenting.

I know of a young CEO of a company heading a high-tech auto-control organisation who, in his newly constructed house, has kept a full-size mirror in his dressing room attached to the bath where he can view his dressed-up body and admire something special in it—may be the hairline or the hairstyle, the height, the glow of health and fitness, the colour of the shirt, or the polka dot tie—something which would attract others' attention and impression. While conducting a high-level workshop in Bhutan which was attended by several parliamentarians and dignitaries including the chairman of the Royal Bank of Bhutan, I was told that the young Bhutanese King makes it a point to get a full view of his decked-up figure in a palace mirror before he addresses his State Parliament during a session. It is apparently a 'SA' and 'SL' habit. It would be ideal if they could be mimicked by the mirror neurons of their teenage kids, if they had any.

Self-Leading

The step next to 'Self-Love (SL)' is 'Self-Leading (S-Ld)'. 'S-Ld' is leading yourself and your teenage kid so that your progress is uninterrupted and undeterred in the prevailing socio-economic scenario which normally would be fast-changing and getting more and more high tech-based—digital devices, AI applications, robotics, lean management and so on.

The whole idea of 'SMART Leadership', in a nutshell, is to lead your life in such a way as to maintain the health, fitness and well-being of the resources that you own as a human, utilising those resources in ways that they had been designed for, although functionally they are wholly or partly replaced due to digitalisation.

Three Case Studies

I have suggested that the 'Pancha Kosha' model to be used for discovering what kind of 'Human Resource (HR)' you are—what ought to be the suitable DOMAIN for you to operate in. In other words, what is your BIRTH DOMAIN—the blueprint with which you were born. Your BIRTH PLAN is incorporated in your genome, the genes that you have inherited, 50 percent from each of your parents. In the genome, all the five (5) Koshas and their propensities are present but in varying proportions.

Some may have the 'Annamaya Kosha (AK)' more predominant than the other four. We do need food 'to live' (that is, to satisfy hunger) but some AK-influenced individuals are at the other end of the spectrum which is 'live to eat'. Their main concern and priority would be food, and their 'Pranamaya', 'Manomaya' and 'Vijnanamaya' Koshas will all be active to satisfy the needs of the AK. Their concern and goal would be to use all the other Koshas to increase the AK inputs. All this takes place at the unconscious level of the mind.

Let me share a case study. SC was born into an upper middle-class family having a very large clan of relatives. So, entertaining them and being entertained by them was a regular affair. The 'Annamaya Kosha (AK)' was thus the major role player. SC studied economics which is a domain related to AK. He qualified in civil service and was posted in a backward State as District Magistrate (DM)—again related to socio-economic development and upliftment which are AK-related. He resigned and joined an international development bank as an economist—again an AK-related assignment. Entertaining guests and being entertained by friends and relations continued in full vigour. Now retired, he is advising his old State (where he was a DM and, thereafter, a departmental commissioner in the State Secretariate) in the area of socio-economic development. It is, again, an AK-related assignment. Entertainment activities still continue with gusto. He exercises on a home-based treadmill. In such cases, bliss does not come through the 'Anandamaya Kosha (AnK)', it comes through the gut.

The hero of my second case study is one PB who is in his mid-twenties. He hails from the South 24 Parganas district of West Bengal whose family profession had been, for a few generations, hair dressing. In underdeveloped countries, barbers would be called upon to perform minor surface surgeries like operating upon a boil or doing a circumcision. Are you not familiar with the tale where the location is an island under British occupation and the aboriginal people used to go to a local native barber for healing? The British Govt. placed a highly qualified white medic with a fully equipped clinic so that the locals benefit from modern medicare. But the natives were too afraid to go to the white doctor; on the contrary, they continued to consult the tribal barber. The British doctor was a very intelligent person.

Instead of getting upset with the local crowd and also Her Majesty's Govt., he befriended the local barber, trained him in antiseptic therapy and left the entire medicare system under his custody after convincing his Govt. that he will visit the island once in every two months to see how things are going on. Our case study hero PB was dissuaded by his father and uncles not to join the family profession but to pursue studies. Post-senior secondary education, PB had some health problem for which he came to Kolkata for treatment. He was treated and cured in a neurotherapy clinic. He was so much convinced about the therapeutic efficacy of this branch of alternative medicine, that he decided to choose neurotherapy as his career. Anything to do with healing and therapy is a 'Pranamaya Kosha (PK)' domain. Is it not a case where the BIRTH DOMAIN has matched with the individual's profession where the incumbent has done exceptionally well within a short period of 5 years?

The third case study centres around one MN, a middle-aged male. Coming from a semi-urban background his father had a small workshop. As it was nothing much to write home about, MN aspired to take up a job and, as his luck favoured, he got a chance to join a public sector oil company in the nonexecutive cadre. MN had a plump body and was a foodie. So, the 'Annamaya Kosha' was the guiding Kosha for him. His oil company purchased crude petroleum, refined it in its oil refinery and marketed the refined petrol, diesel, aircraft fuel and other petro products. Crude petroleum is a fossil fuel and fossils have linkage with 'Annamaya Kosha (AK)'. MN's career progressed well and within a short period, he qualified as an executive and eventually promoted to the Assistant Manager's post. This is again a case where the individual's BIRTH DOMAIN matched with his chosen career.

By now, have you been able to make out whether your BIRTH DOMAIN has tallied with your chosen career?

What More About
The Pancha Kosha Model One Must Know

The 'Pancha Kosha (PK)' model comes from the Taittirya Upanishad (TU) and is said to be one of the most ancient conceptualizations of the human being. PK is discussed in the Brahmanandavalli Chapter of TU which is a part of the Taittitya Samhita of the Krishna Yajurveda.

PK is a hierarchy of human values. I have no idea whether the Russian-American psychologist Abraham Maslow (1908-1970) was influenced by the PK model when he proposed his five-step hierarchy of human needs in the early 1940's. His 1st step relates to the physical survival needs, which is equivalent to the 'Annamaya Kosha'. Maslow's 2nd step talks about safety and security which is somewhat similar to PK's 'Pranamaya Kosha' representing the life force. His 3rd step, social relationship needs, matches with PK's 'Manomaya Kosha'. Can we relate Maslow's 4th step which talks about power, prestige, authority, self-esteem, participation in decision-making to PK's 'Vijnanamaya Kosha' standing for intellect? Nevertheless, his 'Self-actualisation' which is the 5th and final level of the hierarchy, is certainly analogous to PK's 'Anandamaya Kosha' where you experience eternal bliss.

Maslow's idea of step-by-step evolution of needs fits in snugly with the soul evolution concept of PK.

The path of 'Yoga' is said to heighten one's understanding and awareness of the five 'Koshas' or sheaths. Eventually, the aim of 'Yoga' is to move inward, taking a journey through these sheaths and uncovering one's TRUE NATURE, or ATMAN (the inner SELF—the consciousness of 'I'). Then, on experiencing the bliss of the 'Anandamaya Kosha', one discovers the relationship of ATMAN with BRAHMAN—the 'Universal Consciousness'. The five Koshas or sheaths constitute the ANATMAN which protects the ATMAN so that it remains pure and unspoilt, unattached—the unaffected, uncontaminated TRUTH.

Simple prescriptions for taking care of the five (5) different 'Koshas' would be as follows: 'Annamaya Kosha (AK)'—simple freehand stretching-bending exercises, practicing Hatha Yoga; 'Pranamaya Kosha (PK)'—simple conscious breathing activity, practicing pranayama; 'Manomaya Kosha (MK)'—engagement in meaningful tasks not to allow your brain's 'Default Mode Network (DMN)' to be active; 'Vijnanamaya Kosha (VK)'—acquisition of knowledge and knowledge management; 'Ananadamaya Kosha (AnK)'—meditation every day for at least 20 minutes would help you to perceive brief flashes of bliss. While AK is nothing but your 'gross body (sthulasarira)', PK, MK and VK constitute your subtle body (suksmasarira)'. The 'AnK' is your 'causal body (karanasarira)'.

Like the blood flows through visible and palpable arteries and veins, the 'prana' or the 'life force' flows through the 'nadis'—the 72,000 nadis widely spread all over the body, with the Sushumna, Ida and Pingala being the principal ones. 'Chakras' which are invisible energy centres are also involved. Principal 'chakras' are seven in number placed at different levels right from the tail end of the spine to the centre of the skull.

Just with the 'Annamaya Kosha (AK)'—the physical gross body alive, and the 'prana' providing it with the life force—the energy, it can remain active but it will be devoid of any emotions and feelings. It will neither smile or cry, nor it will be happy and joyful, angry or anxious, disgusted or surprised. There comes the role of the 'Manomaya Kosha (MK)' and its emotional manifestations. But no one can continue to live the whole life being an emotional baggage. Emotions must be controlled willfully, circumstances must be looked at logically and analytically for rational decision making. Knowledge and experience have to be acquired and properly managed for leading a wholesome life. For all this, we needed a 'Vijnanamaya Kosha (VK)'.

'Annamaya Kosha (AK)' earns dietary energy (ED); 'Pranamaya Kosha (PK)' earns breath energy (EB); 'Manomaya (MK)' and 'Vijnanamaya Koshas (VK)' do not earn energy (Emotional Energy—EE and Intellectual Energy—EI respectively), they steal, beg or borrow energy. MK collects energy from other people by using 'Intimidatory' and/or 'Interrogative' behaviour. VK collects energy from human as well as non-human (books, journals, internet) sources. But, if MK and VK do not get such opportunity, they can lean on the 'Anandamaya Kosha (AnK)', the Bliss Body to earn some pure cosmic energy. One can attain 'Bliss' through religious, spiritual as well as any 'Peak Performance Experience' in one's own operational domain which may be music, dancing, fine arts, acting, as well as any business or economic profession. Try to get some 'Peak Performance' experience—reach the climax of some activity which you enjoy immensely not only because it is too close to your heart but you also get lost during the performance losing track of space, time, and your ego and such objective and subjective realities. The state to be attained is equivalent to 'Samadhi Sthiti'.

Our 'Karmas' (actions and reactions) and 'Samskaras' (memories and experiences) are stored in the 'Koshas'. They stand up as walls between the individual SOUL and the Universal SELF. During a 'Peak Performance' experience, the 'Atman (soul)' is released from the limitations of the Koshas because the Koshas form the means of bondage for the 'Atman'.

Pancha Kosha Exercises for Digital Age Kosha Fitness

Digital activities are usually dry, unwholesome. They might clash with the healthy vibes of your Pancha Koshas (PK). So, you need to indulge in some special pursuits, from time to time, to provide your Koshas with motivational inputs. Here, I am providing you with some tested tips.

Annamaya Kosha (AK): Your AK is loaded with the 'Dietary Energy (ED)' experiences your ancestors had. You have inherited your AK genome from them. These are related to the cereals, roots and tubers, proteins, fruits, vegetables, spices and herbs that your ancestors were habituated to. Practice 'Effective Management of Change'. Break the habit slowly by trying out new things, one or two at a time. I had a young boy, RV, from Varanasi, UP in my team. His forefathers had migrated from Rajasthan 2 or 3 generations ago to settle down in the outskirts of Varanasi. They were total vegetarians used to only veg and lacto-proteins. Having regular milk proteins is not a healthy habit. Milk, experts recommend for children and old people. Once in a while having paneer or cheese is OK for our climate. I introduced RV to egg protein and it worked out fine. His AK was having an experience of a new kind and it worked well on him.

Pranamaya Kosha (PK): Your breathing activity takes place unconsciously and it changes with changes in your mood, attitude and so on. So, for a change, try out 'conscious breathing'. Inhale by mentally counting at a slow pace, 1 2 3 4, then hold your breath by counting 1, and then start breathing out with a little longer period by counting 1 2 3 4 5 6 so that your PK is breath-free. This will help you to preserve the quality of your 'Breath Energy (EB)'.

Manomaya Kosha (MK): The MK of your near and dear ones may be starving for 'Emotional Energy (EE)' from your MK as you are busy in digital activities. You can try out my '5A' technique to supply 'EE' to their MK. First 'A' is 'Attention' which means you must give them undivided attention as and when they may need it. Establish and sustain positive eye contact and listen to them with full concentration when they are communicating with you. Second 'A' is 'Acceptance'. You must accept them for their plus points rather than criticising them by highlighting their minus points, lapses and failures. Your such unkind conduct will lead to the shrinkage of their MK. Third 'A' is 'Appreciation'. Even for a small work done, offer appreciation which does not cost you anything but means a lot for the person who receives it. Fourth 'A' is 'Affiliation'. Involve and include people if they want to be involved and included. More than one brain is generally better than just one. The fifth and final 'A' is 'Allowing' which indicates providing 'Autonomy' and 'Independence'. Even a little child wants his voice to be heard, opinion or decision to be considered, and many of us, as parents and elders, just shove them off for our own selfish ego satisfaction.

Vijnanamaya Kosha (VK): Decide on your domain where you are most happy to operate. Then use my E (Explore)-Experiment (E)-L (Learn) formula adopting the VARK (Visual-Auditory-Reading and Writing-Kinaesthetic) style to deal with any information related to your chosen field. This will help your VK to develop focused antennas.

Anandamaya Kosha (AnK): Go for 'Peak Performance Experience (PPE)' whenever you can. Your daily activity domain should be chosen in a manner that around 40 to 50 percent of the time there is opportunity available for PPE when you lose track of space, time and economic return on your investment of energy and effort.

Did you ever think that your Pancha Koshas (PK) needed special care now that you are in the midst of digital era?

CHAPTER 4

Digital Impact on Our Brains

'Key' Points: *Our Brain's Adaptation to Digital Use; Brain's 'Seeking System Circuit (SSC)'; Digital Dangers: How Smart Leadership-based Parenting Approach Can Help Teenage Kids; Internet Addiction Disorder (IAD)—Smart Leading and Parenting Tips.*

Our Brain's Adaptation to Digital Use

New age brain research has confirmed that brain is not 'rigid', it is 'plastic'. There is now a big branch of 'Neuroscience' known as 'Neuroplasticity'. So, it is naturally expected that our brains would get adapted to digital use. I will initiate a discussion on this specific issue here.

A million years ago, our ancestors' brain volumes just exceeded 1,000 cc, and by 500,000 years ago, they were within the size range of modern humans (1,100–1,500 cc). In fact, brains tended to be even larger at the end of the Ice Age than today because bodies were also bigger. As the world warmed up over the last 12,000 years, bodies shrunk slightly; and, so did the brains.

Bigger brains come with sizeable costs. Even though your brain constitutes only 2 percent of your body weight, it consumes about 20 to 25 percent of your body's resting energy budget regardless of whether you are sleeping, watching TV or reading this book. Your brain costs 280 to 420 Calories (C) per day, whereas a chimp's brain costs about 100 to 120. Today, in modern times, we can obtain this energy from 1 boiled egg (80C) or, 1 fried egg (110C); and 3 slices of bread with butter (3 × 90C) consumed for the day's breakfast, but a pre-historic hunter-gatherer needed to forage an extra 6 to 10 carrots to earn the same number of calories only to keep his brain energy-happy. These costs are amplified in the case of a pregnant lady and a nursing mother. `

Brain's 'Seeking System Circuit (SSC)'

However, the benefits of increased intelligence outweighed the costs. To obtain those extra 6 to 10 carrots, our pre-historic hunter-gatherer ancestor had to cover a large area of the forest, use the 'Seeking System Circuit (SSC)' of his brain which exists even in the brains of reptiles, birds and mammals to follow the EEL model: Explore, Experiment, and Learn. He had to gather knowledge about the specific locations where he could find wild carrots; how many different varieties of carrots were available, each with its respective taste and convenience of eating in the raw form; whether there was any possibility of any small bacteria or worms to be inside; what had been the past experience of eating those varieties (for this, he had to communicate with his colleagues only in body language and vocal tones as word-based languages had not been introduced still), etc. You can well imagine how powerful is the 'Seeking System' formula EEL for brain development. For a few million years, until agriculture was introduced only around 10,000 years ago, our hunter-gatherer ancestors regularly used this EEL formula for finding their food.

Sadly, we have few direct traces of the brain feats these archaic humans accomplished beyond mastering fire and making more complex tools such as projectile points. Archaeological records cannot help us to detect the biggest benefits of bigger brains which were probably in the area of 'behaviour' such as cooperativeness, mutual trust-building and effective teamwork. Mind you, these brain faculties were developing in members belonging to the same TRIBE or 'KULA' [which is equivalent to modern-day nuclear and extended families (or clans)] who were living together in the same jungle habitat. You cannot expect the same kind of cooperativeness, mutual trust and sound teamwork in any work organisation today and that is the reason why scholars like us are invited to conduct corporate 'Team-building' workshops so often. Only 'Soft Skills' development cannot lead to 'Effective Team Building'.

Today, we do not have to go foraging for food in the hunter-gatherer style. All raw materials to be cooked into edibles for our consumption are available in markets and shopping malls. Home delivery and online purchases are also possible. So, the SSC inside our brains have been sitting idle particularly in our generations (in our previous generations, it was partially active as our fathers and grandfathers used to go to distant markets daily to collect consumables—refrigerators were a rare luxury). Is it thus true that the human brain, unknowingly, was preparing itself for getting adapted to the digital technology era as the modern digital systems do require our 'Seeking System Circuit (SSC)' and the EEL model to be used? Is that the reason why even an illiterate village boy or girl or a rural homemaker can conveniently handle a smartphone, a tablet, or a laptop because the SSC is relatively more active in the Indian rural society. Education and literacy are not needed for SSC to be installed inside your skull. PR, who used to cook for us in our household, had attended school only up to Class V, I suppose; could not write his name properly in English, still could handle his smartphone with the same ease as you and I do. Now that he is not working for us, I still get regular WhatsApp messages from him.

Whether your brain health may be affected adversely if the SSC and EEL models are used for your digital work is a very critical issue which I shall touch upon a short while later. But let us look at its impact on your physical health and fitness. Digital work is sedentary. It does not require you to move. So, physical energy expenditure has come down bringing forth the problems of obesity, high blood pressure, cardiac illnesses, diabetes mellitus, neck-shoulder-back pain and other ailments which keep company with people who are well-fed, well-clothed and well-sheltered. So digitech users who are in the 'Zone of Comfort and Convenience (ZCC)' must go for 'Calorie Restriction' (= consuming little less calories than required) or burning the extra calories (Calorie Input = Calorie Output) by going for planned physical fitness activities.

If you have been putting on extra weight, now you can perhaps attribute sedentary digitech use as one of the root causes. Isn't it?

Digital Dangers: How SMART Leadership-based Parenting Approach Can Help Teenage Kids.

The average adult now spends over 20 hours 'online' each week, 3 hrs. a day roughly to keep his brain's autopilot 'Default Mode

Network (DMN)' engaged outside his 'Work or Task Engagement' hours for which also he uses digital devices. Nearly one-third of that non-task time is spent on social media platforms, with Facebook taking up nearly 60 minutes of each day, which is almost equal to the time we take for eating and drinking. Teens spend much more time engaging with digital media daily. This is the dominant activity in their life today. Under abnormal conditions such as the current Covid 19 pandemic-ridden circumstances, digital use for adults as well as teenagers is considerably more because of the compulsive social distancing.

The teen brain, with its unique feature of PLASTICITY, can get adapted to the digital environment, but how does it get affected in the long run? Can SMART leading approach help in any way for effective parenting of teenage kids? I will take up this issue now.

1. **ATTENTION:** Before the deluge of digital devices, the average ATTENTION SPAN was about 12 seconds. Now, in the digital era, as anyone including a teenager can open multiple windows or turn on multiple devices, one is tempted to multi-task. (Few of us unfortunately know that our brain can perform most effectively on one task at a time.) Multi-tasking takes away our ATTENTION (our digitally invaded ATTENTION SPAN in 2013 was measured to be about 8 seconds only) and, because of poor ATTENTION, the new information to be collected may go to a wrong place instead of to the 'hippocampus' which is responsible for long-term permanent memory storage.

SMART Parenting Tips to a Teenager: If you're studying a serious subject, do not watch TV or listen to familiar music at the same time, on the side, as the serious information will not be led to the right place inside your brain and is likely to be stored in a shallower way. Your learning of the subject will be limited to 'understanding' only; it will not be deep-rooted, so you may not be able to recall.

2. **MEMORY:** The tendency to rely on the 'Internet' as a memory bank increases after each use. The teenager gets tempted and attracted towards it as it conveniently takes him through short-cuts.

SMART Parenting Tips to a Teenager: Strike a balance between your dependence on the 'Internet' and the conventional method of consultation of books, dictionaries, thesaurus and knowledgeable persons.

3. **THOUGHT:** Reading on digital platforms might make a teenage kid inclined to focus on concrete details rather than interpreting information more abstractly, holistically or understand it in theory and essence.

SMART Parenting Tips to a Teenager: Practice developing the discriminatory skill as to where you should go for digital information collection and where else for abstract conceptualisation or looking at the big picture.

4. **EMPATHY:** The more distracted one gets with a variety of data crowded on the same screen of a social site, the less able one is to experience EMPATHY—deep connection with other people. Many of the kids who are growing up in the digital era have not developed conversation skills or learnt to read social cues. As a result, many of them miss out on major aspects of natural communication.

SMART Parenting Tips to a Teenager: Wherever and whenever possible in social and work roles, exchange handwritten notes which have now become almost obsolete. Such notes and correspondence serve as links of EMPATHY between the writer and the reader. Ensure establishing and sustaining positive eye contact while talking and listening to others including parents and elders. Get educated with the help of live examples and videos on the nitty-gritty of body language and tonal quality so that you develop empathy and emotional intelligence which most of today's teenagers are found lacking.

5. **FOCUS:** The more you get used to the technology and the constant rush of information that it produces, you become less able to figure out what is important to FOCUS on.

SMART Parenting Tips for a Teenager: Do not spend more time on digital media than what you essentially require where digital technology is really helpful. Sit quietly from time to time to practice full deep breathing with slow, soft instrumental music being played in the background and FOCUS on the music. Periodically, shift your FOCUS from music to your breathing activity. Such alternate FOCUSING practice will most likely help you.

6. **LOSS OF TOUCH WITH REALITY:** Your eyes fixed on the small screen increases depression, anxiety and aggression and can even lead to psychotic-like features where the digitech user loses touch with reality. [Digital addiction is more likely to happen if adolescents lack interest in studies and feel cynicism towards school and adults do not enjoy their family life or work role and do not take pride in what they do, and in the organisations where they are engaged.] The worst of all, digital technology has built-in gratification that stimulates the 'pleasure centres' (viz., the 'Reward Circuits') of the brain, keeping the digitech user coming back again and again for more 'Dopamine (D)' or the 'reward' molecules.

SMART Parenting Tips for a Teenager: There is a possibility, if one gets digitally addicted, of the brain's frontal lobes which are responsible for executive functioning including impulse control getting affected. So, you as a teenager, should engage yourself, as a regular practice, in making plans, working out checklists and 'To Do' lists to keep the Prefrontal Cortex (PFC) activated.

Internet Addiction Disorder (IAD): *SMART Leading and Parenting Tips*

Digital devices are providing the user with comfort as well as convenience. So, following my 'Zone of Comfort and Convenience (ZCC)' concept, there is, shall we say, a 'Zone of Digital Comfort and Convenience (ZDCC)' for all digital users. Immediately outside this ZDCC, there is a 'Digital Danger Zone (DDG)' which means your digital use habit has crossed the ZDCC and exists in the most vulnerable stage of approaching towards the 'Zone of Addiction (ZA)'.

Should you already be in the 'Digital Danger Zone (DDG)', the dangers can be averted if you are a little CONSCIOUS about the negative signs and symptoms that I have talked about. But if you have crossed the DDG border and walked into the 'Zone of Addiction (ZA)', then you have to be extra careful.

Physical hazards of digital age may be carpal tunnel syndrome, headaches, back or neck aches, dry eyes, strained images, sleep disturbances and, what I want to highlight here, is the 'unexplained weight gain or loss'. The last-mentioned problem is becoming common, health professionals claim, as an outcome of 'Internet Addiction Disorder (IAD)'.

IAD, as a general term, is supposed to cover: cybersex addiction (unavoidable addiction to porn sites); cyber-relationship addiction; net compulsions (compulsive use of online gaming, online auction or shopping sites); information overload (obsessive web surfing or database browsing); computer addiction (obsessive use of the computer). IAD-afflicted people get drawn towards fat-rich diet because the brain needs more energy to cope with their addictive behaviour. One possible eventual health hazard for middle-aged adults is early development of Alzheimer's symptoms beginning with loss of working memory.

Incidentally, the human brain is nearly 60 percent fat. If you are a fish eater, you must have experience of dealing with the oily stuff in the fish brain of all sizes. You might have also been exposed to chick brain and might have seen goat and lamb brains on display in meat shops. The healthy dietary fat income range in adult humans is 20 to 35 percent of the total calorie intake. For a total input of 2,000 Calories a day, the fat quantity should be 44 to 77 gm. If you are practicing 'Smart leading and parenting' for the digital era, then you should concentrate upon 'monounsaturated' fat and its intake should be 15 to 20 percent. These fats come from: olive and peanut oil; nuts and nut-based butters; and olives. 'Polyunsaturated' fat intake should be 5 to 10 percent, obtainable from: safflower, sunflower, corn, soybean and cottonseed oils, and nuts. 'Saturated' fat should be avoided by digitally engaged modern sedentary individuals; 'Saturated' fat sources are junk food items like: hamburgers and hot dogs; pizzas; cream and ice cream; processed meat (ham, bacon, salami and sausages); butter and lard; coconut and palm oil; products from bakeries and confectioneries (cakes, pastries, cookies, croissants); Indian sweets and savouries (including samosas, bhujias, kachuris, puris and dalpuris); fat dairy products like cheese; street food (like chow mein and rolls). 'Transfat' should be altogether avoided (margarine, powdered coffee cream, condensed milk, pre-packaged baked goods).

SMART parenting would mean planning the daily diet with: non-veg protein (largely fish including of sweet water/bony and salt water/oceanic varieties, occasionally lean poultry, one egg per day); veg. protein (lentil, dried beans, soybeans, rajma and dried peas); milk protein (yogurt and paneer); avoidance of fried food, red meat (goat, lamb, cow, pig) and ghee; earning vitamins A, E and C, Omega 3 fatty acids and DHA from vegetables, fruits and fish.

An excess intake of dietary fat translates into increased lipid (= fat molecules) content of brain tissues, which is likely to have significant (and probably negative) consequences for brain function. Abnormal build-up of fat droplets in the brain may cause or speed up Alzheimer's symptoms. The brain stem cells which normally repair brain damage become inactive with fat deposits. (Based on: Findings at the Research Centre of the University of Montreal Hospital, Canada; and, Gary L. Wink, Ph.D., *Your Brain on Food*, Oxford: Oxford University Press, 2010).

Alzheimer's is not a normal part of ageing. The most common early symptom is difficulty remembering newly learned information which is a common occurrence with too much of digital work habit—technically known as 'digital overload'. These fat deposits are triglycerides (a type of fat or lipid found in your blood and stored in your fat cells) enriched with specific fatty acids which are also found in animal fats and vegetable oils.

In this context, let me point out that external appearance and constitution of a person are, at times, misleading. Thin and lean people are not necessarily fit. I am talking about people who belong to the 'Thin Outside Fat Inside' ('TOFI') category. In their case, they hog junk foods and their fats get deposited around their organs and not under the skin (which is known as 'subcutaneous fat'). I know two such 'TOFI' type young men in their early twenties. Both are smartphone addicts. They have little appetite and tend to skip their breakfasts off and on. The SMART diet that was recommended for them included: raw vegetables in salad form, plant-based and nutrient-rich items. Also recommended was frequent physical movement which has an aggressive effect on visceral fat (excess intra-abdominal adipose tissue accumulation) and helps keeping the body healthy and fit IAD may alter the volume of the brain, not in all but, in some cases. The brain changes are similar to those produced by alcohol and drug addiction. IAD shrinks the brain's grey and white matter fibres which results in changes to brain functioning, particularly emotional processing. As long as the addiction continues, the brain will continue to get altered and affected negatively.

Now that you are aware of the hazards of 'Internet Addiction Disorder (IAD)', do you feel you have already identified someone who has become or moving towards becoming a victim of 'Digital Overload'?

CHAPTER 5

Digitalisation of Teenage Kids

'Key' Points: *Smartphone: A Teenage Kid's Extended Self;' Hallucinatory Digital Addiction (HDA)'; Symptoms of HDA; Teen and Technology; Search for Passion Domain; Digital Technology as a Calming Device; Can Digital Technology Be a Killer; Digital Work and Dietary Brain Fat; Digital Technology and Disturbed Sleep; Digital Engagement and Brainpower Erosion.*

Smartphone: A Teenage Kid's Extended Self

Our ancestor prehistoric hunter-gatherers were often hungry as they were generally healthy and fit. They managed to get enough food through a combination of intense co-operation between the members of their tribal group and manual work, including some hours of walking, running, digging and carrying as long as the sun was out. Besides, if you were a hunter-gatherer, you did not have to work more than necessary to satisfy your own and a portion of your associates' daily needs. Once that was ensured, you would benefit from resting and devoting time to social activities such as gossiping and enjoying the company of your fellow tribesmen. Whatever little environmental stress would be generated due to forest-dwelling, you could manage to handle with the freeze-fight-flight circuits available handy in your hind and mid-brain.

Many contemporary stressors of modern times—commuting, the threat of losing your job, getting your children into good schools, supervising their education, taking care of your old ailing parents, and saving for retirement—can make you readily realise why digital devices today are your best pals, serving you like oases in desert lands. But added on to all these typical modern age stressors, is the tension caused by your teenage kid's unparalleled attraction towards your smartphone. A couple of live case studies will exemplify.

Hallucinatory Digital Addiction (HDA)

Arjun does not own a smartphone but wishes to own one. He imagines as if his dad's smartphone is his own. So, without telling his dad, he has shared his dad's number with his friends. The outcome: while at work, Arjun's dad Saroj gets calls from Arjun's pals. Arjun has a lot of friends in school, in the swimming club, in his cricket coaching centre and, of course, in his locality where he is an active member of the boys' club. Saroj gets calls at all odd hours—when in office, while travelling, while in his dentist's chamber, and while shopping consumables on his way back home from work.

Mayuri is another one who has shared her mom's smartphone number with her friends in her school, in her music and art class, and in her tutorials. Subhadra, the mom, holds a senior position in the IT sector and, although she keeps the device switched off at work, when she switches it on in the lunch room, there are several missed calls and she gets totally confused.

Both Arjun and Mayuri have the same behavioural manifestations, related to their smartphone attraction. Both run to their respective parents to grab the gadgets to check the messages and missed calls when their parents return at night after the whole day's toil. On top of the load of stressors that they carry back from work, Saroj and Subhadra have to face, most unprepared, their kids' smartphone related hysterical activities. It is an emerging problem with kids in Indian middleclass homes today and, I call it, 'Hallucinatory Digital Addiction (HDA)'. 'Hallucinatory' because the kids suffer from a hallucination that they are the owners of their parents' smartphones. The kids live with such hallucinations. The smartphone today has become their extended selves.

Symptoms of HDA

What are the Ill-Symptoms of HDA?

First is 'Sleep Disturbance'. Your teenage kid has poor sleep quality with 'Rapid Eye Movements' (known as REM sleep which means the sleep quality is not deep and sound enough to provide complete rest to the growing brain which is essential for developing concentration and solid memory power).

To be a SMART leading parent take the following remedial steps. Prevent your teenage kid from using the gadget at least one hour before going to bed. Do not allow him (no gender bias; my use of masculine covers feminine also) to keep the device by the side of or under his head pillow. After he has gone to bed, switch on some slow and soft flute recital which will help to bring sleep quickly; or, you can sing a lullaby.

Second is 'Anxiety and Depression'. The whole day, when the phone is out of his reach, he will be anxious about the missed calls and messages. Being depressed, his adrenalin glands will secrete the stress hormone 'cortisol' which affects working memory and increases the oscillations of his brain cells affecting his attention span, concentration power and mental focus. His academic activities will suffer a lot deteriorating his task performance. A SMART leading parent will make the kid join him in performing simple stretching-bending physical activities and deep breathing exercises regularly with slow, soft background music that the youngster loves to listen.

Teen and Technology

Shamin is eighteen and a fresher in college. He is a single parent child. His parents are not divorced but separated from each other. Shamin lives with his mom, but visits his dad in a nearby locality every day after college. He has genetic affinity towards both but, most sadly, is torn in between. His best friend has a digital personality—his smartphone.

His mother is away the whole day running her own alternative health care practice. Both of his parents being in station yet being away from him physically throughout the day, Shamin, looking at his case from my 'Neuro-management (NM)' point of view, I diagnosed it as one of partial 'Oxytocin (O)' deprivation.

'Oxytocin (O)' is one of the basic happiness chemicals which needs to be present in a growing kid's brain in balanced quantity for his well-being. I must thank Dr. Paul Zak who has been championing the cause of 'Oxytocin' for the last couple of decades.

It is Dr. Zak who has pulled out 'Oxytocin' from the dark vaginal alleys of gynaecology and obstetrics. 'O' used to be known only to medical doctors, especially gynaecologists and obstetricians as a hormone which is secreted when a pregnant lady suffers from severe labour pain to make the vaginal passage adequately wet and slippery to facilitate normal delivery. With the Caesarean Section becoming popular as a short-cut technique, O had taken a back seat. Dr. Zak, an industrial economist with special training in neuroscience has identified O's link with love, bonding, mutual trust and cooperation without which any business or industrial organisation cannot excel in quality and productivity. He has highlighted that O is produced in the brains of both the nursing mother and the child who is being breast-fed to develop mutual trust and bonding between the two. The male version of 'O' is 'Vasopressin (V)' which is the hormone for bonding between the father and the child.

For Shamin, his smartphone works as the 'O' and 'V'-provider as he uses it for chatting with his friends and keeps it as his closest companion even at home till very late at night.

How can such problems get sorted out? You cannot expect a teenager to be a SMART leader. A teenage brain is not mature enough to have strong and permanent SMART leadership (SL) circuits in the frontal lobes of the forebrain or neo-cortex. Their parents have got to use their SL circuits.

Search for Passion Domain

As a SMART leading parent, find out your teenage kid's passion, which magnetically attracts him. Teenage is the period of life when an adolescent must set his career goal, select the domain where he would like to operate the rest of his life. When the youngster enters into his PASSION DOMAIN, everything disappears. Time, place, relationships—all get lost and he gets totally engaged in the activity that he loves and adores from the core of his heart.

Shamin is a multi-talented teenager. He can paint, he is good in sculpture and craftwork, he can compose lyrics and provide melody, he can sing and play the guitar. He can stage-act very well; and, he is very keen on his subject—philosophy. Now, start the process of elimination. Painting, sculpting, craft, artwork, or music cannot be an economic domain for him unless he turns out to be extraordinary. He is opting out from stage-acting as it takes a lot of his time and his academic activities get affected. So, motivate him to zoom on to philosophy and specialise on some aspect of philosophy—a path which not many have travelled so far. Once he can discover that territory, he would enter a DOMAIN of no return and that will keep him absorbed totally. If ever he felt bored, he could fall back on painting or craftwork or creation of music.

If you have faced a similar problem with a youngster in your family, do you feel you have some clue now on how to reduce or totally eradicate the problem?

Digital Technology as a Calming Device

This incident took place a few years ago. I was totally taken aback by a rushing sound approaching my room. For a split second, it reminded me of little JOY, a snow-white British terrier, a puppy that was growing up healthily at our home before it got lost one evening in the late autumn of 2015.

I raised my head from my laptop, turned it right to see what was happening. It was a little boy, around 6/7 yrs. in age bursting into my office. He was quickly followed by a couple in their mid-thirties. I opened my Time Planner and found that I had given appointment to Rajib and Soma Das who wanted to consult me regarding their son Romit.

Romit had been a victim of 'Attention Deficit Hyperactivity Disorder (ADHD)'. ADHD is a brain malfunctional problem which is brought from the mother's womb. ADHD patients have tremendous difficulty in mental concentration. They cannot concentrate on any study material in school, at home as well as in the tutorials. As an outcome, they get stuck in following any lesson. On top of that, they are physically restless. They must move about restlessly. As a matter of fact, within minutes of their appearance, Romit was not to be found anywhere. Finally, we could trace him in the courtyard at the back of my ground floor apartment where he was running after stray cats.

All of a sudden, something strange and totally unexpected happened, which I got exposed to for the first time. Rajib, who is an IT professional and runs his own enterprise, took out his laptop from its case and put it in front of Romit. And, there was magic, or shall I call it a miracle! Romit not only calmed down, but his 'ADHD' problem totally disappeared out of the open windows. He lost his hyperactivity—he could sit still on the bed, totally poised working on the laptop like a professional. I had never come across any such case before in my very long professional career dealing with brain and behaviour.

Rajib and Soma asked me: 'Doctor, we have come to ask you specifically if we are doing something wrong. Instead of remeding his ADHD problem, our use of digital technology as a calming device—is it going to increase his problem or have his brain circuits grow in an abnormal fashion.'

I shut my eyes for a few moments to ponder, and then said, my SMART parenting tips would be the following:

> When a growing child is in temper tantrums or crying due to frustration, the care-giver quickly hands over a smartphone or a tablet to calm the child, such instances are commonplace now-a-days in our culture. But, such 'distraction strategy' may negatively affect the child's opportunity to learn how to self-soothe and self-regulate in those moments. And, once the child gets habituated to this strategy, he would expect the same behavioural action on the part of the care-giver to earn his 'Dopamine (D)'—the 'feel good' brain chemical as he would feel that he has 'CONTROL' over the care-giver. So, let it not be a habit. You can use this strategy occasionally when there is no other way. Instead, teach the child something which he likes and to learn it he has to follow a prescribed procedure. ADHD affected children are usually sensitive to sound and music generally soothes their brain. So, for one ADHD child who loved the sound of percussion instruments, I had recommended taking lessons in tabla and within a few years of practice, he got almost normal. Another ADHD affected teenager who loved the sound of string instruments learnt sarod and his brain problem got remedied in two years.

I asked Romit's parents to try out some string instrument and dissuade him from using the laptop at high rate. Digital technology, used at a high rate, may make the child's brain adopt an internet approach to thinking—quickly scanning and processing multiple sources of information. Brain in children exposed to high volumes of technology may adapt to frequent visual stimulation, rapid change and little need for imagination. This technical process matches very well with the fast-oscillating ADHD brain. So, Romit's attention should be diverted from high technology to a musical instrument (may be keyboard) which he can control at will and which will produce sound as an outcome, releasing 'Dopamine (D)' molecules inside his brain.

The parents followed my advice and today, after five years, at the age of 9, Romit who has been practising music on a keyboard is moving towards almost zero-ADHD brain condition. His academic attainments are also much better than earlier.

Have you ever come across any case where digital technology has been used by parents as a calming device to quieten down an outraged kid?

Can Digital Technology be a Killer

Can digital technology be a 'Killer'? Yes, it can be; but unfortunately, very few of us are aware of it. Let me elaborate on this issue looking from a 'Body Engineering' angle. 'Body Engineering' is viewing the human body from the perspective of 'Engineering'.

Most mammals vocalise and make sounds using the body's 'Vocalising System', but the human 'Vocal Tract (VT)' is special for two reasons. One is that our brains are exceptionally skilled at rapidly and precisely controlling the movement of the tongue and other structures that modify the shape of the VT. Additionally, the distinctive short and retracted or withdrawn (as opposed to 'protruded' or 'extended') face of modern humans gives our VT a unique configuration with useful acoustic properties.

The VT in humans consists of two equally long tubes—one vertical and another horizontal. In modern humans, a short and withdrawn face causes the oral cavity to be short thus requiring the tongue to be short and rounded instead of long and flat as in the case of our pre-historic ancestors. Nevertheless, the uniquely configured VT of modern humans carries a substantial cost from the point of *Bioeconomics* (= economic aspects of biology).

In all other mammals including apes, the space behind the nose and the mouth (the 'pharynx') is divided into two separate tubes: an inner one for air and an outer one for food and water. In a dog or a chimpanzee, food and air take different pathways through the throat. But in humans, unlike any other mammal, the 'epiglottis' (a gutter-shaped flap of cartilage at the base of the tongue) is a few centimetres too low to contact the soft palate. By dropping the 'larynx' low in the neck, humans lost the tube within a tube and developed a big common space behind the tongue through which food and air both travel to get into either the 'oesophagus' (food pipe) or the 'trachea' (wind pipe). As a result, food sometimes get lodged in the back of the throat, blocking off the airway.

Humans are the only species that risks 'asphyxiation' when we swallow something too large or imprecisely. So, in this context, Smart leading parenting would mean avoiding the use of any digital device including TV while eating, drinking or even taking a capsule or a pill. This should be specially remembered by parents and caregivers while feeding a growing child who is calmed or where attention is diverted with the help of a smartphone or a tablet. The child can choke itself if you are careless.

So, having something to eat or drink or swallow and chatting with friends or using a digital device, you are engaged in twin tasks: speaking with great clarity, or viewing or reading something on the small screen with full concentration and swallowing a morsel of food or a few drops of water, beverage or a drink—a little dangerously, at a big risk to your own life.

Although your teenage kid might have faced choking problems from time to time, did you know that it could be so serious now in the digital era where the gadgets pull teenagers like magnets?

Digital Work and Dietary Brain Fat

You would not be required to travel as far as the Kalahari Desert in Africa. Just take a trip to the Andaman and Nicobar Islands in the Bay of Bengal to trace the tribal hunter-gatherers of modern times. An average male tribal hunter-gatherer weighs 51 kilograms (112 pounds), walks 15 kilometres a day (about 9 miles), and also has to climb trees, dig roots and tubers, carry food and perform other physical tasks on a daily basis. His total energy expenditure is about 2,600 Calories a day. Since 1,100 of those Calories sustain his body's basic needs (his basal metabolism), he spends 1,500 Calories a day being physically active, amounting to nearly 30 Calories per kg of body weight per day. His body is trim, devoid of subcutaneous fat which is the surplus body fat that gets deposited just under the skin in people owning a plump body.

In contrast, a typical post-industrial 'digital age' male, from the middle to affluent executive or business class, weighs about 30 percent more and works 50 percent less, expending just 12 Calories per kg per day on physical activity. In other words, a tribal hunter-gatherer works about 2.5 times as much per unit of body weight as an Indian well-to-do individual. This explains a lot about why cardio-respiratory disorders and diabetes mellitus are called "rich men's diseases" in the Indian health parlance. This is indicative that plenty of money, affluence, comfortable and luxurious living do not make one HAPPY. One main factor providing 'HAPPINESS' is 'Physical Well-Being (PWB)'.

The Calorie input-output profile that I have painted above with respect to a well-to-do Indian would be one where there is a strong possibility of accumulation of 'fat'. 'Fat' is a very interesting constituent of human biology. Firstly, the components of each molecule of fat can come from digesting fat-rich foods, but, at the same time, our bodies also synthesize fat just as easily from carbohydrates if you have a carb-rich diet. This is the reason why fat-free foods still make you fat if you are high on carb. Secondly, fat molecules are useful, highly concentrated reserves of energy. A single gram of fat stores 9 Calories, more than twice the energy per gram of carbohydrate or protein. After you eat each meal, hormones cause you to convert sugars, fatty acids and glycerol, obtained from the dietary input, into fat within special fat cells, of which you have 30 billion. Then, when your body needs energy, other hormones break down fat into its components, which your body can burn.

Humans, of all creatures, have a special need for lots of fat right from the moment of birth, largely because of our energy-hungry brain. An adult human's brain consumes between 280 and 420 Calories of energy per day, 20 to 30 percent of the body's basal metabolic budget, when you're not doing anything the whole day and night—just idling and resting. Since brains require sugar incessantly, having plenty of fat ensures our brains an unending, reliable supply of energy.

There are 'good fats' and 'bad fats'. The 'good fats' are the 'lipids' which are called 'fatty acids'. 'Essential Fatty Acids (EFAs)' that are good for your brain, include Omega-3 which is available from: cold water fish (herring, mackerel, salmon, sardine, rainbow trout, tuna, sword fish and white fish), sea fish (pomfret), olive and olive oil, flaxseed and flaxseed oil, peanuts—peanut butter and peanut oil.

Without lots of fat, human brains could not be so big. And 'lipids' or fat molecules are particularly important in the brain because they enable electrical signal transmission amongst 'neurons' or brain cells. The human neo-cortex or the forebrain has accumulated about three times more lipid changes than the same part of a chimpanzee brain has since we split ourselves from our common ancestor. As human cognition evolved, the types and amounts of fat in key brain areas were rapidly shifting and mutating—and this growth was crucial to the development of our complex abilities.

Due to evolutionary pressures, many of us are now too well adapted to craving and storing fat. Such people can consume a lot of fat-rich food and also have the capacity to store them in the body with a corresponding proportionate increase in their body weight to fall back on it whenever required under typical circumstances like lean season, flood, famine, fasting for a cause or to follow a religious ritual, serious illness when you lose your appetite etc.

Body's total energy budget is expressed in terms of 'Basal Metabolic Rate (BMR)'. A typical pre-historic hunter-gatherer weighing 60 kg would have a BMR of roughly 1,500 Calories a day. If a modern human has a smaller intestine as well as smaller teeth, that would mean that he has descended from the pre-historic hunter-gatherer stock who had high quality diet with lots of meat and lots of food processing after fire was invented and cooking came into practice. In such cases, a greater portion of the BMR will be allocated to the activities of the brain.

For a modern sedentary individual engaged in digital work, the total fat in the diet should not exceed 30 percent of the total calorie intake. Thus, for him, if the daily 'Total Energy Expenditure (TEE)' is 2,000 Calories, a SMART leader should ensure that his 'Daily Energy Production or Acquisition (DEP)' does not exceed 2,000 Calories, and the fat content of the DEP must not cross 600 Calories.

Do you realise that for a digitally engaged sedentary person, who does not have time available for physical fitness activities every day, a low-fat, vegetarian or, at the most, a fish-protein diet would be a wise choice for personal well-being?

For a modern forest-dwelling tribal, the 'Total Energy Expenditure (TEE)' ranges between 2,000 and 3,000 C. He is moderately active—lives by walking and sometimes running long distances, carrying children, digging for plants, roots and tubers, processing food and performing other daily chores without assistance from any machine or beasts of burden. For him, the 'Daily Energy Production or Acquisition' ('DEPs') are generally higher than the TEEs. Studies have shown it to be 3,500 C per day, resulting in a daily surplus of 500 to 1,500 C. For a chimp, TEE average is about 1,400 C a day. Why a vegetarian diet is preferred? It is preferred as the 'Cost of Procurement' is less and 'Return on Investment' ('ROI') is high for honey, tubers, nuts and berries.

Digital Technology and Disturbed Sleep

Many digital gadget users experience intermittent sleep disturbances or just plain, lousy sleep (and some, even insomnia). They don't realise the culprit may be the computer screen or smartphone. These displays emit blue spectrum light, which suppresses the brain's natural release of 'Melatonin (M)'—the sleep-inducing brain chemical. M is produced in and secreted by the unpaired 'Pineal Gland (PG)' inside our brain. With daylight appearing in dawn, the eyes of our ancestor hunter-gatherers would receive the signal to be carried through nerves to the PG which will shut down M production as one had to get ready for work activities. Again, at dusk, the signal of the setting sun and darkness approaching would reach the PG and M production would be switched on.

Industrial Revolution provided us with bright electric lights to extend the working hours, introduced in quick succession—the radio, gramophone, television, tape recorder, VCR and other electronic gadgets for entertainment. All these stimulated us well beyond an evolutionary normal bedtime hour. From limited operating hours, technology blessed us with 24 × 7 of TV and FM radio programmes. Subsequently, digital gadgets like laptops, tablets and smartphones came into use bringing bright light invading our biologically limitedly capable eyes at hours when our visual activities ought to be drowned in sleep. Many digitech users are short of sleep for extended periods of time making the body's hormonal system responding in several ways that used to be adaptive only during 'stress'. Sleep deprivation curtails the surge of growth hormones that are scheduled to be released during the phase of deep, sound, undisturbed, dreamless sleep [known as the 'Non-Rapid Eye Movements (NREM)' phase as opposed to the 'Rapid Eye Movements (REM)' phase representing light, disturbed dreamy sleep.] Instead, inadequate sleep induces the body to produce more of the stress hormone 'Cortisol (C)'. High C levels switch the body's metabolism from a state of growth and investment into a state of fight and flight by raising alertness and shuttling sugar into the bloodstream. Chronically high C levels depress immunity, interfere with growth, and increase the risk of type 2 diabetes.

Chronically insufficient sleep also promotes obesity in those who have such proneness. During normal sleep, the body is at rest, causing levels of one hormone 'Leptin' to rise, and another hormone 'Ghrelin' to fall. Leptin suppresses appetite and Ghrelin makes you hungry, so this cycle helps you avoid getting hunger pangs during sleep. However, when you consistently get too little sleep, your Leptin levels fall and Ghrelin levels rise, effectively signalling a state of acute appetite in the brain, regardless of whether your stomach is full, half-full or empty. Sleep-deprived people thus have more cravings, especially for carbohydrate-rich foods like biscuits, shortbreads, cookies, pastries and donuts.

There are several live case studies in my collection. I will talk about a recent one. Anik Roy is a graduate engineer preparing for the civil services exams. However, he is more interested in film studies. He was pushed into electrical engineering by his dad who rose up to the post of an electrician in a factory and wanted to realise his own unfulfilled dream through his only son. Anik puts his study materials away after dinner and watches films of all sorts on his smartphone till late at night. Since his Melatonin (M) balance gets disturbed due to the bright light from the small screen, he does not get sleep early when he retires. He leaves his bed, starts searching for jars containing biscuits and cookies and, once he finds some, eats the stuff up in plenty. Since he has a genetically thin and lean, skinny-bony constitution, the carbohydrates from the biscuits do not add any fat to his body; instead, makes him acutely constipated, sometimes leading to 'Irritable Bowels Syndrome (IBS)'. Unless pushed out of bed by his mom, he does not get up before forenoon.

What a Smart leading parent would do? He would retire from digital work at around 9 pm; have his dinner, stroll around a little inside the living space listening to slow, soft, instrumental music—may be a flute recital (a wind instrument like flute acts liking a sleeping pill); then lay down his body in the supine posture (that is, yogic sabasan) with his head placed on a pillow not thicker than 2 inches (5 cm), so that blood pressure and blood flow in the body and brain do not interfere with his falling into deep, sound sleep. Believe me or not, within 5 to 7 minutes, fairies will take his consciousness away into the land of un-interfered, non-REM sleep.

Digital Engagement and Brainpower (incl. Memory) Erosion

Obesity is linked to brain shrinkage, deficits in memory and power of imagination. Today, amongst city and metro-dwellers, one person may be obese because he is sedentary, digitally engaged, does not take any exercise and eats a lot of junk food. Another might be obese for genetic reasons but actually eats really well and does lots of exercise. Yet, there could be one more who is obese because he has insulin problem. These were the findings of Lucy Cheke and her colleagues at the Dept. of Psychology, University of Cambridge, UK who were trying to find out the links between obesity, memory loss and dementia. The Cambridge team suggested that obesity may contribute to the development of neurodegenerative conditions. The higher a person's 'Body Mass Index (BMI)'—the measure of your weight relative to your height, the worse would be your performance on memory tasks.

Obesity activates 'microglia', the brain's resident immune cells to strip 'synapses' (cell-to-cell connections) from the brain's long-term memory store—the 'hippocampus'. Most interestingly, attention and memory control our appetite and eating behaviour. If the attention and memory mechanisms of our brain are functioning properly, then we would remember when we had eaten, what all and how much we had eaten. And, if the reverse happens—there is a dysfunction in these systems, then it could lead to weight gain as you would not readily recall, consciously, your last eating experience.

That memory plays an important role in eating behaviour came from a 1998 study showing that patients with severe 'amnesia' (that is, 'loss of especially episodic memory') will readily eat multiple meals one after the other, because they could not remember that they had eaten just a little while ago.

When we are deciding how much to eat, we are not just basing those decisions on physiological signals about how much food there is in our stomach, but also on cognitive processes like memory, says experimental psychologist Eric Robinson of the University of Liverpool in UK. If (i) your memory is impaired; or (ii) you are deficient in remembering things; or, (iii) there may be nothing wrong with your memory but your attention is not on the eating activity but somewhere else, then you might overeat.

In a 2011 study Robinson made half of the study participants play Solitaire on a computer while eating their lunch. As expected, they had hazier memories of their luncheon episode and went on to eat significantly more biscuits later on than those who were simply eating their lunch and were not engaged in any such altogether different activity.

How would a Smart leading parent learn from these research investigations? He would make it a point to ensure his teenage kid does not engage in any digital activity (like watching the TV, working on the computer, or fiddling with the android phone) while eating a main meal or even having a snack.

I distinctly recall what me and my team members would indulge in after coming back to our room in the Mega Thermal Power Station guest house after conducting workshop session for the whole day. We will order plates of onion pakoras and tea and switch on the TV to listen to the newscasts. When the guest house serving staff brings the snacks, we will continue with our engagement with the digital device and go on eating the snacks without any attention on the eating activity. As a result, we will not feel that we need to control and stop; we will call the bearer again and order for a second round. When we had to stay for a whole week, we would return with heavier bodies.

Robinson and his colleagues have developed a smartphone app that makes people conscious of what they are eating—both quality and quantity-wise. The idea is to create vivid memories that will make the eaters less likely to eat during the day.

[*Reference:* Mo *Costandi*, "Obesity alters brain structure and function", *The Guardian*, International edition, 23 November, 2016, 18.30 GMT.]

CHAPTER 6

Digital Technology and Happiness

'Key' Points: *Digital Happiness Set Point; Too Much Digital Use Kills Happiness; A Theory of Digital Gratification; Digital Addiction—Is There a Chemical Cure; Balancing Physical and Biochemical Algorithms.*

Digital Happiness Set Point (DHSP)

Every one of us wants to be happy; we tend to avoid unhappiness. And, 'Happiness Set Point (HSP)' is the point at which most of us find ourselves, existing, on a regular basis; it is a genetic endowment, inherited from our parents and, to a certain extent, grandparents. HSP is the measure of 'Happiness' that we deserve, being guided by our nature, our natural propensities to be happy. It is the 'default' location on the spectrum of your 'Well-Being (WB)'.

Since, modern life is digitalised to a great extent, I am taking this opportunity to introduce the concept of 'Digital Happiness Set Point (DHSP)' which is the result of all the emotions you are feeling at a certain point, related to the use of your digital devices and digital experience.

There are three DHSP forces—forces that drive your thought patterns and ultimately determine how much digital happiness you will earn.

The first DHSP force is: JUDGMENT. We tend to categorise everything as good or bad, right or wrong. We do not realise that we ourselves create this good-bad, right-wrong divide. This constant state of judgment has helped us through our evolution to quickly detect threats so that we can remain in our 'Zones of Comfort and Convenience (ZCC)' and avoid our 'Zones of Discomfort and Inconvenience (ZDI)'. Evolutionary forces have wired our brains to focus on, to be more aware of the negatives than positives, that we are facing or experiencing at the present moment. (We do not foresee what would be the future negative consequences of what we consider positive, comfortable and convenient at present; we are near-sighted, not farsighted—a strategy adopted to satisfy our need for 'Survival and Replication').

In modern life, while having chilli chicken, we focus on the hardness of the chillies than the softness of the chicken pieces occupying the space in our mouth. In digital use, we focus on the most irritating ads (which can be skipped leaving a toxic taste) than the absorbing discourse on the YouTube channel. A Smart leader who has a high 'Digital Happiness Set Point (DHSP)' leads himself towards the main positive experience being indifferent to the trivial negative ones thus conserving cerebral energy. Facebook had conducted a research during the period June 2018 to June 2019 on multi-screeners (those who use more than one digital device at the same time) and according to Sandeep Bhusan, Director and Head of Global Marketing Solutions, Facebook India, across eleven markets in the country, more than one in every two people have been observed to use their phones during commercial breaks in the serials and shows while watching TV. [Reference: Times News Network, "Marketers need to look at human brain not as 1 organ but 2 organs", *Times of India*, Kolkata edition, 20th February 2020, p.16.] This is an example of Smart leading indeed!

The second DHSP force is: ATTACHMENT. When we judge something to be good, naturally we get attached to it. But many or too much of 'goods' could be 'bad' for us too, such as: nicotine, alcohol, too many cups of tea or coffee, pain killers, paracetamols, narcotics. We consider them as good because they give us transient pleasure. We tend to cling to such things as we want the pleasure to be permanent and not just temporary. Digital devices fall into this group of 'bad' goods which are habit forming and could be time-wasters in many cases. Smart leaders segregate digital use into two distinctly different categories: (i) work-related digital technology use; and (ii) non-work-related technology use—just to overcome loneliness and depression and satisfy social-emotional needs. Average Smart leaders develop the habit of using (i) and (ii) in 80-20 proportions (although the target of the Smartest leaders would be 100-0).

The third DHSP force is: RESISTANCE—the opposite of ATTACHMENT. It is the driving force to get away from bad. We resist change when it involves uncertainty, when there is a risk involved. We resist the idea that something bad can happen to us if we do not welcome change. Too much use of digital devices can lead to so many health problems; but most of us resist this idea and do not want to change our digital habit. [I have already dealt with this aspect while elucidating on the first DHSP force—JUDGMENT.]

I have found a positive way of increasing my DHSP. The trait most strongly associated with long-term increases in life satisfaction is, in fact, a persistent commitment to pursuing altruistic goals. That is, the more we focus on compassionate action, on helping others, the happier we seem to become in the long run. I implement this strategy in two ways with genuine compassionate feeling: I use the WhatsApp and the mobile messenger to wish a select few people (numbering around 60) in the morning and night and I do thank those and express gratitude who share important or interesting photos, messages, information and videos with me. I profusely thank those who send me floral and seasonal (for example, springtime) tributes as I love flowers and natural phenomena. Those who are ill or has some sudden illness in the family, I make it a point, not ritualistically, to enquire about the health and recovery status. Above all, I post informative articles on the Facebook, LinkedIn and Twitter which are read, commented upon and shared by many; so much so that if I stop such posts for a week or two, regular readers miss the experience and enquire what has gone wrong. Such digital activities enhance my self-esteem.

Too Much Digital Use Kills Happiness

Any addiction kills happiness. The American Society of Addiction Medicine (ASAM) recently released a new definition of addiction as a chronic brain disorder, officially proposing for the first time that addiction is not limited to substance use. All addictions, whether chemical or behavioural, share certain characteristics including salience, compulsive use (loss of control), mood modification and the alleviation of distress, tolerance and withdrawal, and continuation despite negative consequences.

Between 2010 and 2015—just in 5 years' time, worldwide internet use has increased by 1,000%. At the same time, the following terms related to digital technology use have been added to the mental health vocabulary, which many of us have not been familiar with although some of us may display some of those signs and symptoms.

NOMOPHOBIA: the fear of not being able to use your phone due to very low charge, lack of Internet connection and the like.

FOMO: 'Fear Of Missing Out' anything on social media. This might happen if you want to 'like', 'love', 'comment', 'post' or 'share' anything as soon as possible and do not want to miss doing it.

IGD: 'Internet Gaming Disorder'. IGD occurs when you are obsessed with online games and send requests to other social media users to join in the play, even if they are not interested.

IAD: 'Internet Addiction Disorder'. IAD is a terribly unhealthy condition when your daily schedule is all about spending waking hours in the virtual world.

FAD: 'Facebook Addiction Disorder'. This takes place when you are obsessed with posting pictures and you eagerly await posts from your friends on Facebook. One main reason of your such obsession is rating your pictures according to the response of your Facebook friends.

SELFITIS: The obsession to post 'Selfies' is a genuine mental disorder (representing 'narcissism'). This may happen if you click and post more than 5 selfies in a day. In this, you make different types of faces to display your different moods.

SMA: 'Social Media Addiction'. You might have this disorder if you constantly check updates on social media and thus are always 'online'. You use your phone even in the toilet.

PVS: 'Phantom Vibration Syndrome (PVS)' is a disorder in which a person feels a sense of vibration, even if his phone is not around him.

DP: 'Digital Pouting' is an escape route taken by a person who wants to avoid getting involved in a specific situation. These happens with many adolescents these days when their parents talk about their marks scored in an exam and, to avoid this, they plug their earphones or direct their eyes towards the digital screen.

These nine (9) disorders are not yet listed in the mental health professional's international standard handbook, the 'Diagnostic and Statistical Manual of Mental Disorder (DSM)' as yet. However, these are most prevalent among working males and females in the middle to high income groups and also in those who exhibit certain psychological traits like anxiety, neuroticism, impulsivity and loneliness. These are becoming visible in teenage kids too, who are in high schools, colleges and universities and un-employed youth who are frustrated for some reason.

A Theory of Digital Gratification

In the early 1970's Dr. Walter Mischel, a psychology professor at Columbia University and his research colleagues conducted a study on little kids which has earned him a place among the forerunners of modern psychological theorists. Mischel and his team took a group of 50 children (mean age: 4 yrs. 6 mths.) and offered them a choice between one small but immediate reward or two small rewards if they waited for a period of time. During this time, the researchers left the room for about 15 minutes and then returned. The reward was either a marshmallow (a confectionery made from sugar, water and gelatine coated with corn starch) or a pretzel stick (slightly sweet, chewy, dark sticks) depending on the child's preference.

In follow-up studies, the researchers found that the children who were able to wait longer for the preferred rewards tended to have better life outcomes, as measured by their SAT (Scholastic Assessment Test required to be taken for admission to under-graduate courses in the US), educational attainment, Body Mass Index (BMI) (body weight in kg divided by square of height in metres), and other life measures. So, it is a question of instant, immediate or short-term gratification versus delayed, deferred, long-term gratification.

Anticipation of a reward on reaching a goal starts producing the neurotransmitter 'Dopamine (D)' inside the brain. This enhances the motivation to take action to move towards the goal. When the goal is reached, there is another round of 'D' released inside the brain. 'D' is the motivational chemical for which an individual becomes hungry for maintaining emotional happiness and well-being.

In family, social and friend circles, a teenage kid gets his supply of 'D' from 5A: Attention (positive eye contact and sustained uninterrupted listening); Acceptance (being credible to others despite faults, shortcomings and deficiencies because of love or for some special unique strength absent in others); Appreciation (small things done for others being acknowledged); Affiliation (allowed to participate or to be included in a group instead of being prevented); and, Autonomy (getting enough independence rather than being controlled by others). Today's children are deprived of opportunities for 'D' generation via 5A due to the following environmental circumstances.

In the middle to high income class: academic pressure, rote learning, boring-poor-uninteresting teaching in school and in tutorials; lack of enough time spent by parents with them (whatever time is spent is filled with adverse criticism and mental punishment—parents may spend money but not emotionally rewarding quality time); being academically driven rather than motivationally inspired.

In the low income class, the demotivating factors are: aimlessness; future uncertainties; both parents engaged in the unorganised sector; one or both of them suffering from some chronic ailment or life-threatening disease due to poor lifestyles, addictions etc.

So, for today's kids, the 'D' hunger does not get satiated from the home or social environment which leads them to digital gratification.

A 2011 brain imaging study of a sample from the original Marshmallow study participants when they reached mid-life showed key differences between those with high delay times and those with low delay times in two areas: the Pre-Frontal Cortex (PFC) (more active in high delayers) and the ventral striatum (more active in low delayers) when they were trying to control their responses to alluring temptations.

PFC brain circuits take time to develop. A child has to wait until his late teens (post-high school, college level) for his PFC circuits for 'Impulse Control' to be generally ready. So, it is a primary responsibility for the child's parents and care-givers, teachers and tutors to train the child in impulse control by using some tailor-made special exercises and games. Competitive games that stimulate impulsive behaviour should be replaced by yogic exercises, pranayama and meditation.

Digital Addiction: Is there a Chemical Cure

Post-mortem brains are needed to study: causes, treatments and cures for Parkinson's and Alzheimer's diseases, mental illness, depression, Down's syndrome and many others including AIDS. There are also areas like stress, injury and post-traumatic stress disorder (PTSD).

Many researchers are also looking into the consequences of addiction to alcohol, drugs and other narcotic substances. Dr. Deborah Mash is in the forefront of those addiction researchers. She is a top neuroscientist holding, at the same time, a few important posts including the directorship of the University of Miami Brain Endowment Bank—one of only three general brain banks in the USA supplying preserved brains to brain researchers in different parts of the country.

According to Mash, addicts first indulged in chemical recreation during the 1960's and 1970's. Drug abuse studies in particular required brain tissue from the age 40–55 crowd. Digital recreation is much more recent as the explosion of consumer-oriented digital technology has started taking place from the tail end of the 20th and dawn of the 21st century. Neuro-imaging studies have indicated that the impact of 'Internet Addiction Disorder (IAD)' and other digitally addictive behaviour is same as addiction to alcohol and narcotics except for the externally induced chemical changes inside the brain.

Finding treatment and a cure for addiction has been one of Mash's main professional crusades and her research in this and other areas of neuroscience have been widely published and acclaimed. Mash's research has been centring around IBOGAINE ('I', in short) which has consciousness-altering properties. It is derived from the roots of a shrub native to equatorial Africa, where hunter-gatherers have long used it in small doses to remain alert while hunting, and in larger amounts during sacred rituals. Since the 1960's, addicts have found that using 'I' causes them to lose their craving for the drugs they were addicted to, and it is achieved without any withdrawal symptoms.

'I' is a psychoactive drug, but not a hallucinogen like LSD. How it works on the brain is most interesting (Mother Nature has so many unexplored wonders!!). It puts you into a 36-hour waking dream state (your brain's 'Default Mode Network—DMN' gets engaged in the dream, which is an 'altered state of consciousness'). During this brain state, you are prompted to relive your childhood experiences, get to the root cause of your addictive behaviour. That means, 'I' works on the long-term memory store—your brain's 'Hippocampus ('H')'. Amongst the root causes, a primary common one has been observed as emotional deprivation during childhood which affects the balance of your brain's happiness chemicals EDSOM [E: Endorphin—brain's own internally generated stress manager; D: Dopamine—anticipatory reward chemical; S: Serotonin—'feel good' mood management chemical; O: Oxytocin—love, bonding, trust and relationship-building chemical; M: Melatonin—restful sleep-inducing chemical].

In the African hunter-gatherer society, 'I' was used for clearing of the old unhappy memories to make way for a depression-free adulthood which would be an essential prerequisite for success in the hunter-gatherer role. It acted as a preventive to get rid of the childhood emotional baggage so that you do not end up in adulthood with emotional dysfunction that could lead to many unhealthy situations.

According to Mash, 'I' could be used to re-programme an addict's life. She had begun the human safety trials of 'I' in 1994 but the progress has not been fast due to funding problems. Hopefully, Mash and her team would be able to get over the funding hassles for their 'I' projects and would succeed in establishing the substance's efficacy for the cure of 'Internet Addiction Disorder (IAD)' and other digital technology addictions.

[*References:* 1. Nina L. Diamond, *Voices of Truth* (Chapter Twelve: Deborah Mash), New Delhi: Full Circle, 2001, pp. 362–414; 2. *Wikipedia*: 'Ibogaine'; 3. Scientific papers by Deborah Mash and colleagues published in the *Annals of the New York Academy of Sciences*.]

Wouldn't it be a god-sent thing if 'Ibogaine (I)' gets really established as an anti-addiction drug through proper clinical safety trials? If it happens then it would be most convenient for parents and care-givers to mix 'I' in powdered form with milk or a health drink and serve it to kids to prevent them from getting addicted to digital recreation.

Balancing Physical and Biochemical Algorithms

"In recent decades life scientists have demonstrated that emotions are not some mysterious spiritual phenomenon that is useful for writing poetry and composing symphonies. Rather, emotions are BIOCHEMICAL ALGORITHMS that are vital for the survival and reproduction of all mammals."

Yuval Noah Harari, *Homo Deux: A Brief History of Tomorrow*, 2018: New York: Harper Perennial, p. 83.

The digital age is dominated by ALGORITHMS—physical, electronic. It has little space for biochemical algorithms. 'Algorithm' is a methodical set of steps that can be used to make arithmetical calculations, make decisions, and solve problems. It follows a systematic method: Step 1, Step 2, Step 3 and so on. You can build a machine that embodies this algorithm and pursues it automatically. A very common example is a tea or a coffee vending machine. The purpose of the biochemical algorithms controlling humans is to work through sensations, emotions and thoughts.

Consider a problem. You are driving a car on a narrow yet busy street. It being the location of a popular polyclinic, cars are parked on one side, making it only one lane. Your speed was slow but suddenly when you applied your brakes, it didn't work. What may happen now? It boils down to a mathematical problem of calculating probabilities:

Probability 1: Your car will crash against the slow-moving car in front of yours.
Probability 2: You can apply the handbrake to make the car stop.

Probability 3: You lower the window pane and shout for help.

There could be a few more probabilities. However, to take a decision, you need to take into account a lot of data. How far are you from the car in front? What was the speed of your car when you applied the brakes? Is the handbrake in proper shape? What would be the reaction of the driver in the car ahead of yours? How many cars are behind yours? etc. etc. In order to weigh and balance all these variables and probabilities, you require far more complicated algorithms than the ones controlling automatic vending machines. And yours would be biochemical algorithms, not physical.

An anxiety-prone person whose biochemical algorithms over-estimate danger will 'freeze' in fear; and, his out-of-control car will hit against the car in front with a big bang and, in his frozen state, he would face the music coming from the front car driver. A rash person—one whose biochemical algorithms underestimate danger would start shouting and arguing with the driver whose car has been hit. A sane, happy person—whose biochemical algorithms behave in a balanced manner, will come out of his car and not only apologise to the front car driver but also offer to get his damage repaired. He will also admit his fault that he ought to have checked the brake oil level after he got his vehicle serviced just a couple of days ago.

Today, in the digital era, if you're too much digitalised, then your biochemical algorithms are not getting opportunity to be used much; so, the cells become dry not being bathed regularly by the neurochemical molecules, and the circuits get rusty. Smart leading entails balancing both algorithms: physical-electronic as well as biochemical consciously. Those who will overestimate dangers of digital habits will keep themselves away from enjoying the blessings of the digital era. And, those who will underestimate the dangers of digital habits, will become addicted and fall prey to physical and mental health problems. There was a news item in the *Times of India*, Kolkata edition of 20th January 2020, which read as 'Phone addiction makes students lonely, anxious'. The British (Swansea University) and Italian (Univ. of Milan) joint research study has found that students who use digital technology (smartphones, internet) excessively for social networking (40%) and information seeking (30%) are less motivated to engage with their studies, and are more anxious about tests. The effects may be worsened by increased feeling of loneliness due to poor face-to-face social interaction one-to-one, one-to-two and in groups which help to release happiness chemicals EDSOM (Endorphin, Dopamine, Serotonin. Oxytocin and Melatonin). Detailed discussions on the most critical biochemicals EDSOM are to follow soon.

Thus, don't you think that those who will strike a balance will get the cream of the digital era and shall not be a victim of overuse?

CHAPTER 7

Digitalised Teens

'Key' Points: *The Teen Brain; Brain Development in Kids; Smart Leading and Parenting of the Turbulent Teens; The Teen's Brain Biology Is Ancient; Digital Shelter for Confused Teens; The Role of Sex Hormones in Teenage; Identification of the Sex Hormonal Mix in the Teenage Kid's Personality; Teenage Sleep in Digital Age.*

The Teen Brain

Teenagers do not think with the same part of the brain as adults. There is not much of a difference between the number of nerve cells ('neurons') that a kid's brain approaching teenage and an adult brain has. The difference is in the neural network—the neuron-to-neuron connections which start developing as the teenage kid gets exposed to different circumstances. A village girl or boy, thus, has the same number of neurons as her or his metro counterpart, but the difference is in the connectivity between the neurons. The metro kids' brains are more neuro-webbed compared to those of the rural and semi-urban kids.

Brain Development in Kids

Connections in children's brains develop from the back to the front; and those brain sectors important for higher-order thinking (that is, logical-imaginative and not irrational-impulsive) continue to form and strengthen as they grow into their twenties. Inside the mother's womb, the first sensory power to develop is auditory and a growing child including teenagers have good connectivity up their ears. They are very sensitive to sound including the tonal quality of other persons' voices. Most of them get addicted to digitalised music; you will find them lying down, sitting, standing, walking, jogging or working out with earphones plugged in. This auditory sensitivity has a crucial midbrain (= the paleo-mammalian portion) link which is driven by the 'Biological Imperatives (survival and replication)' innate in the nature of all living creatures. Teenagers are emotionally hyperactive for this basic reason which is evident from their sexual sensitivity and instinctive emphasis on learning and memory building in relationship with the environment—particularly social.

As teens transition into adulthood, connections in the front portions of their brains (frontal lobes of the forebrain or neo-mammalian neo-cortex) are strengthened, while those in other regions (which were essential for earning the care of parents and other elders during growth and development) are pruned. A fully developed frontal lobe is essential for planning, decision-making, problem-solving, impulse control and risk avoidance.

Today's teenagers, in every income segment of our society, are under 'stress'. Let me share three examples. One teenage girl and a teenage boy in a multi-crore income business family are so much stressful that they do not have even eye contact with their parents; both are addicted to smartphones. One teenage boy from a middle-income family with both parents working has no smartphone but most strangely, suffering from emotional deprivation for 12 hours (from 9 am to 9 pm) does not jump on his parents' bodies for a hug or a kiss when they come back dead tired, instead grabs his dad's smartphone and locks himself up in the toilet with the gadget in hand. A teenage boy from a humdrum farmer's family came to Kolkata to spend a vacation ran back to his village not because he missed his parents, grandma, sister or local peers, but he was missing his smartphone which had been left in his local mobile shop for repairs. Stressed adolescents lose the 'plasticity' of their brains—their ability to prune, form and strengthen the cell-to-cell connections in every nook and corner of the living tissue. This makes those adolescents especially susceptible to addiction to everything. In today's Indian families having different ranges of income, the addictive substances include tobacco, alcohol, narcotics, dendrite (very common with rag-picking kids on railway platforms) and, on top of all, smartphones.

Smart Leading and Parenting of the Turbulent Teens

Smart leading and parenting would mean giving teens a 'Frontal Lobe Assist (FLA)' by helping them to plan, prepare and even rehearse for situations that require higher judgment. Whenever and wherever feasible, the teenagers should be involved in some technical or creative projects—alone, or in pairs or groups. The domain may be music, dance, drama, creative writing, painting, art and craft work, sculpture, modelling, gardening and so on. Smart leading parents who would pick up the basics of brain development from this piece as well as from other sources and know their kids best would be better placed to choose the project domain for the teenagers. The goal: to allow the kids to use digital devices to the extent that those help in their studies and cognitive development and not to get addicted to those electronic appliances. I came to know of a case recently where a teenage boy studying in 2nd year college got addicted to his smartphone after he was refused dating by three pretty girls within three months of his joining college. What a root cause for getting addicted digitally?

My recent experiences also included the following:

One mom thinks: "My sober-natured son had, all of a sudden, started appearing unfamiliar from the tenth grade in school–tonal quality changing, body hair appearing. He has just cleared his board exam to get to the eleventh and currently his behaviour is so unpredictable—happy and jovial at times, pensive and depressed at some other times, and occasionally he has strange stormy outbursts."

One dad thinks: "My sweet little daughter is suddenly getting transformed into a lady—physically morphing into hitherto unseen and unknown local profiles. She has promoted herself from school tops and skirts to her college dress—kurta-salwar suit. She changes her dress, fittings, fixtures and accessories often to appear more attractive to her male peers."

This mom and that dad are not SMART leading parents; because a SMART leading parent knows that such changes are not only external—the internal, invisible changes are eternal following our creator Mother Nature's biological laws. The boy and the girl are growing whole hog to establish their independent identities totally separate from their parents—getting FIRMLY ESTABLISHED (which I call 'GROUNDED') as full-fledged biological devices—who have the ability to 'reproduce'.

In the Yogic 'Chakra System', the 'Muladhar' (the 'Root' Chakra) at the base of the coccyx is reaching the end of the process of maturation along with the next higher chakra—the 'Swadhisthan' (the 'Sacral').

The Teen's Brain Biology is Ancient

Your teenage kid's brain biology is ancient. If you think it has changed in modern times, you are grossly mistaken. The innate skills, intelligences and talents show up during the teens to make oneself acceptable to be included as a 'key' member of the tribal team. Teens reflect the ancient hunter-gatherer biopsychology. Thanks to the genes he has inherited, the kid is adapted to a varying extent for certain activities, food, climatic conditions and other aspects of his environment but not to all. An uncle of mine whose ancestors never left the terrains of Bengal was posted in Shimla, Himachal Pradesh. His daughter and son, my cousins, who were born and brought up there had perennial skin problems as their skin could not adapt to Shimla's freezing cold.

So, if your teenage son cannot do without his smartphone, his brain is getting adapted to the digital technology; but at what cost—at the cost of his brain function. Mismatches are caused by stimuli that are too much, too little or too new. If you tell him that the listening to music so closely using earphones will interfere with his auditory physiology and natural brain function and may create disruptions in his power of concentration affecting his working memory, the teenage lad will either argue or avoid and the distance between you and him will grow instead of being bridged. In order to develop bonding (with a good release of the bonding hormone Oxytocin) between you two, you have to request him to lend his smartphone with the earphones to listen to the music that he was listening. You listen to his preferred music for a little while, appreciate his taste (ensure that you do not criticise which would stimulate his reactive 'adrenal glands'), request him for one or two more of his favourites, listen also to those when he puts those on—appreciate those; and now tell him not to use the gadget continuously so that he allows his ears and auditory cortex to get some rest. You may quote some latest research on this to him. This kind of SMART leading approach, being soft and tactful, may lead to some better response. Teenage brain is a work-in-progress and, therefore, the normal direct handling would not click.

Digital Shelter for Confused Teens

So much confused are the teenage kids generally that quite often they are preoccupied with 'Self'-related trains of thoughts. But, in such ponderings, so tiresome it is for them to remain grooved into their brain's 'Default Mode Network (DMN)' (= the idle brain's devil's workshop—when the brain is idle, the DMN becomes auto-active bringing 'Self'-related past and future thoughts, mostly useless and unproductive) that they tend to take shelter in the digital world: playing games, watching movies, listening to music, and the like. During the turbulent teenage, kids from all parts of the world and all cultures become grossly disorganised with their thoughts as well as physical belongings and personal things being scattered here and there. A semi-urban, urban or metro kid attending senior school or college is seen amidst piles of books, copy books, loose plain or ruled sheets, handwritten or typed notes on the desk, dumped clothes on the clothes rack or on the chairs—his body reclining most casually on the laundry pile with both ears plugged with earphones.

The Role of Sex Hormones in Teenage

'Testosterone (T)' is the male sex hormone and 'Oestrogen' and 'Progesterone' '(O-P)' are its female counterparts. The teenage brain experiences the turbulence of these hormones for the first time. The incomparable yet inexperienced biological equipment housed within the cup of the skull bones has not yet figured out how to modulate the body's response to this new influx and surge of powerful chemo molecules. These sex hormones trigger physical changes in adolescents such as deepening of the voice and the growth of facial and body hair in boys and the development of breasts and beginning of periods in girls.

In boys, 'T' finds friendly receptors in the 'amygdala'—the part of the paleo-mammalian brain that controls the fight-or-flight response. In girls, both 'O' and 'P' are linked to chemicals in the brain that control mood and temperament.

Sex hormones are produced by the gonads associated with the 'Swadhisthan (Sacral)' chakra of Yogic Sciences. They have 'creative' properties and are particularly active in the 'Limbic System (LS)' which is the emotional centre of the brain. That explains, partially though, why adolescents not only are emotionally volatile but may even seek out emotionally charged experiences in the western world during 'dating' where, in the conservative (not so ultra-modern) Indian society, smartphones have a big role to play in fulfilling such primitive physical needs through its versatile applications. Brain is highly flexible in teens and is the work-in-progress. It is about 80 percent of the way to maturity. So, it is full of possibilities with an increased capacity for remarkable innovative accomplishments. It is a Smart Leadership challenge for the parents to channelize that large volume of raw energy into the right kind of streams.

Identification of the Sex Hormonal Mix in the Teenage Kid's Personality

Irrespective of the gender, each teenager has both the male and female sex hormones present in the kid's biology. A Smart leading parent endeavours to find out the proportions of testosterone 'T' and 'O-P' in the teenage child. T's characteristics include: generally, goal-directed-hard-working nature, tactless approach, assertiveness, competitiveness, risk-taking tendency, restlessness, carelessness, aggression, physical strength and action orientation. O and P's characteristics are: cool temperament, patient and attentive listening power, caring and organised nature, slow to medium pace of working, loving-kindness, empathy and compassion, participative behaviour, persuasiveness, carefulness, consciousness about wastage and loss prevention, frugality.

Once you know your kid's personality profile, you are in a better position to monitor his digital habits. You must be wondering: how to figure it out whether your teenage kid has the right proportions of 'T' and 'O-P' as per his gender. Follow the teenager's oral communication! A 'T'-strong child will say: "I want one more piece of the fruitcake" (it is the MALE EGO expression with a commanding tone). In the same context, an 'O-P'-strong child would say: "May I have one more piece of the fruitcake please?" (It is the FEMALE POLITE expression with a requesting tone). And, this will be irrespective of the child's gender—whether it is a teenage boy or a girl.

Could you ever imagine that you could make a rough assessment of your teenage kid's sex hormone dominance from the way she/he speaks? [This is what 'Neuro-management (NM)' opts to find out for you].

Teenage Sleep in Digital Age

You just cannot get digital age teenagers to follow the 'early to bed, early to rise' golden rule of Benjamin Franklin. You simply cannot make them go to bed at a decent hour every night and get out of bed in the early hours of the morning. I regularly get such complaints from working mothers who visit my 'Winning Child' clinic for parenting-related problem-solving.

Why such irregular sleeping habit is a daily companion of almost every teenager barring rare exceptions? I could ultimately clear the mist. Sleep patterns, called 'chronotypes' vary from one stage of life to another. Infants and children are 'larks'; that is, they wake up early and go to sleep early. Adolescents are 'owls', waking late and sleeping late. If teenagers are forced to follow the adult 'chronotype', they may wake up early as otherwise they will miss their high school or college. But, unfortunately, the gap does not get filled by an early bed time; the teen brain does not adjust at the other end of the day. Thus, most teenagers suffer from a 'sleep debt' due to the shrunken sleep period. And, for many teenagers, weekends are no exceptions as they have to go for their early morning tutorials or, some—for cricket coaching, tennis practice, gym, or music, dancing or martial art lessons. The outcome—a chronic sleep deprivation syndrome with manifestations such as: irritating and aggressive behaviour, weak memory power, poor concentration, lack of appetite, constipation, sluggish stomach, irritable bowels syndrome, skin problems and the like.

Adolescence is the rapid learning phase as the teenager is being made ready to face the realities and to survive and grow in the ever-changing world full of hidden opportunities and covert threats. For consolidation of daily learning and both short- and long-term memory development the optimum sleep requirement in teen age is nine and a half hours daily, latest research says.

A fact, apparently veiled from common knowledge, is that beginning and after 10 to 12, young people's biological clock shifts forward making them more active by about 7 and 8 pm in the evening and creating a 'no sleep' zone at 10 to 12 pm, just when their parents are starting to feel drowsy. One reason is that 'Melatonin (M)'—the sleep hormone secreted from the brain's pineal gland is released 2 (two) hours later at night in a teenager's brain than it is in an adult. That makes most teenagers stay awake past midnight when their activities cannot be monitored by their parents who are deeply asleep under the influence of 'M'. This is an excellent opportunity for digital engagement freely without any interference from anybody.

How a Smart leading parent would take advantage of a teenager's 'no sleep' zone at night? Allow the kid to have his digital foraging in the late evening between 8 and 10 pm without any peeping in or helicoptering, so that enough of the brain's reward chemical 'Dopamine (D)' is released inside his brain satiating the 'D'-hunger. As a result of such 'D'-balancing, the 'no sleep' zone: 10 to 12 pm can be effectively utilised for solid academic work. I have used this technique for such a 'time management reversal' most successfully in the case of a Standard XI girl student whose academic performance was deteriorating day by day because of her intense useless digital engagement from 10 pm well into the wee hours of the morning. After the reversal was stabilised, her physical and mental health as well as academic performance vastly improved. Of course, the girl had a first-class brain; otherwise the improvement would not have been so vast and fast.

CHAPTER 8

Getting 'Grounded': Smart Leading and Parenting of Digital Age Teens

'Key' Points: *Excessive Dopamine-hungry Teenage Brains; The Science of Addiction; A Teenager's Brain State: Hard to Study; Teen and Tridosha; Teen and Triguna; Smart Leading and Parenting Application; Teenage Myopia; Digital Responsibility; Set An Example; Raising Balanced Teenagers in the Digital Age; Digital Engagement vis-a-vis Teenage Emotional Processes; Nature and Nurture in Teenagers; Taming of Teenage Turbulence; Grounded: Is Teenage Still the Trigger in the Digital Era; The DDD – 3D Approach for Smart Leading and Parenting of Digital Age Teens to Get Grounded.*

Excessive Dopamine-hungry Teenage Brains

Teen brains are EDSO-hungry (Endorphin for stress reduction, Dopamine for reward anticipation, Serotonin for mood management and Oxytocin for bonded relationship-building). Reason: teenagers crossing the teen threshold into youth are keen to ensure their preparedness for fulfilment of the 'Biological Imperative (BI)'—survival and replication. It is for this purpose only that they have been delivered from their mothers' wombs; that is the social belief. Here, I will talk about the excessive 'Dopamine (D)'—hunger found in the bulk of the teenage population.

'Neurons' (or, brain cells), in general, are much more restless and active in teen brains compared to adult brains. They fire at much higher rates, making them ready to learn and develop. Amongst the things to be learnt, before the dawn of civilisation and origin of language and education, were negative activities like seducing the opposite sex, bullying weaker members of the tribe, and 'addictive behaviour'.

The Science of Addiction

What is the 'Science of Addiction'? 'Addiction' is really a specialised form of memory of 'pleasure' except that the activity is not in the big memory storage 'Hippocampus (H)' located in the 'Limbic System (LS)' of the Paleo-mammalian mid-brain, but in the 'Nucleus Accumbens (NA)' and the 'Ventral Tegmental Area (VTA)'—which are the key territories for the brain's 'Reward Circuit'. Any pleasurable stimulus strongly activates these synapses. These respond by strengthening their connections which causes more 'Dopamine (D)' to be released in response to each stimulating trigger.

Although 'addictive behaviour' had been a major problem in the western world for long, the waves have started reaching the Indian shores in the case of the new gen kids in the educated middle and upper middleclass societies. I know of a college girl who had been smoking pot since she was in Standard XI to drown her frustration as she cannot simplify identify with her dad. Another college boy that I know had tried out nicotine (smoking and chewing both), alcohol, marijuana and similar addictive substances and had finally got stuck to nicotine which provides solace from his stress. I will run out of counts as so many addicted teenagers I know of. And, while writing I got the same story of widespread addictive behaviour in teenage kids and youth from a clinical psychologist student of mine who is in daily touch with such population.

If you include 'Digital Addiction' in the list, it is rampant in every home now. I came across the 'Calcutta Times' supplement of *Times of India*, 12th March 2020 edition, which carried a fleshy report titled "Always staring at your phone? It could be screen time overload" (pages 1 and 4). The activities of NA and VTA can be controlled, as I had told you earlier by the frontal lobes of your brain—if you are an adult, but if you have a teen brain the neural circuits in the frontal lobes are still under construction.

A Teenager's Brain State: Hard to Study

How harmful a common addictive substance tobacco could be for the brain (it causes cancer, emphysema and COPD is common knowledge)? Nicotine exposure during the teens damage the pathways producing 'Serotonin (S)' and 'S'-deficiency is one of the leading mechanisms of depression as any neuro-psychiatrist that you know will tell you. That may explain why depression is more frequent in people who had been heavy smokers as teens. Signs of depression are hard enough, for instance, to detect in teenagers you are around with all the time. With digital devices being their constant companions, normal teens today seem withdrawn compared with teens twenty years ago, making it much harder to distinguish between a shy, introverted teenager and a seriously depressed one.

Finally, I would say that the human brain is priceless—it is equipped with so many tools and techniques for survival, replication and socialisation. The 'Anterior Cingulate Gyrus' in the human brain's 'Anterior Cingulate Cortex (ACC)' is the human brain's 'Error Detection Circuit (EDC)' which makes an adult brain normally conscious if we have made a mistake. This fault-finding tool is still being hardwired in the teenage brain so adolescents face difficulty in learning from their mistakes even though they are made aware by their parents and elders.

Teen and Tridosha

Teenage is the age of turbulence, as I have already discussed. It is a time when mood swings and behavioural ups-and-downs are a regular affair, and also, most unpredictable. In terms of the ancient Indian system of medicine, 'Ayurveda', teen is the time when 'Vayu' or 'Vata' amongst the three bodily substances (i.e., 'Tridosha') is most active in the biology. The three bodily substances ('Tridosha'), which must remain in balance to produce sound physical as well as mental health, are: 'Vayu/ Vata' (representing 'Air'), 'Pitta' (representing 'Fire'), and 'Kapha' (representing 'Water'). During teenage, the 'Tridosha' loses its balance.

Signs of 'Vata' imbalance include: psychological: dry and lightness of the mind (not serious about anything)—restless thoughts, feeling ungrounded (lack of any burning passion and life's aim—goal ambiguity—not clear about the direction to move forward—confused), anxiety; physical: poor circulation, muscle twitching-spasm or constriction, pains and aches, roughness of skin and lips, respiratory problem; body language: fidgeting, restless body, excessive movement.

Teen and Triguna

Let me bring in another Vedic concept, which is relevant in Yogic philosophy—the 'Triguna' theory (the theory of three qualities), where the 'Triguna' are 'Sattva' (purity and simplicity), 'Rajas' (energy and activity), and 'Tamas' (darkness and impurity). Teenage is typically a combination of 'Rajasik' and 'Tamasik' propensities. These two become predominant in the nature (that is, 'Prakriti') of the teenager—the 'Rajas' driving the kid towards 'Tamas'.

Smart Leading and Parenting Application

In the dynamic digital era, it is thus more important for parents, guardians, and teachers to be aware of the emotional needs of the adolescents, especially in times of crisis and stress, when their vulnerability to mental health problems is at its highest.

There are two rules of thumb—care-givers and elders should remember. Number one: behavioural changes that seem to cluster or are associated with other symptoms should raise your level of suspicion that you might be dealing with something more than just a difficult phase that the teenager is going through. And, number two: it is better to be safe before than sorry after. If you identify any radical changes (than otherwise normal for that age) are happening to your kid, then you must take the right steps to visit and consult a specialist yourself with the case written down systematically (point by point) as the child may not be willing to face a neuro-psychiatrist because to him, the symptoms are nothing unnatural. 'Real' mental health problem must be diagnosed at the right time before it reaches a stage when it cannot be managed.

Just to share a very critical case that I handled long ago was that of a teenage boy who used to imagine that he had an inborn musical talent although in reality he did not. When this 'imagined feeling-reality' mismatch (= 'delusion') crossed the normal threshold to be regarded as abnormality, the case was referred to me and when I could smell the possibility of 'schizophrenia',

I asked the boy's dad to consult a reputed psychiatrist and the psychiatrist confirmed my suspicion.

There are two general characterization of adolescent behaviour that can help in making the distinction between 'normal for this age' and 'abnormal for this age'. There may, however, be an intermediate state which I call 'subnormal'. 'Subnormal' is the warning signal, it is the 'lull before the storm'. These are: severity of mood; and, change in function. Any exaggeration or deepening of a teenager's mood swings or a predominance of one mood over another—especially anger, sadness, or irritability, and especially if it lasts longer than two weeks—is a sign of possible psychiatric problems.

Changes in eating and sleeping habits, a tendency to act out more than usual, taking more risks, and spending less time with friends and families are also warning signs. So are sudden 'avoidance' or 'away' signs—such as not accompanying parents to a social get-together or a religious or cultural gathering which the kid used to look forward to until just a few weeks ago and an abrupt conspicuous absence from extra-curricular activities (not because of academic or any other work pressure which requires him to be busy at home).

Teenage Myopia

In the old days, people with poor distance vision probably were less able to hunt animals or gather food effectively, and they were less capable of spotting predators, snakes, and other perils. Individuals with genes that contributed to 'myopia' probably died younger and had fewer kids. The development of the first eyeglasses took place in Northern Italy in the second half of the 13th century.

Near-sightedness is a complex trait caused by many interactions among a large number of genes and multiple environmental factors. However, since people's genes have not changed much in the last few centuries, the recent worldwide epidemic of 'myopia' would have resulted primarily from environmental changes. Of all the factors identified, the most commonly tracked culprit is 'Close Work': intent focusing for long periods of time on nearby images such as words, pictures or diagrams on a page or a screen.

Some studies have found that teenagers who spend less time outdoors and more time on digital screens are most likely to get 'myopia'. Additional factors identified include diets rich in starch and early adolescent growth spurts.

Experts recommend turning off the bright LED light on the computer screen about an hour before bedtime to relax the over stimulated eyes and the brain. A research study in a reputed institute in New York found that just a 2-hour exposure to self-luminous backlit displays of smartphones, computers and other LED devices suppressed 'Melatonin (M)' by about 22 percent. Stimulating the human natural sleep-wakefulness rhythm like this before bedtime could definitely affect sleep and distant vision—especially in teenagers!

Now, if you are a parent, try to impose the 'LED Lights Off' rule on your teenage child and you will face the music as Sekhar Gupta, General Manager of a public sector undertaking faced before he approached me for help. The Guptas have a single child—a teenage daughter Ruchika. She was studying, then, in Standard XII in a reputed Kolkata English medium school. But her digital engagement would start after dinner from 10 pm and continue well into 2.30/3.00 am. The engagement comprised mostly of exchanging text messages with some of her best school friends. Time for selection test was drawing close and she was too addicted to reduce the long time spent on that habit. Her parents fell victims of 'Learned Helplessness (LH)'.

[Note: 'Learned Helplessness' (LH) is a state that occurs after a person has experienced a stressful situation repeatedly. He comes to believe that he is unable to control or change the situation, so he does not try even when opportunities for change become available. The LH concept was developed by well-known psychologist Martin Seligman and his colleagues at the University of Pennsylvania in the late 1960s, as an extension to their work on depression.]

A SMART leading parent does not fall a victim of LH. Sekhar and his wife were given some Smart parenting tips by me which they gainfully implemented and got the results. When Ruchika came back home from her socialising activities, her mother Joyeeta will serve her a snack with a health drink and would sit with her in the lounge (instead of watching the TV as that would have alienated the daughter from her mother—the TV will be switched off so that they could interact). Joyeeta will begin by sharing with Ruchika something interesting that had happened that day in her office (she is a working mother). Ruchika will also open up with her friends' stories and this will continue for 10 to 15 minutes.

Once both of them had EDSO (Endorphin-Dopamine-Serotonin-Oxytocin) balance and beta-positive wave brain state, Joyeeta will propose a 'TO DO' list to plan ahead the activities for the evening. The list will make sure to complete all digitech-based activities by 9/9.30 pm. They would finish their dinner by 10 pm and then Sekhar took out Ruchika for a stroll in the nearby park; walk 3 to 4 rounds, and be back by 10.30 pm. For one solid hour, Ruchika would do some writing work like answering question papers, or preparing special notes on some critical topic, and so on. Writing would keep her brain focused and attentive. For such study-related work, she would use her desk and use the bed only for sleeping. She should wind up positively by 11.30 pm every night to wake up by 7.30 am in the morning. Her school timing was from 11.30 am to 4.30 pm from Monday till Friday. On Saturdays, the school closed at 1.30 pm after only 2 periods of classes.

Both the parents seriously pursued this Smart parenting practice for a month and good results were forthcoming. But they continued this family culture, did not break it as otherwise everything would have gone back to old square one.

Digital Responsibility

It is our responsibility to use modern technology in a way that:

1. we become attached with detachment—which means we become dependent on it but do not get panicked when it is not available [our 'Zone of Comfort and Convenience (ZCC)' must be plastic like the plasticity of our brain—it must have the flexibility for expansion or outstretching—must not be rigid];
2. we are aware of the impact that it has on our health, environment and society at large;

3. we do not become 100 percent habituated to it so that we lose our natural powers [one example is 'handwriting'—writing with your right hand stimulates the language-related circuits in your left brain; so, giving up writing with hand and getting habituated to digital typing instead may have some adverse impact on the brainpower, which needs to be investigated, of course!].

Set an Example

Set an example for your growing kid by adopting the following 'Smart leading and parenting' practices:

- Examine your 'motivations' for using digital technology. Try cutting down on the number of posts or status updates you make each day. Ask yourself whether you are posting for 'narcissistic' reasons or with a meaningful purpose.
- Take breaks, both large and small. A technical break can be as small as stepping away from your desk to take a short walk across the room or as large as declaring a technology blackout for an entire day each week.
- Devote some time in improving the places where you spend so much of your day. Reorganising your desk space, your books and other documents, stickers, framed photos, paintings, souvenirs, trophies, decorative pieces, flower vases, plant pots and so on.
- Use your dining space for having your meals. Keep yourself away from all digital devices while dining. You can have some slow, soft, instrumental music on the background. Try to refrain from talking while eating. Speak only if absolutely necessary.
- Allocate some time (for yourself during weekly off-days and for your kids every day) to get engaged in some creative activities such as sketching, drawing, painting, craftwork, sewing, embroidery, reading poetry, creative writing, listening to music, even socialising (for those who like it) which have shown to preserve and also, to an extent, improve cognitive abilities.
- Set aside the digital gadgets for a few hours every day. Keeping yourself away from such devices and consciously contem-

plating on your future priorities will go a long way towards improving the quality of your life.

- Create both 'digital' and 'non-digital' TO DO lists—the alternate tasks of planning your work schedule in such a way that after being 'on-line' to complete a 'digital' work for an hour, close shop and get up to do some 'non-digital' work.
- Turn off the lights—all of them. To avoid disrupting your sleep rhythms, turn off all your screens an hour two before you go to bed and give yours eyes a rest.
- All of us are aware that calling up someone or receiving a call on the smartphone while driving is dangerous as we can easily understand the direct nature of the hazard. But there is an indirect hazard, a hidden risk is involved if you're using the smartphone while riding in a car, a cab, an auto or a public transport. It is desirable to keep your mobile in the silent mode while travelling as well as in public places where mobile use is forbidden.

I insist that you, as a parent, follow these and other prohibiting rules strictly. Then there would be a strong possibility that your kids would follow suit as growing children tend to use their brain's active mirror neurons which work by copying the elders particularly the elders and other care-givers. If you do not follow them but only prompt them to do, your tips will be left uncopied as today's digitalised youngsters do not copy those who only preach but do not practice.

Raising Balanced Teenagers in the Digital Age

For taking good care of infants, toddlers, pre- and primary schoolers, practical tips from your experienced mothers and grandmothers are good enough. To get a glimpse of the theories at the back of those practical tips, you can—if you wish, glance through the pages of my best-selling book, *The Making of A Winning Child* (New Delhi: Allied Publishers, 2012) or, if there is a critical problem, contact me freely.

But raising of balanced teenagers in the digital age poses tough hurdles. Because, as I have said earlier, the teenage brain, being a work-in-progress, is in a state of constant flux. Lot of the old circuitry which had served well from infancy up to the Standard VII/VIII in school are being pruned to be replaced by new neural webs as biologically the teens constitute a period of turbulence. During the teens, the kid's brain gets engaged, most often in the 'Default Mode Network (DMN)' when thoughts revolve around the 'Self' in the bygone past and the forthcoming future scenarios, ignoring the present. And, a today's teenager takes shelter in digital engagement to avoid the stressful experience of the DMN which flashes mostly negative pictures on the mind's screen making the child hopeless, pessimistic and cynical—frustrated for no reason whatsoever killing his dormant potentials.

I am sharing some proven tips for balanced teenage parenting which have worked well for other digital age parents who have been consulting me from time to time.

First of all, develop an effective 'bonding' [based on the love and trust molecule 'Oxytocin (O)'] with your teenage child by finding out certain 'likes' and 'dislikes' that you have in common with her/him. [Do not ever enter into the realm of 'likes' and 'dislikes' that are not common between the two of you as it may lead to conflict.]

Then, sit with the child (when he volunteers—'volition' is the 'key' not 'compulsion') to prepare a general 'To Do' list for the child, to include activities such as:

- Taking care of the younger siblings, grandparents and parents (including doctors, medicine etc.); taking initiative in household work for the whole family; going to the local market occasionally on weekly off-days and holidays; getting provisions from nearby shops, keeping track of datelines for all payments (monthly, quarterly, half-yearly, yearly) for example: electricity, internet, cable TV, tuitions, school/ college, mobile, domestic help, cricket/tennis coaching, music/ dance class, social club, gym, income tax, municipal tax, car registration, car insurance, life/health insurance etc.; taking full responsibility for organising personal clothes and other belongings, educational and study materials and stationeries; spending time on digital engagement (for educational activity, personal development and entertainment purposes—decide on the specific time limits mutually);

spending time for physical fitness activities (exercise, sports, games); breathing exercise and meditation; time for socialisation in family and with friends; time for 8-1/2 to 9 hours sleep; etc.

- Preparing 'To Do' list every night for the next day, right from the 'Waking Up' to the 'Going to Bed' time to include: self-study, institutional study, study under tutelage.
- Occasionally, may be once in 3 (three) months doing a 'Time Audit' to identify 'Time Wasters' (for which the kid her/him-self is responsible and thus can be curtailed), 'Time Killers' (where another person—may be an emotionally dependent friend who is responsible for killing the kid's time), and 'Time Stealers' (which normally cannot be avoided) such as being caught up in a traffic jam or getting an attack of flu or diarrhoea—such events steal your time and are generally uncontrollable. As you're aware, digitech over-using teenager's physical and mental health are both most vulnerable making them more prone to trivial health problems; so balanced digital use with planned balanced diet, planned physical fitness activities and planned sound sleep will eradicate this specific type of 'Time Stealer' problem.

Now, this kind of 'Effective Time Management (ETM)' culture will be sustained if, along with your teenage kid, you also prepare a list of your responsibilities as a parent (in the 'To Do' form)—in general and also daily and do a quarterly 'Time Audit' with him so that the kid realises that it is not just an one-sided game, it is a participative activity. One-sided parental activities will not work out with a teenage kid in the digital age—generally as today's teenage kids are SMART. So SMART parenting is a both-sided game. However, helping the confused teenage kid to manage his time more effectively is just a 'paracetamol', it gives temporary relief and does not hit at the root cause. To get at the root of the problem, we would need to know about the 'Primary Emotional Processes' which are deep-rooted in the developing brain. Although all the processes are commonly present in all teenagers but the guiding emotion(s) varies from one teenager to another.

Digital Engagement vis-à-vis Teenage Emotional Processes

The word 'emotion' is derived from the Latin verb "emovere" meaning "to move out". Basic emotions and their accompanying affects have the capacity to move animals and humans to action in ways that promoted their survival. You must realise that it is 'emotions' that prod all of us, humans, to 'Act' in order to fulfil our 'Biological (= survival + replication) and Social (= bonded relationship-building) Imperatives' (in short 'BSI').

These 'Actions' are, as established through decades of pains-taking research by neuroscientist Jaak Panksepp [founder of the new domain of 'Affective Neuroscience (AN)'] to: move out for resources (SEEKING—Explore, Experiment and Learn); compete for and defend those resources (RAGE – aggression/fight); escape from and avoid danger (FEAR – anxiety/freeze and flight); identify potential mates and reproduce (LUST – libido); nurture the offspring (CARE – love, affection and compassion); engage in fun-filled activities (PLAY – gaming); and, use powerful separation distress signals for maintaining social contact and bonding (PANIC – acute stress).

These seven (7) primary-process Emotional Action Systems, which serve us as survival guides, reach their peak level during teenage. It is important for us to know that the nerve circuits associated with these systems are located in the brain regions below the 'Neo-mammalian Brain' or 'Neo-cortex' which is the 'Forebrain' as the circuitry in the cortical regions are still under construction. So, as I had said earlier elsewhere that, teenage children are no better than bundles of BSI-related emotions.

Nature and Nurture in Teenagers

A child is born with almost all the sub-cortical (= below the 'Neo-cortex') circuits in place—which constitute its primary 'Nature' whereas its 'Neo-cortex', despite having all the brain cells or 'neurons' ready, the cell-to-cell connections—the inter-cellular network is formed entirely as a result of the child's interaction with its environment—this is the 'Nurture' part, which provides the child, as it grows, with the wherewithal whether to or not to 'control' the seven primary emotional processes arising from below the 'Neo-cortex'. These primary-process emotions require no learning; instead, they are innate, instinctive.

In the primitive hunter-gatherer society, before reaching the teenage threshold, boys and girls were dependent on their care-givers for their survival resources, particularly food. Out of the seven (7) primary emotional systems, most active for them would have been PLAY and CARE. Only occasionally, RAGE, FEAR and PANIC would undergo stimulation. During full teenage adolescence, LUST which was dormant so far would raise its head and teenage boys and girls have to use their 'SEEKING SYSTEM CIRCUITS (SSC)' to mobilise resources for themselves, old, infant and pregnant members of the tribe. In the case of modern humans, these emotions become more diversified because of cortical intelligence and cognitive powers, linguistic ability, capacity for imagination and visualisation.

In today's modern society, there is no question of a teenager using his SSC for mobilising resources as he is still dependent on the care-givers for survival resources. Instead of remaining idle, the youngster's SSC gets engaged by digital technology. That is fine if the teenager utilises the digital platform to 'Explore, Experiment and Learn (EEL)'—the SSC model for academics and general knowledge/current affairs acquisition. Instead, according to the personality profile of the teenager (which varies from one to another), the kid utilises digital gadgets for satisfying personal emotional needs as: LUST – pornography; PLAY – games; CARE: social sites, chatting, WhatsApp; FEAR, RAGE, CARE, LUST: film watching.

Today, the teenager is a 'Cost Centre' in his family unit – a source of expenses for his care-givers. In a few years' time, he has to develop himself into an 'Income Centre' because in today's economic world, resource for survival is CASH in exchange of which you can get everything why only food. A SMART leading parent's NURTURING challenge is how to divert the digitally negatively engaged mind of a teenager to get channelized into the 'SEEKING SYSTEM CIRCUITRY (SSC)' to identify his preferred DOMAIN in which he can have his DREAM translated into REALITY by reaching his PEAK PERFORMANCE and get the supply of 'Dopamine (D)' which he is getting currently from his digital engagement.

DOMAIN is an area or territory where your kid would love to operate. DREAM is the VISION of one or a set of 'Work Activities' that he visualises to get totally absorbed in and would like to get that experience again and again for motivational reinforcement of his DRIVE. 'Peak Performance' is the level of performance where all the personal skills, intelligences and talents (the source being his body-brain-mind-and-soul powers) are optimally utilised.

Let me share an example. One teenage boy identified, as his DRIVE, entertaining people and making and keeping them happy. He selected as his DOMAIN—film-making. It came readily to his mind. Now, once the first two steps have been taken, he has to identify his DREAM, which could be making: feature films (on social themes—tragedies, comedies, art films—old stories/remakes, modern stories, war films, horrors, crime fictions); religious films; non-feature films (documentaries, corporate films, events). He could make out, amongst many choices, that he would get maximum mileage from his skills, intelligences and talents if he went into non-feature films, so he selected non-feature as his DREAMLAND—his VISION.

Taming of Teenage Turbulence

Life is not primarily a quest for 'pleasure' (as Sigmund Freud, MD, 1856–1939, the father of 'psychotherapy' thought) or a quest for 'power' (as Alfred Adler, MD, 1870–1937, an expert on individual psychology surmised), but an arduous SEEKING for 'meaning'—a 'purpose' which for many, boils down to realising a DREAM. Viktor Frankl, MD (1905–1997), Austrian neurologist who had survived the tortures of a concentration camp during World War II because he kept himself alive by DREAMING at one point of lecturing after the war about the psychological lessons to be learned from the Auschwitz experience. His best-selling book *A Man's Search for Meaning* first published in 1946 has gone into many editions.

Should you want me to call you a SMART leading parent (who can tame teenage turbulence) the first question you need to ask yourself is: has there been a meaning and purpose in your life, or have you been living just to enjoy your life by eating, drinking, entertaining and satisfying your gross physical and materialistic desires? If your answer happens to be 'yes', then there is every possibility that, apart from your biological genes to be inherited automatically, your kid may copy your thought-genes by his (I have chosen to use the male gender to denote both male and female, for brevity's sake) 'mirror neurons' which get very active when the neo-cortex nerve circuits are developing.

'Mirror neurons' are located at various places on the surface of the neo-cortex. As you very well know, and I have been telling you again and again, that Mother Nature (aka 'Evolutionary Forces') has created you for the purpose of survival and replication and social bonding ('Biological and Social Imperative'—B.S.I) for assured support. These driving forces are there in the sub-cortical structures of your brain like for any other mammalian species. But you are different as you have been provided with a thick 'Neo-cortex' to think beyond the B.S.I. and find a meaning and purpose to your life.

I feel it is never too late to find some fresh meaning and purpose at this stage of your life but that is not the point here. Since we are talking about SMART parenting, let us restrict our discussion to that realm only.

Your teenage kid is still under the firm grip of his brain's 'Emotional Processes'. In order to channelize his powerful emotional energy properly, you need to adopt your SMART Leadership behaviour 4L: Look (establish and sustain positive eye contact with him and talk to him in such a way that he also does not avoid gaze), Listen (lend him your ears for uninterrupted hearing), Love (feel loving-kindness for him, hold his hand or put your hand softly on his shoulder), and Learn (keep your mind open to receive from him inputs hitherto unknown to you—he can also become your teacher) instead of using the age-old parental style of 4C: Command (order about or make strict impositions), Control (monitor his habits closely as you do not trust him), Coerce (force him to give output/obey your instructions), and Coax (with no results forthcoming, appeal for his cooperation). You study your child's attitude, thoughts and behaviour to find out the following:

Is he guided by the 'SEEKING SYSTEM CIRCUITS (SSC)'—Explore, Experiment, Learn? [Does he search the Internet or watch channels like 'Discovery' to find out answers to the questions arising from the exploratory thoughts with which he gets preoccupied often? If his questions are answered, he gets a rush of the reward brain chemical 'Dopamine (D)'. Do you realise that he gets glued to the digital device because you have no quality TIME for him?]

Or, does he 'Create/Produce' something—either tangible or intangible [like a poem, a lyric, or a piece of art or takes a photo and posts it on the Facebook. The moment he gets a 'like' or a 'love' response, 'Dopamine (D)' is released inside his brain. [Do you realize that he has become dependent on Facebook because he had never been appreciated at home for his 'Creative' outputs? 'Creativity' is the noble face of LUST. Selfless 'Creativity' can originate PLAYFULLY also.]

Or, is he guided by the emotion of CARE—wants to provide his friends with 'Comfort and Convenience' in some way or the other and his medium of 'CARING' is Facebook, WhatsApp or Text Messaging [Do you realise that he has become emotionally closer to his peers as you never sought his 'Love' and 'Affection' and did not earn his 'Emotional Proximity'?]

Don't you recognise that Dr. Jaak Panksepp's 7 (seven) 'Emotional Processes' are like the 7 rays of the Sun which, in a teenager, can form a 'rainbow' with a SMART leading parent's golden touch? Don't you feel that they are like the 7 basic notes of music ('Saptaswar') which, with the golden touch of a SMART parent, can be transformed into a sonorous melody.

An aimless teenager who has not been able to discover any meaning or purpose in his life, with the guidance of his parent(s) is in a state of homeostatic imbalance—sort of hunger not being adequately satiated—not feeling 'Grounded'.

'Grounded': Is Teenage Still the Trigger in the Digital Era?

From infancy to teenage, every kid is dependent on others for his 'Dietary Energy (ED)' input—which ensures his survival and growth of reproductive power. Until the stage of 'ED Independence', he is not qualified to be considered as 'Grounded'. A 'Grounded' male is guided by his brain's 'Seeking System Circuitry (SSC)' to adopt the role of a hunter-gatherer. A

'Grounded' female has to play the role of an organiser of roots, tubers, consumable plants-shrubs-herbs, fruits and berries until and unless she has happened to get into the 'Reproductive' role and starts moving in the family way. This standard system and culture was auto-followed in the pre-historic, pre-language, hunter-gatherer society of primitive humans. 'Teen' was thus the 'trigger' for an opportunity to get 'Grounded'.

That was the socio-cultural aspect of a teenager being 'Grounded'.

'Grounding', most interestingly, has a link with a biomechanical/ bio-structural support factor. Extremely slow and gradual evolution from 4-leggedness to 2-leggedness has raised the human body's 'Centre of Gravity (CoG)/Centre of Mass (CoM)'. Before attaining teenage, the CoG/CoM of a boy or a girl was closer to the ground level like that of 4-legged mammal of equivalent height. Teenage—the gateway to adulthood, suddenly raises it much above the ground, making the growing adolescent physically unsteady and unstable particularly if he had a lean constitution. It takes him some time to get adapted to this feature and to adopt a steady standing posture (free from fidgeting movements—side-to-side and forward-backward). Until his stance is steady and he feels well-supported, he is not 'Grounded'.

This is perhaps the reason why in India, in the Vedic age, the Yogic Sciences had prescribed a whole battery of postures ('asanas' involving stretching and bending) for attainment of bipedal stability and erectness. Those habits would help the teenager to get 'Grounded' and ready for utilising his brain's newly wired 'Seeking System Circuitry (SSC)' for fulfilling his 'Appetitive Motivation'—organising food ['Dietary Energy (ED)'] for self and others in the tribe.

Teenage body is like teenage brain—both are work-in-progress, still under construction which will not be complete as per the evolutionary biological schedule as we have violated Mother Nature's instructions imprinted in our genes. We have given up our million-year-old lifestyle of mobilising our own 'Dietary Energy (ED)' by hunting and gathering; instead we collect our provisions from markets and shopping malls and depend on digital gadgets instead of using our natural powers available in our bodies and brains. There is a mismatch between our biology and our sedentary digitalised lifestyle. So, teenage is no longer the trigger for getting 'Grounded'.

Mobilising 'ED' was a must for survival—the topmost priority in the pre-historic days as much as it is today. Those who lead a hassle-free life realise this truth only when food is scarce during fire, flood, war or a lockdown due to an epidemic. In the context of 'ED' which constituted the DOMAIN—in the pre-historic days, every teenage male hunter would cherish one or more of the following DREAMS (= VISION), the DRIVE (or 'Motivational Urge') being 'ED Mobilisation', to be: an ace hunter (or fisherman), a skilled tool designer-maker-repairer, an ace game carrier, a top strategist, an ace tree-climber. The female teenager would dream of being the best collector of roots, tubers, wild fruits, berries, herbs and spices, firewood, dry branches and leaves.

A SMART Leader's job is to help the teenage kid to discover his preferred DOMAIN and the specific DREAM that he would like to be translated into reality. An example will help you to understand what I mean. A teenage girl from a business family, Sruti Kanoria, was referred to me for guidance regarding identification of her DRIVE, DOMAIN and DREAM. My analysis revealed Sruti's DRIVE to be 'Dietary Energy (ED)' as she was a foodie and her DOMAIN to be 'Bakery Products'. We both had a few sessions together to ultimately ZOOM into 'Gluten-free Bakery Products' to be her DREAM. She joined an expensive course in Bengaluru and enjoyed it so much that her rank in the finals came as number 1. She was campus interviewed to be picked by a multi-national 5-star hotel in Bengaluru itself. This is just one example amongst many success stories that I have where DDD—the 3-dimensional match was the 'KEY' to success.

DDD—The 3-D Approach for SMART Leading and Parenting of Digital Age Teens to Get 'Grounded'

'Grounded' for a teenager means that he is on a stable footing—ready for using his brain's million-year old 'Seeking System Circuit (SSC)' for mobilisation of resources for the survival of self and dependents, if any. In other words, he has been able to find a suitable DOMAIN (= terrain or territory of operation) where he can fulfil his DREAM (= what he aspires to be—what his VISION is about his future) utilising his DRIVE (= motivation). This is what I describe as the DDD—3D approach. If the teenager is unable to zoom onto DDD, his SSC will be overtaken by digital gadgets. Digital engagement will make his brain's reward circuits active to release the anticipatory neuro-chemical 'Dopamine (D)' and 'feel good' hormone 'Serotonin'—deprivation of which leads to restlessness, switching on of the brain's 'Default Mode Network (DMN)' and, eventually, anxiety disorder and mental depression.

SMART leading, in this context, would mean, first of all, identifying the teenager's DRIVE factor. My connotation of the DRIVE factor is somewhat different from what the Western scientific literature has documented from the days of bifurcation of 'Psychology' from mainstream 'Philosophy'. I was fascinated to be exposed to the Upanishadic concept of 'Pancha Kosha'—the 5 sheaths that envelop the 'Atman' (Soul) that each living person has—the gross body (SthulaSarira) represented by the 'Annamaya Kosha (AK)'- requiring 'Dietary Energy (ED)' input; and the subtle body consisting of, in successive sequence, the 'Pranamaya Kosha (PK)', 'Monomaya Kosha (MK)' and 'Vijnanamaya Kosha (VK)' requiring 'Breath Energy (EB)', 'Emotional Energy (EE) and 'Intellectual Energy (EI)' respectively. Finally, there is the 'Karana Sarira' or 'Causal Body' which is the cause of all the Koshas that I have talked about so far. It is the 'Anandamaya Kosha (AK)'—requiring the 'Creative Cosmic Energy (EC)' for 'FLOURISHING'—meaning 'Basking in the Sunshine of Happiness' resulting from your 'Peak Performance (PP)' by utilising all your skills, intelligences and talents. It is equivalent to the Russian-American psychologist Abraham Maslow's 'Self-actualisation'.

Let me show you the procedure as to how you SMARTLY lead a teenager to zoom or focus using the DDD—3D approach. Find out if the teenager is specially interested in 'Dietary Energy (ED)'. If he is not, then he does not have any strong 'Likes' and 'Dislikes' about food and other dietary inputs. In case he is DRIVEN by 'ED', then what are the signs and symptoms? He will be fussy about the quality, quantity, looks, smell, and other features of the dietary components which are linked with his sensory experience. Then his DRIVE (= motivation) is related to the AK. If that be so, then there could be several DOMAINs to choose from: Dietetics and Nutrition, Hotel and Hospitality

Management, Food Technology. Now, how do you help him to identify what his DREAM is? His DREAM could be to help people avoid obesity (then the DOMAIN ought to be 'Dietetics and Nutrition Science'). His DREAM could to prepare such items that those leave lasting impressions on the consumers' brain—like Hyderabadi Biryani (then the DOMAIN would be Hotel and Hospitality Management with specialisation in Food—Muglai cuisine). If his DREAM is to innovate a more efficient technology for preservation of cooked food, then the DOMAIN would be Food Technology and Biochemical Engineering with specialisation in 'Preservation Technology'.

A second example now! With this sudden invasion of COVID -19, one young teenage girl DREAMs of inventing some preventive vaccine. Then her DRIVE is related to the 'Pranamaya Kosha (PK)' which is related to the life-force and life-sustenance. The DOMAIN becomes 'Pharmacy' or 'Biochemistry' and the DREAM of course is inventing vaccines for preventing virulent viral attack.

Now let us go for a third example. A young teenage girl, chubby, chirpy and chatty is getting her DRIVE from the 'Monomaya Kosha (MK)'. She is 'People and Social Engagement (PSE)' type. She wanted to have power and authority over people—so her DOMAIN was chosen to be 'Human Resource Management (HRM)' but her DREAM was not to CONTROL people but to INFLUENCE people so she went for her MBA degree, but specialised in HRD and took up employment in the HRD function.

I hope you are now clear about my DRIVE-DOMAIN-DREAM or 3D approach to help teenagers to get 'Grounded'!

Just check, whether in your own career selection, you took, UNCONSCIOUSLY, the 3D approach. If that was the case you now know the reason why you feel very stable and GROUNDED—happily settled in your living and working.

PART–2

Brain Tools

Hand Tools

Man's nearest relative, in the animal world, is chimpanzee. Man and chimpanzee have 98.5 to 99 percent common genes. Chimpanzee is a 2-legged creature like man. 4-legged creatures evolved into 2-legged ones to make the forelegs free so that those could become hands fitted with fingers to provide functional versatility.

Human hands and fingers have diversified functions: pushing, pulling, holding, gripping, pointing, tearing, thumping, screwing, bending, brushing, twisting, throwing, grooving, hole-making, catching, cupping and what not!! All the hand tools used for cooking and dining and, of course, for technical, engineering, medical and surgical applications are nothing but extensions of our hand and finger functions. Dr. Rudolf Drillis of the Engineering Faculty at the New York University (NYU) had spent his lifetime in relating different types of tools to our versatile hand and finger functions. I had seen his great work while lecturing at the NYU in the late 1970's.

And, as a matter of fact, while talking about the versatility of our hands and fingers, there is something most interesting in the design of our brain that you may not be aware of. The cerebral cortex of our brain, if you look at it from the top (that is, you take a top view of the plan), we have the somato-sensory cortex and the motor cortex, respectively representing the sensory organs attached to the body and the body parts which are 'motor'—which we can move. These two are laid out like bands going right across from left to right—the right side of the body being represented on the left and vice versa. In these two, space has been allocated according to the utilitarian importance of the body parts. And, most interestingly, more space has been allocated for hands and fingers than legs and feet establishing their critical importance.

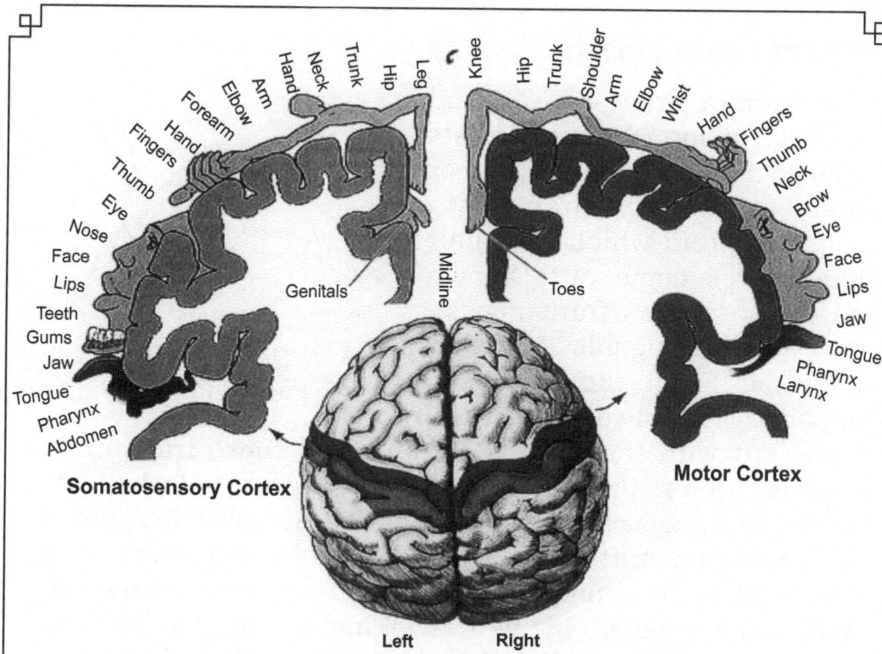

Fig. 4: Top View of the Human Brain (Somato-sensory and Motor Cortices)

Brain Tools

In my long human science career, I had felt that for SMART leading and parenting, certain 'Brain Tools' would be required and it had always been my endeavour to develop such tools, try them out in practice and, if found effective, share those with others. There is a reason why I call them 'Brain Tools'. Human brain, like our hands and fingers, have various different functional potentials like: Thinking, Decision-making, Planning, Calculating, Language Application, Visualisation and so on. For putting each functional potential into practice to get results, there are procedures. Like for decision-making, you can go for a gut-level decision ('gut feeling'), a heart-level decision (a decision out of love, empathy or compassion), a logical-analytical-rational decision, an emotional/impulsive decision, or a creative decision. Each of these procedures represents, in my opinion, a 'Brain Tool'.

Smart Brain Habits

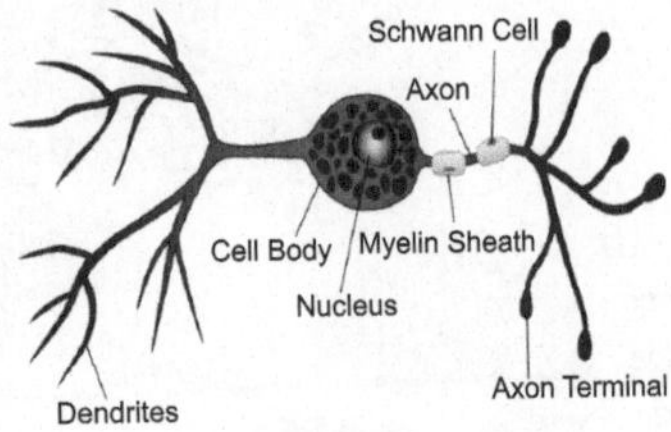

Fig. 5: A 'Neuron' (Brain Cell) and its Parts

The human brain has around 10,000 million (some scientists claim 8,500 million) neurons or brain cells. The neuron has a cell body from which long hair like nerves come out, known as 'axons' for transmission of electrical signals to other neurons. From the cell body appendages called 'dendrites' come out with the purpose of receiving those transmitted signals. An axon meets a dendrite at a 'synapse' where the electrical signal is converted into chemical molecules (known as 'neurotransmitters' and 'neuromodulators') which form messages to be conveyed to the main cell body or neuron. Axons are covered by white-looking myelinated sheaths forming the 'Glial Cells'. Our brain, thus, has 2 types of cells—grey-coloured 'Neurons' which are responsible for the functions I have talked about just now and the white-coloured 'Glia' which protect the neurons. Both these are known as the grey and the white matters respectively.

Now, you may be fortunate to have very healthy and active neurons and glia but that will not make you SMART unless the neuron-to-neuron connections through 'synaptic joints' form effectively helpful networks. Academic exposure through school, college, university education in India or even abroad provides you only with just enough knowledge and information to answer different subject-related questions. Such exposures do not prepare you to take SMART decisions and actions and solve the problems that you face SMARTLY. For which you need special circuits to be formed through brain habits. Those special circuits I call 'Brain Tools (BT)' and since the area of application for us now is Teen Motivation and Management we can call them SMART Leading or SMART Parenting Tools (SLT or SPT). However, henceforth for brevity's sake, I will use the term 'Brain Tool (BT)'.

BRAIN TOOL 1

BUD

'Key' Points: *The Messy Teen Brain; The BUD Brain Tool (BT); Installing BUD Inside A Teen Brain; How I Got BUD Installed in My Brain.*

The Messy Teen Brain

A teenager's brain is in a total mess. It is cluttered with garbage from the Facebook, Instagram, Twitter, YouTube, WhatsApp and what not, in addition to prescriptive sermons from parents, elders, teachers and tutors and tips from peers. On top it, some serious teens have academic overloads. This is what is happening on the front stage. In backstage, inside the teen brain, the neuronal circuits are not so systematically organised like a spider web as they should be; instead they are in a higgledy-piggledy condition. Thus, I am sure, you are realising how important it is for the teen brain circuits to be properly cobwebbed which needs a SMART handling. There are simple 'Brain Tools' that I have developed to help the scatter-brained teenagers and put them on the path to reach the peak of 'Success'.

Brain Tool (BT) 1: BUD

Thinking BIG, Thinking Unique, Thinking Different

While running my own tiny HRD workshop boutique, I could never make my team members to 'Think Big', which is one of the prerequisites for planned and earned 'Success'. Was it my failure? I used to think that I was at fault; perhaps I could not motivate them. But now, after a few years of delving deep into the realm of human brain, I understand that those boys did not have the BUD circuitry developed inside their brains. Brains have in-built circuits for survival, replication and bonded relationship-building but not for 'Thinking Big', 'Thinking Unique', and 'Thinking Different'. Take the first letters from these three types of thinking and you get BUD. If you have to be ahead of others and also yourself—doing better than your past performance ('competitive') and eradicate your 'Deficiencies' by fighting with your 'Weaknesses' ('combative'), you have to be a BUD-dy.

Installing BUD Inside a Teen Brain

BUD, like the bud of a flower, represents a teenager's DREAM. When the teenager starts using his 'Seeking System Circuitry (SSC)' (to 'Explore, Experiment and Learn'), the bud blossoms into a flower—he realises his DREAM. 'SSC' had been installed in the human brain millions of years ago to help humans to survive and reproduce; and, it has stayed put ever since. Every human infant is born with the 'SSC' in place in its brain, the BUD circuit has to be installed by following a simple discipline.

A SMART leading parent, caregiver or mentor must motivate a teenager to keep his eyes and ears open to detect anywhere in his environment something 'Big' (like a big word, or a big man, or a big house, a big butterfly or a big dog), something 'Unique' (like the cluster of clouds morphing into a unique shape, or a unique embroidered design made by his mom or grandma, or a unique flower arrangement in a local florist shop, or a unique oyster shell while collecting shells on the seashore), and something 'Different' (like a conjoined twin banana, or a lady with six fingers on her right hand, or a newly born with a cleft-palate, or like my salt-and-pepper hairstyle). Motivate the teenager to note the BUD findings daily in a diary. My experience is if the teenager does it for 3 to 4 months with full sincerity and faith, the BUD circuitry will get formed in the mammalian brain due to reinforced learning and will start giving automatic BUD-influenced outputs to make him Think 'Big', Think 'Unique' and Think 'Different'.

How I Got BUD Installed in My Brain

I realise now, at this advanced age, that this is one circuit which my mother had helped to install in my brain when I reached my teens and being from a Hindu brahmin family had my sacred thread ceremony. She would nudge me to spend some time in the back garden or front portico of our family house or sometimes in the local park to identify Bigs, Uniques and Differents; and note them down in a special ornamented diary which she had gifted me on my first teen birthday. Having been groomed under the umbrella of such a SMART leading parent, the outcome was I stood 1st both in English and Bengali in the West Bengal Board School Final Exam in 1955 creating new records in scores. I got series of release of the reward chemical 'Dopamine (D)' in the form of awards, medals, certificates, book prizes and hugs and kudos from parents, grandparents, tutors and teachers including from J.M. Banerjee, MA (Oxon) our headmaster whose own grandson and daughter in-law MIT-based Abhijit Vinayak Banerjee and Esther Duflo got the Nobel Prize for Economics in 2019.

BRAIN TOOL 2

GUT Feeling (GF)

'Key' Points: *The GUT Brain and GUT Feelings; An Example; Internal Equilibrium or Homeostasis; GUT Feelings in Animals.*

The GUT Brain and GUT Feelings

GUT means the intestines housed in our 'Digestive System (DS)'. In the 'GUT' and its associated parts of the 'DS', a 2nd Brain has been identified by modern brain scientists. They call it the 'GUT Brain'. Why? Because there are a few million neurons (= brain cells) present in our 'DS' which can sense stimuli, process them and take decisions. We have often experienced that our GUT can feel and it is commonly known as 'GUT Feeling (GF)'. GF is strong in pre-teens and teens.

An Example

One pre-teen boy is a keen swimmer. He had reached the finals in his school's under-13 swimming competition. He was present at the finals but did not participate. When he came home and his mother asked him: "How did it go?", the answer was "Mom, I didn't compete as I had a GUT feeling that I was going to have fever". The same night, the boy had a high temperature and he suffered badly for the next 6 days.

Internal Equilibrium or Homeostasis

All living creatures follow a system of internal equilibrium which physiologists have called *'homeostasis'*. Humans are no exceptions. The GUT neurons are highly sensitive to the body's internal temperature, pressure, humidity and sò on. Any minute deviation from the standard is sensed by them and the information is transmitted to the brainstem in the lower or hind brain.

A boy, in his late teens, studying in the 2nd year college, is being mentored by me for more than a year. One Monday morning, he had an appointment with me at 11.45 am. At 11 am, I got a call from him that he was unable to come as he was feeling uneasy—he may become sick at any time. He had gone eating out with his friends late the previous night and had a disturbed sleep whole night and now had a 'GUT Feeling (GF)' that his stomach may misbehave. So strong was the GF that he had dropped the idea of visiting me for a mentoring session. He really suffered from a loose bowels the same afternoon.

GUT Feelings in Animals

Animals have very strong GF. I have a first-hand experience with dogs as I had been a dog-lover and dog-keeper since my boyhood days. We had a pet dog Lucy, a local terrier, who was very loyal to me. She was in the family for 7 years. One day suddenly she stopped taking her food. She won't eat even from my hands which she used to relish in the past. She did not touch a morsel of food for 4 days, laid on her bed with sunken looks and passed away on a stormy evening in the midst of a heavy downpour. Lucy had a strong GF that she was going to die. And, since she wanted to have a peaceful death, she went on fasting as otherwise if she had eaten, her stomach would have betrayed.

BRAIN TOOL 3

Neuroception

'Key' Points: *Neuroception; The Pancha Kosha Facts; Annamaya and Pranamaya Koshas (AK and PK); Monomaya Kosha (MK); Vijnanamaya Kosha (VK); Anandamaya Kosha (AnK); More About Neuroception; The Scientific Basis of Neuroception.*

Neuroception

Perception of anything using your brain's logical, rational and analytical power is what I call 'Neuroception'. Intelligently used, it can serve as a very powerful Brain Tool (BT) for KOSHA and 3D (DRIVE-DREAM-DOMAIN) analysis for a teenage kid.

The Pancha Kosha Facts

The 'Pancha Kosha (PK)': Is easy to remember. How? Tag the 5 Koshas with the 5 fingers of your hand. Analogous to the 'Thumb' is the 'Annamaya Kosha (AK)'—the 'Dietary Energy (ED)' which I've already introduced to you with two illustrative live case studies.

Annamaya and Pranamaya Koshas (AK and PK)

Everything to do with food, clothes and accessories, shelter and comfortable lifestyle is within the 'Annamaya Kosha (AK)' sheath. It is visible, palpable—present in the form of the 'sthulasarira' (gross body). The next layer, subtle, invisible, non-palpable, present in the subtle body or 'sukshmasarira' is the 'Pranamaya Kosha (PK)' which represents the 'life force'—the 'Breath Energy (EB)'. It stands for all things related to life, vitality, energy, health, physical fitness, immunity, safety and security—directly (taking care of own) and indirectly (taking care of others). It is analogous to the 'Index Finger'. Just like AK and PK both are the basics of a living body, the 'Thumb' and the 'Index Finger' both together can do several things even if the other fingers are not there. Now, a case study would be illustrative.

A young boy from the Sunderbans region of 24 Parganas in South Bengal used to suffer off and on from cough and cold, fever, stomach problems and his father would always treat him with allopathic medicine. And this boy used to wonder if there could be any alternative medicine—any alternative therapy for treating such ailments. His DREAM (which had its roots in PK) was to find out some alternative route for cure and prevention of diseases other than the western style allopathic medicine. The DRIVE came from PK—life force, health, fitness, healing, prevention. He came to Kolkata after his senior secondary and went for treatment in a Neurotherapy clinic sheer by chance. It clicked and, eventually became his DOMAIN. Because of the 3D synchronisation, he has done very well within just 4 years. He has not only developed a high-class therapeutic skill but has also shown so much of managerial acumen that he has been given full charge of one complete centre.

Monomaya Kosha (MK)

The next layer is 'Monomaya Kosha (MK)'. Analogous to the 'Middle Finger', it deals with 'Emotional Energy (EE)' and represents anything to do with the give-and-take of EE covering the very broad human emotions spectrum starting with the Valentine's day celebrations and ending with reminiscing on a departed soul—in between there is the whole world of EE give-and-take. MK covers: sketching and painting, sculpture, architecture, interior decoration, novels, stories, poems, lyrics, music, dancing, drama, theatre, movies, interest in sports and games, public relations, human resource management and development, journalism and mass communication. Those who are involved in such activities are getting their REWARDS in terms of emotional satisfaction, so also are those who are being exposed to the outcome of those. MK, like PK is a part of the subtle body or 'sukshmasarira'. Pursuance of MK activities is not devoid of hazards, the main RISK being the battle of EGOs as MK breeds competition.

Vijnanamaya Kosha (VK)

The fourth sheath, analogous to the 'Ring Finger', is the 'Vijnanamaya Kosha (VK)' which relates to 'Intellectual Energy (EI)' and is the conscious tip of your mental ICEBERG. It does not allow you to get carried away by your emotions and tries to find out a logical basis for everything. It is a sign of VK activation when one goes deep into anything with the analytical faculty of the mind. While the REWARD is obvious, the main RISK is the possibility of 'Paralysis by Analysis (PbA)': you get lost in the cobweb of your analytical thought process.

Anandamaya Kosha (AnK)

The fifth and final sheath, the 'Anandamaya Kosha (AnK)', is analogous to your 'Pinky'. It relates to the 'Creative Energy (EC)' which you experience when you have got an insight or an inspiration or have created, invented or innovated something, or even have found out a shortcut or bypass to the main route. 'REWARDS' comprise the 'Eureka' feeling and the main RISK is getting carried away ignoring and neglecting your worldly duties and responsibilities.

Most people are a combination of three sheaths—AK, PK and MK. But, there are also people who are governed and guided by two sheaths: one primary and the other secondary and usually they are AK and MK, AK and PK, or PK and MK. Intelligent use of the 'Brain Tool (BT) -3': 'NEUROCEPTION' would help to do the 'Kosha Dominance (KD)' analysis for anyone. A SMART leading parent would use it, without fail, for the KOSHA and 3-D analysis of his teenage kid.

More about Neuroception

Each of us, you and me included, is a collection of several biological systems serving different purposes and performing different functions. There is the 'Circulatory System' where your Heart is in charge. Then, there is the 'Respiratory System' which is headed by the 'Lungs'. We have the very important 'Digestive System' which is governed by the 'Gut Brain (GB)' about which we had a very long and elaborate discussion, scripted in the Appendix. We cannot miss out the system which makes us mobile—the

'Muscular-Skeletal System'. All these systems function with the help of nerves; and, we have the 'Nervous System' divided into two parts: the 'Central Nervous System (CNS)' consisting of the brain and the spinal cord; and the 'Peripheral Nervous System (PNS)' which is serving the entire body.

'Neuroception' that is, 'Neuro' + 'Perception', means how the brain perceives or senses through its nerve circuits a possible hazard where 'risk' is involved. It is our brain's Safety Valve mechanism. It is present in reptiles, birds, amphibians as well as all mammals. But since its circuits are present only in the hind brain (reptilian complex) and the mid-brain (paleo-mammalian complex), its scope is limited to environmental situations like safeguarding oneself against a ferocious animal or a dangerous, negative human being. That scope suits a small child who can protect himself against a barking dog or a negatively motivated human. As he is under the protection of her care-givers, they take care of all other hazards like playing with a sharp object (a knife/a razor blade) or putting the finger into a flame and so on. As the child grows and reaches his teens, he has to face many more hazardous situations which do not occur during childhood, boyhood or girlhood. A teenager has to do many things independently outside the protective umbrella of his parents. So, it is the responsibility of a Smart Leading parent to make him aware of those hazards by expanding the scope of the 'Neuroception' Brain Tool by involving the logical-analytical faculties of the 'Neo-mammalian Brain'—the Neo-cortex.

This is what I meant by the responsibility of a 'Smart Leading (SL)' parent.

The Scientific Basis of 'Neuroception'

Now for those readers who are not convinced with such simple explanation, but would love to have the scientific basis, I am writing the rest. Those who feel overwhelmed by technical stuff can skip this portion. Nevertheless, I would recommend that you read it slowly or more than once as then it will be really convincing for you.

An indispensable part of our 'overall' nervous system ('overall' because it involves the CNS and the PNS both) is the 'involuntary'

'Autonomic Nervous System (ANS)' ['involuntary'....so 'Auto..']. ANS is our personal surveillance system, always on guard, asking personal safety-related questions.

ANS is made up of two branches, the 'sympathetic' and the 'parasympathetic' and responds to signals and sensations via three pathways, each with a characteristic pattern of response to ensure our safe survival.

The 'sympathetic' branch is found in the middle part of our spinal cord and represents the pathway that prepares us for action when we smell danger. It triggers the release of 'Adrenaline'—the fuel for the fight-or-flight response. In the 'parasympathetic' branch, the remaining two pathways are found in a nerve called the 'Vagus' (it is the 10th cranial nerve, meaning 'wanderer') which travels from the brain stem in two directions: downward through the lungs, heart, diaphragm, and the stomach; and, upward to connect with nerves in the neck, throat, eyes and ears.

The Vagus is divided into two parts: 'Ventral (front)' responds to the cues of being 'Safely Engaged' and 'Socially Connected'—that is, to use my language, being in the 'Zone of Comfort and Convenience (ZCC)'. In contrast, the 'Dorsal (back)' responds to cues being in the extreme end of the 'Zone of Discomfort and Inconvenience (ZDI)'. Under such circumstances, we feel extreme discomfort and inconvenience, get frozen and numb. The 'Dorsal' response is most primitive and is the oldest pathway, as in the case of the Reptilian Complex part of our brain. The 'sympathetic' response—'fight-or-flight' is related to the Paleo-mammalian brain and was the next to develop in the evolutionary history. The 'Ventral' response brings pattern of 'Social Engagement' and is the latest to develop. It functions in the forebrain—the 'Neo-cortex'.

In the 'Ventral' vagal pathway, you're in 'Social Engagement', that is, the 'Zone of Comfort and Convenience (ZCC)'—feel safe and warm while chatting with a Facebook friend in the messenger, discussing things that both of you like, say movies or music. There is no scope for any argument or disagreement as, for both of you, the tastes are identical. Suddenly, your friend shifts his gear and raises an issue which is very sensitive and personal.

Your neural switch tends to switch from the 'Ventral' to the 'Dorsal' ('Sympathetic') as you are being pushed from your ZCC to the 'Zone of Discomfort and Inconvenience (ZDI)'. You feel like arguing (Adrenaline activated), but you stick to the 'Ventral' and stimulate your 'Parasympathetic' and beg to be excused on the plea that you have a very important meeting to attend to. This is a sign of 'SMART Leadership (SL)'.

The SMART leading parent develops his 'Neuroception' sensitivity so much that before the 'Dorsal' vagal pathway is activated, he changes direction. This is good 'Neuro-Management (NM)'. If you are neuro-managed, there is a strong possibility that your teen-age girl or boy will also be neuro-managed by following your good example.

BRAIN TOOL 4

Can Do

'Key' Points: *The Hammer and the Nail; A Real-Life Case Study; 'Can Do' and 'Cannot Do' Brain Circuits; Examples of 'Can Do' Brain Tool Installation; A 'Can/Cannot Do' Exercise for You; A Vital Application: 'Early to Rise'; Rewards of Getting Up Early; The Bad Habit of 'Getting Up Late': Behind the Curtain; Use 'Wake Up' Medicine to Get Up Early; Delaying Gratification; The 5 Psycho-social Hungers of Teenagers.*

The Hammer and the Nail

The American psychologist Abraham Maslow (1908–1970) had once said: "If the only 'tool' that you have is a 'hammer', you tend to treat everything as a 'nail'." The world is full of 'nails' which need 'hammers' to be driven by, but there are many other problems the solution of which need 'Tools' other than a 'hammer'. In the same sense, BUD (Thinking Big, Thinking Unique and Thinking Different), Gut Feeling and Neuroception are not the only Brain Tools which can help a teenage kid in everything. There are so many other Brain Tools (BT) that are available and must be recognised by teenagers. Here I will talk about another such very useful BT.

A Real-Life Case Study

I shall use a real-life case study to introduce this BT. It involves one of my most favourite students. Imagine his name is R. When R was the General Manager (GM) of a renowned company, his boss—the Managing Director (MD) was looking for a SMART executive to head a group company. He called R to get ready overnight to board a flight to Germany along with 2 of his colleagues who were also holding GM posts in other functions in the same Company. They disembarked at Frankfurt International Airport, Germany and from there were taken by road to a small village about 50 km away. After a quick snack and coffee, they were placed in front of an extended bed of burning charcoal. The German examiner asked them to take off their shoes and socks, fold up their trousers and walk straight across the hot bed from one end to the other. One of R's colleagues P looked overenthusiastic; he took the first chance and the moment he stepped on fire, he screamed and stepped out with burn injury under his feet. Same was the fate of the other colleague Q. R was the last to try. He concentrated all his energy to visualise 'SUCCESS', quickly nurtured a 'CAN DO' attitude in his mind, stepped into the fire bed, did not stop or look back, and succeeded in crossing it uninjured. Subsequently, he crossed it 14 times without any injury or any other hassle. The German examiner connected R to his MD to report about his success. The MD not only congratulated him but also told him to pack up things immediately on his return and take up the new assignment of MD and CEO of XYZ Co. in the group.

'Can Do' and 'Cannot Do' Brain Circuits

If you are a SMART leading parent, do not influence any teenager that he Cannot Do, like many parents do. I have a teenage Standard X student whom I gave a task which I knew he will be able to complete although he might take a little time; the moment I finished talking to the boy, his mother who accompanies him to my 'Winning Child' clinic would intervene: "This he 'Cannot Do' Sir" instead of telling "He has never done it Sir, however, let him try." This lady is a 'Cannot Do' mother having a 'Cannot Do' circuit installed in her brain. While 'Can Do' is a positive 'Brain Tool (BT)', 'Cannot Do' is a negative one. So, you see, there are positive BTs and negative BTs. Parents having negative BTs installed in their brains develop kids with negative BTs only (of course, there are exceptions—but that is the general rule as growing kids copy their parents with highly active 'Mirror Neurons', meant for copying others, built into the upper layers of their brain).

Examples of 'Can Do' Brain Tool Installation

'Can Do' Brain Tool represents your willpower the circuits for which are in the Frontal Lobes of the brain, the wiring of which takes place at a rapid pace during the teenage. So, teenage is the time when the parents must set 'Can Do' examples for their kids in teens.

First example. I was overweight as I approached my teens and never cared to shed a few kilos. My mother took me one Sunday to the Anderson Club at the Dhakuria Lakes in South Calcutta, held my hand until we reached the edge of the swimming pool and literally pushed me into the pool water. I started swimming with a dog stroke to save myself from drowning. Mr Nalin Malik, an ex-Olympic swimmer who was present there exclaimed: "Maam, he 'Can' swim. Don't you see, he 'Can' swim." Thinking in retrospect, I now feel that was when I got the 'Can Do' Brain Tool installed inside my brain.

Second example. Being tempted by the idea that I can get my driving licence at 18, at 17 I started taking driving lessons. My father engaged an expensive Anglo-Indian elderly driving coach Mr. Tom. On the very first day, after the routine lessons, Mr Tom came out of the car and told me: "Now you drive." As I pressed the accelerator to speed up Mr Tom jumped in front of my car and I abruptly applied the brakes. The car stopped with a jerk. Mr Tom exclaimed: "Boy, you 'Can' drive and you 'Will' drive."

A 'Can/Cannot Do' Exercise for You

Make a List of What Things 'You Can Do' and 'You Cannot Do': minimum 5 and maximum 10 of each.

A Vital Application of 'Can Do': 'Early to Rise'

I hope you remember the 'Cannot Do' mother of a 14-year old Class X boy Rahul who attends my 'Winning Child' clinic regularly to be mentored by me. Last year towards the end of March she complained to me that Rahul cannot get up early in the morning. He wakes up when mom has gone to the kitchen but keeps on lingering—turning left and turning right alternately for almost half an hour; then after repeated reminder, leaves the bed most reluctantly. I, as Rahul's mentor, took up a challenge to convert him into a 'Can Get Up Early' character. In fact, it is difficult for a teenager to get up at dawn unless there is a compulsion (punishment??) like: he has to get ready for the first trip of the school bus; or, the Maths tutor would come on dot at 8 O'clock—or there is a 'Reward' forthcoming. I asked his dad Samarjit to get a seasonal membership of a swimming club in the Dhakuria Lakes in South Kolkata and also a well-fitting swim shorts for Rahul. Once these were done, I told Rahul to keep his clothes and strap shoes ready by his bedside at night. Incidentally, Samarjit was a swimmer and could teach Rahul not to be a champ but at least to save himself from drowning.

The next morning at 5.30 am sharp, Samarjit called Rahul and told him that they were going to the club for a swim. Star-struck Rahul jumped out of bed, finished his wash fast, got ready for a cup of Horlicks and left for the club on his dad's two-wheeler. After a few dog strokes in the Lakes followed by a shower, Rahul got his 'Rewards' in the form of happiness brain chemicals E (Endorphin) - D (Dopamine) - S (Serotonin) - O (Oxytocin) and happiness neuro-electricity (Beta-positive). On return, his brain was ready for 2 hours' solid study before he sat for his pre-school morning meal. He had enough time to leave home at 10.30 am. The school hours were from 11 am to 4 pm.

The impact of the 'Rewards' was such that Rahul himself insisted on implementing and following the 'Early to bed and early to rise' rule. He felt good as he could 'control' himself (actually, the Rewards started controlling him). Indirectly, he got another Reward: the 'Power of Self-control' which is an 'Asset' for anyone. April, May, June—the Swimming Club's seasonal membership was for 3 months—just the right time period to develop a 'Habit'; and once you develop a 'Habit', you need not look back.

What are the other 'Rewards' of getting up early after a good night's sleep:

> No heaviness in the head and the eyes; fresh and clear mind; healthy and fit body; action orientation (you leave the bed promptly without lingering on unnecessarily); well-functioning Gut Brain and good gut health; good appetite; no rushing and running against time—lot of time available and, therefore, also opportunity available; development of the 'Can Do' circuit inside the brain.

From sleep to wakefulness is a 'Change'. In the pre-historic hunter-gatherer tribal society, this 'Change' was a part of daily living and working as it was controlled by the circadian rhythm (natural day-and-night cycle). The 'Pineal Gland (PG)' inside the brain will stop production of the sleep hormone 'Melatonin (M)' the moment the sun was out, for daytime was the time for hunting and gathering (to fulfil the need for survival) and would restart it again at dusk after the sundown. Today, for a teenager who is not a habitual early-riser, this 'Change' is unwelcome as it is not always controlled by the PG if the boy is sleeping in a room where sunlight cannot enter as the shutters are down or the curtains are drawn. Besides, if the boy is sleeping with his face down or covered under a sheet. If you suddenly try to wake him up, the 'Change' is a 'Punishment' for him unless you replace it with a 'Reward' which will make him jump in joy and his brain will be flushed with happiness molecules.

Rewards of Getting Up Early

No theories, to start with, in this. Only 4 case studies culminating in a theory.

The Great Hero never took off his dark glasses while talking to me!! Mahanayak Uttamkumar!! When I was a 12-year old kid in Class VIII, I would have a little chat with him every day around noon time. Uttam's driver Nyapa's wife Suma used to cook for my Thama (grandmother). The octogenarian widow would relish Suma's veg. preparations. So would Uttam. At 12 noon, his Dodge Kingsway limousine would stop by the side of the boundary wall of our house and Nyapa would take Uttam's tiffin carrier to Suma to have it filled with veg. cuisine. My Thama had a soft corner for Uttam. One day I asked the hero: "Uncle, what time do you get up in the morning?" "Oh! At 5.30 am sharp! Whether on the previous day, I've had whole day, whole evening or whole night shooting in town or outside somewhere, no exception! You know why? Because the moment I get up I visualise the scenes to be shot that day and I practice the dialogue what I've to say. I'd get into the personality of the character that I was playing that day. And, I feel so good!" Mahanayak had a REWARD to look forward to which will make him get up early. Now I think that was one of the reasons why nobody has been able to beat him in Bengali cinema still!

When I was a student in St. Xavier's College, Calcutta, Satyajit Ray's Pather Panchali got released in the Basusree cinema hall in Calcutta. Since he was known to our family (Satyajit's wife and my mother were in college together), I was keen to watch his first movie. I bunked college with a couple of friends and took a bus to Basusree. The hall was empty—no takers. But by the time the film ended, I was full of emotions—simply overwhelmed. I nudged my mother to ring up Bijaya (Satyajit's wife) and went to their Mudiali apartment the very next day. We had been invited for breakfast. We reached at 8.30 am and I asked Bijaya aunty: "Uncle is up or still resting?" "Oh, Babul (my home name), he gets up at 5.00 am." When I met Satyajit after 10–15 minutes, I asked him: "Why do you get up so early?" "Because". He said. "I look forward to the dawn when nobody will disturb me and I can concentrate on my work. Come with me." He took me to his studio and unrolled scrolls of paper with beautiful ink sketches. "I am an artist and I direct my actors by drawing every scene, every movement in detail. And when I draw, I get totally lost. That is the best period of my day." That was Satyajit's REWARD every morning which he used to look forward to.

Fast forward to 1962 when I reached London. I was a guest in Prodyot Sen's (a friend of my father, Mr. Sen used to work in a senior position at the Indian High Commission in London) small apartment in Finsbury Park. He had a whole house but had converted it into small apartments given on rent; had kept a small one for himself, his wife (a senior nurse in a reputed London hospital) and their 6-month old daughter Srabani. On the 2nd day after my checking in there, Mr Sen suddenly said: "Babul, Pt. Ravi Shankar is coming. He will be our guest on the way to the Edinburgh Festival. Don't feel inconvenienced as he is a very early riser as he does his *Riyaz* (music practice) from 5.30 to 8.30 am. If you want to listen, sneak into his room quietly (he knows you'll be here with us), sit on the carpet, do not talk or ask him any question." Panditji arrived quite late at night when I was fast asleep. As I woke up at 6.30 am, after a quick wash, I went straight into the room where he was practising, totally immersed in Raga Darbari. As he finished and opened his eyes, I asked him: "Panditji, what do you get by waking up so early?" "I get cosmic energy from my *Riyaz*—that prepares me for the whole day and evening. If I do not get up early, how do

I get so much time?" That cosmic energy was perhaps behind his worldwide success as an extraordinary musician who took Indian classical music to the Western audience.

Another fast forward to 1975. I was the CEO of the prestigious professional management body—the Calcutta Management Association (CMA). I was close to many top managers of Indian, foreign and multi-national companies. One such person was Mani Shankar Mukherjee (alias 'Shankar' the famous Bengali novelist) who was then a senior manager in Dunlop India Ltd.—at that time a British company. One afternoon, we were having a business lunch together in a Chinese restaurant near his office along with a friendly chat. He was already at the peak of his literary career. I asked him: "You're a senior manager of a British company, you hold an important office in the Public Relations Society of India, when do you get so much time to write?" Straight came the answer: "Very early in the morning. When the eastern sky has just started getting golden—the sun is about to rise, I'm there at my writing desk. I pour out everything that I feel right from the depth of my mind and that is the time when I'm most productive. My best stories and novels are all composed very early in the morning. I look forward to that experience."

I have given you four case studies of highly successful people who were early birds. They could get up early as they had their 'Missions' and 'Goals'—fulfilment of which led to 'Rewards'.

Are you not convinced still that one of the qualities or traits that make individuals (I differentiate between 'individual success' and 'group/team success') treading the path of success in life is the 'Can Do' 'Brain Tool (BT) -4' applied to make 'Getting Up Early' possible? (And, this habit must be nurtured by SMART Leading parents in their teenage kids instead of spoiling them.)

The Bad Habit of 'Getting Up Late': Behind the Curtain

Getting up late is a bad habit. Many teenagers and their parents may not take it so seriously. But there is certainly a science behind what is apparent. Sleeping till late does not allow your brain's extremely important 'Pineal Gland (PG)' to follow the circadian rhythm (the natural day and night cycle) violating its design principles. You're compelling the PG to be kept open beyond sunrise which is anti-Nature inviting physical and mental health RISKs. Besides, by getting up late you are not taking advantage of your brain's 'alpha' wave (7 to 14 cycles/ sec or hertz) which is an auto-event if you rise early. 'Alpha' wave is responsible for your brain's creative flashes, intuition, gut feelings and innovative problem-solving. I always keep a notepad handy by my bedside to note down 'alpha'-generated new and novel thoughts and ideas before I leave my bed early in the morning. I hope I was able to convince on this in the last piece where I shared the live cases of early-rising celebrities.

MIT in USA is an institution where some pioneering research on the 'Science of Habits' had been conducted. Charles DuHigg (*The Power of Habit*, New York: Random House: 2013), James Clear (*Atomic Habits*, New York: Penguin Random House, 2018) and B.J. Fogg (*The Tiny Habits*, New York: Virgin Books, 2019) today are topmost experts on HABITs. I have gone through their works (although cursorily) but I have hardly found any mention about the bad habit of late rising in teenagers—on which I have some experience to share!

1. A teenager lingers on despite his (no gender bias) sleep has broken waiting for a parent—especially the mother to call him a few times so that he has the feeling that he can 'control' her. This is the 'Control Hunger' of a 'Rebellious Child (RC)' of Dr. Eric Berne (Refer to his *Games People Play* book (London: Grove Press, 1964) and his Theory of 'Transactional Analysis (TA)'. While behaving in such a manner the teenager's RC 'Ego-state' is active. An unruly, manipulative, problematic child's psychology is to behave in this fashion so that he can control the parent and the parent succumbs to his tantrums.

   Remedy: Let the kid sleep on. Don't call him—don't give him any attention. If he misses the school bus, let him miss. If he is late for the tutorial, let him be late. Let him learn self-control and develop the 'Can Do' Brain Tool (BT). [I have reversed the habit of two such teenagers in recent times.]

2. The teenager boy sleeps with the mother (or the girl sleeps with the father or the kid in the middle of the parents)

and according to the founding father of 'Psychotherapy' Dr. Sigmund Freud, the boy may suffer from 'Oedipus complex' (the adolescent boy is sexually attracted towards the mother). Freud's protégé Dr. Carl Gustav Jung conceptualized the 'Electra Complex' in the case of a girl child (the adolescent girl is crazy about her father). These are problems of the civilised societies as in the era of the hunter-gatherers, at the onset of puberty the kids will automatically move separately from their parents driven by the urge for independence. In today's society, many parents still treat adolescents as small kids and do not allow them to grow psychologically although physically and physiologically they have all signs of growth and maturity. So, in such cases, although the parents have got up, the teenager will still linger on with 'theta' wave inside the brain imagining physical contact with the elder.

Remedy: Make the teenager sleep separately from the parents at the onset of puberty. [I've freed 2 boys during the last two years from such bad habit. They were carrying it into their twenties when they approached me for help.]

3. If you are an Unsmart Parent and expect too much from your teenager kid—much more than he can deliver, he may confront and fight or avoid you during waking hours but during sleep will develop 'Muscular Armouring (MA)' [Reference: *Bioenergetics* by Alexander Lowen, New York: Penguin Compass, 1994 based on the theories of Dr. Wilhelm Reich]. MA represents a situation when the muscles are tensed affecting the bones, tendons and filaments also, leading to eventual joint pain.] Such teenage kids will not be able to get up early because of lack of sound, undisturbed sleep. A small percentage of such teenagers—both male and female develop 'Dromomania'—which stands for running away from home. They feel being tortured at home and want to free themselves from that environment. [I had done some studies on 'Dromomania' with around 50 teenage boys.]

   Remedy: Handle them in a balanced manner. Do not micro-control them like a helicopter or drone parent.

Use 'Wake Up Medicine' to Get Up Early

I had a smooth transition from pre-teen to teen, as I had already begun to nest a DREAM—to be 'Different' from others—to be a 'Change-maker'. In the pre-historic times, most of the teenagers would live with a DREAM—to be an ace hunter, a record-breaking gatherer, a risk-savvy climber or a skilled tool-maker. Today, a teenager does not have to get ready for hunting or gathering, but there is a space still left in one corner of his (no gender bias) mind to nurture a DREAM. Nevertheless, in most cases that DREAM does not develop as 'self-generated/self-created' as it was in my case. It is usually environment-triggered: stimulated either by the parents or family elders ("We want you to be a doctor, or an engineer, or a chartered accountant, an MBA or an IAS/IPS")—or influenced by a peer ("Chum! Come let us join the law course in Bengaluru").

Having a DREAM well-nested in the mind of a teenager is a pre-requisite for getting up early, according to the 'Theory of Habits (ToH)' that I'm working on. According to ToH, there has to be a 'Cue' first. Let us assume, the teenager had set an alarm at 6 am. The alarm rings giving him the 'Cue'—which is the wake-up call. The 'Cue' is followed by 'Action' or 'Behaviour' (some Habit experts call it 'Routine') which could be either (i) he promptly gets up or (ii) he does not get up, he still lingers on and gets up only when he gets a 'Reward' (that may be, his mother or grandmother calls him a number of times—he gets her 'Attention' and feels that he could 'control' her—that is the 'Reward' or 'Incentive'. My point is that a teenager who does not get up unless coaxed, cajoled, called again and again or punished, is not DRIVEN by a DREAM. He needs a DREAM to be DRIVEN to jump up from the bed and rush to the wash room to get ready. This was my case during my teens. I used to sleep alone in a separate room. I will wake up as I get the 'cue' (the wake-up alarm), I will take 'Action' to jump out of the bed and rush to the wash room anticipating the 'Reward' or 'Incentive' [having a rush of 'Dopamine (D)' inside my brain] that I will get after I put down on paper the little poem that I was creating inside my mind. Every morning, I will create something or look at my study materials from a different angle and note down such thoughts to discuss with my teachers and tutors and they would not only give their approval but appreciate my endeavour [leading to another rush of 'Dopamine (D)'].

Now, let me share a fresh case study with you. I have been mentoring a young lad—Arka Ghosh Chaudhury for the last 3 years. One remarkable profit that he had derived from my mentoring sessions was to crystallize a DREAM—to be an automobile designer. Once he got the kick, he started collecting lot of factual data on sedan cars by searching the net, watching videos and TV programmes on scientific and technological channels. He began developing his own WORKBOOK on 'Automobiles' with newspaper and magazine cuttings. But so much of his time was spent till late at night on such activities, that he could never rise early. He had to be called several times by his mother or grandmother before he could manage to leave the bed at around 8.00 am.

Nevertheless, my 'Wake Up Medicine' worked on him. What is this 'Wake Up Medicine'? Finish dinner by 9.30 pm. Until 11 pm, work on something that you enjoy—such as practising maths, or answering questions on your liked subjects. Sharp at 11 pm, move to the bed. Either sit erect on the bed or lie down supine (sabasana). Start full conscious breathing deeply (in, hold, out) at a slow to moderate pace, repeat the breathing cycle 9 to 10 times so that your brain wave gets transformed from beta to theta (light sleep) moving through alpha. At this stage, just like you swallow a pill, Arka was taught to swallow a wake-up pill by saying "I must wake up at 6.00 am to get ready to work on my automobile design sketches (Arka is a skilled artist by nature and draws beautiful sketches which constitute his REWARDs). And every day, I must develop some new design feature" and then lie down. Arka practised this technique for 2–3 days and thereafter he never had to look back. The wake-up medicine would make him up every morning between 6.10 and 6.20 am without fail.

Delaying Gratification (DG)

The biological purpose of all living beings is to survive and reproduce. We, humans, are no exceptions to this Law of Nature. For fulfilment of this purpose, our brains are hardwired in a certain standard manner. When survival (and not replication) is the prime need, right from the moment of severance of the umbilical cord, the newly born infant is guided by the 'Instant or Immediate Gratification (IG)' circuit, already pre-installed in the hind (reptilian) and middle (paleomammalian) portions of its brain. He (no gender bias) expresses his frustration if he cannot reach the nipples of his mom when he is hungry or thirsty. He cannot withhold his body waste—he has to get rid of his urine or faeces the moment his bladder is ready or the anus is prepared to release the stool. He soils his pampers and screams until it is changed and a fresh clean one is put on. Gratification leads to the release of happiness chemicals and oscillations of happiness electricity inside the infantile brain. Today, with modern brain imaging and brain wave recording technology available, you can measure such occurrences.

The infant's entire physiology is designed for IG. As the infant grows into his childhood, the IG circuit brings within its fold his psycho-social behaviour. It manifests in his desire for quick results (Expression: "I want my *Cadbury* just now"), fast solution to his problems ("I can't open my zipper"—he tries hard, fails and then screams) and immediate satisfaction of his needs ("I want that toy." Mom says: "That is Rohit's, not yours"; the boy says: "Get me one like that just now"; Mom says: "How and wherefrom can I get you one like that just now? You've to WAIT till next week when we go to the toy shop. We'll see if we can get a similar one"; the boy throws up temper tantrums and says: "I can't wait." This means he does not have a 'Delayed Gratification (DG)' circuit in his brain—'Waiting' means 'Delaying or Deferring Gratification'. 'Gratification' will take place—but it will be 'Delayed/Deferred'. As he enters the school campus, his expectation is for immediate feedbacks. So, he likes oral questions-and-answers session rather than written tests where he cannot get immediate feedback regarding his performance; he has to wait until the teacher examines and gives his marks. A SMART leading parent would have noted this and gets his growing child get habituated to the DG phenomenon in academics as the big tests like Board and University exams are all DG events and teenage is the right time to get the DG circuit firmly installed inside the teenage brain.

I would request you to recall, along with me, the classical Marshmallow Test in a Stanford (USA) school by world's leading expert on 'Self-Control' [= 'Delayed Gratification (DG)'], the

Austrian-American psychologist Walter Mischel (1930–2018). I had written about it in an earlier chapter. Mischel had proven, by following a group of school children from childhood to their youth moving through TEENAGE mid-way, that the ability to 'Delay Gratification (DG)' was most critical for a successful life, predicting higher SAT scores, better social and cognitive functioning, a healthier lifestyle and a greater sense of self-worth. And, he had proven that DG can be taught.

The crucial factor in DG is the ability to change your perception of the object or action you want to resist. Are you trying to avoid the junk food (a piece of cream cake that you love) in front of your nose? Put a frame around it in your mind, as if it were just a picture and not real—to make the temptation not 'Instant' or 'Immediate'. Are you trying to avoid lighting a cigarette? Put up in your mind the picture of a lung cancer patient that you saw recently in a video undergoing most painful therapy? Trying to avoid getting affected by the Corona Virus? Try to retrieve from your memory the video which showed the dead body of a Corona-affected person—how it was disinfected thoroughly by the clinical health workers in a morgue, then undressed and wiped, put into a plastic cover, then zipped and sent to the crematorium (if you want this movie I can share with you—it was forwarded to me by a medical doctor friend of mine).

One case study from my 'Case Basket'! In the summer of 2019, a 18-year old (DOB: 13/11/2000) boy Monotosh came to my 'Neuro-management Group (NMG)' office for his mentoring session with an umbrella. He was perspiring like hell. I asked: 'Why do you need an umbrella? Does not look like raining outside." "Sir, it is the terrible heat! Without umbrella, I cannot tolerate the mid-summer heat. Look Sir, how I've perspired!". I immediately asked him to sit and get relaxed. Then I taught him the Mischel technique to change the perception of the situation. He had to imagine that it is not that iron hot, it is tolerable; in fact, quite comfortable. His mental perception would move fast (although following a circuitous route) to his skin.

[The stimulus would be worked upon by his 'Parasympathetic' instead of his 'Sympathetic' part of his 'Autonomic Nervous System (ANS)' This is what the Yogis practice. If you find this portion jargonistic, just skip it—you won't miss much I can assure you].

The boy came back after a week without the umbrella and not perspiring. But it was an equally hot day. He had practiced and mastered the technique of 'Altered Perception' which was Mischel's proven way for developing a DG circuit in the brain.

Question: Don't you think if you are a parent, you will be tempted to apply this technique to get rid of some of your Bad Habits before you teach your teenage kid to use it for his benefit? If you are more focussed on your teenage kid's balanced development, would you first identify if he has developed a DG circuit (Self-control) or is still a laggard with an IG circuit only?

The 5 Psycho-Social Hungers of Teenagers

DG involving 'Self-control' is a vital prerequisite for climbing up the ladder of success in life. And here, parents have a very big role to play while bringing up children—particularly teenagers by satisfying their 5 Psycho-Social Hungers. While opening up the discussion on 'Delaying Gratification', I had introduced the topic and explained how from the moment a child is born, all along its growth and development over the years, it is guided by its 'Instant or Immediate Gratification (IG)' circuit for its survival in any environment. As a part of its upbringing process, responsible parents devise strategies for installing the 'Deferred or Delayed Gratification (DG)' circuit—an important event being 'Toilet Training'. At one time of my career, I had come across Prof. Gourango Chattapadhyay of the Indian Institute of Management, Calcutta, Joka (who had been trained in the famous Tavistock Institute of London) who had emphasized the importance of the impact of childhood toilet training on adult behaviour.

Here, I will just go through, very quickly, a few more situations in our day-to-day living and working which are vital thrust areas and teenage is the right time when SMART leading parents should remember my tips and take action.

A human child having such a big and highly networked brain compared to its evolutionary predecessor chimpanzees (genetically 98.5 to 99% similar to humans but with a smaller sparsely networked brain) has several hungers apart from the biological hungers for food (and sex; for 'sex' read Freud's Theory of a Child's Psycho-sexual Development) which relate to his psycho-social realm.

These are:

Structure-Hunger: Strong need for gainfully (leading to a 'Reward') structuring the 'Time' available in hand (I had cited this as one of the main reasons for late rising in the case of a teenager—he can get up on a school or college day but not on a holiday or during lockdown because there is nothing for him to structure his time if he gets up. Here the parent has to guide and schedule some activity which leads to the release of 'Reward' chemicals in the brain).

Attention-Hunger: The teenager was talking to the mother and suddenly a call comes stealing mother's 'Attention' from the child who gets upset. A SMART mother has to handle it tactfully. How? The mother has to say: 'Oh! He should not have called me now when I'm busy with you? Beta, should I attend or not?" Or "I will just tell him that I'll call him later and get back to you in a minute."

Stroke-Hunger: The teenager's brain's reward circuitry needs stimulation or strokes—meaning 'Appreciation'. A SMART parent should set guidelines to the teenager as to when he can expect appreciation. For instance, a father who goes to the market on Sundays was not feeling well, so he asked the teenage son to go to the market to get fish, fruits and vegetables. When the son brings the provisions and settles the accounts, he gets a 'Thank you very much' appreciation. So, the son gets the 'Cue' what action or behaviour on his part will bring the 'Reward'.

Acceptance-Hunger: Teenagers are extremely sensitive to criticism as 'criticism' means 'Rejection' (Rejection = I'm not liked/ I'm not loved). Criticism could be direct: "What have you done stupid!" "How could you do this nonsense?"; or, indirect (comparing with others): "Your friend Leena is doing so well in studies, why are you lagging behind Ratna, I don't understand?" or "Look how neatly your sister has made her bed; and, look at yours; it's like a garbage dump." Instead, a SMART parent should use what I call the 'Sandwich' technique. Lay the first slice of bread with a positive stroke means 'appreciation' "Leena you are so good in dancing! Your dance teacher is full of praise and she appreciates your quick grasping power." Now, come with the butter, or cheese, or salad, egg or mayonnaise or honey to be put on that 1st piece of bread: "Leena, it's not that you don't have the material. I can see it being applied when you have done so well and with a lot of grace. Why don't you apply it to your studies?" Look at Leena's face. She would lift her sunken face to make eye contact with mom. Now, the mom should put the top slice of bread by making body contact (either hold her hand or touch her shoulder to give a pat) with Leena and say: "I have full confidence on you Leena, that if you apply yourself you 'Can Do Well' in your studies also. If you need any support from us, please tell; don't hesitate."

Affiliation-Hunger: Today's teenage children want to feel an integral part of the family. In our Indian culture, many of us use it totally wrongly. Mother feels teenage son will be scared of ghosts so she sleeps with him (leading to the son's possible trigger of 'Oedipus Complex'—the son gets sexually attracted towards the mother). The teenage daughter wants to sleep with the father and the father allows it (leading to the daughter's possible trigger of 'Electra Complex'—the daughter getting sexually attracted towards the father beginning to hate the mother, going to the extent of hitting and abusing her). Instead of such 'Physical Affiliation', Smart Parents should practice 'Social Affiliation': dining together, vacationing together, taking the teenage kids to parents' friends places, calling them when friends of parents visit your house and introducing them, etc.

BRAIN TOOL 5

Change Management (CM)

'Key' Points: *Changes while Growing Up; Five Psycho-Sexual Stages; Active 'Seeking System Circuit (SSC)' during Teenage; Changes are Opportunities; The 2S-5M Formula for Practical Application of 'Change Management (CM)'; Your Working Life Space: Your Career; A Case Study.*

Changes while Growing Up

From infancy to adolescence, a human child undergoes a lot of physical changes well-reckoned by parents from all walks of life and all cultures. Reason: these changes are 'Gross' and noticeable. Similarly, the 'Gross' changes in attitude and behaviour—manifested via expressions and communication are also noticeable to parents—all and sundry. 'Subtle' changes are in the child's psycho-sexual development for which we have to knock at Dr. Sigmund Freud's epitaph and get connected with his departed soul. Freud proposed that psychological development in childhood takes place during five psycho-sexual stages.

Five Psycho-Sexual Stages

ORAL: 0–1 year-old children derive pleasure from oral activities. Including sucking and tasting—they like to put things in their mouth; **ANAL:** 2–3 years old; children begin toilet training; **PHALLIC:** 3-6 years old: boys are more attached to their mother, while girls to their father; **LATENCY:** 6 years to puberty; children spend more time and interact mostly with same sex peers; **GENITAL:** beyond puberty—it starts at the teen and continues further into youth; individuals are attracted to opposite sex peers (barring lesbians and gays having inborn deviant orientation).

In this context, SMART leading parenting would mean not only recognizing such changes in the kid, phase by phase, but also regarding the corresponding behavioural manifestations as 'NATURAL' and not thwarting the natural propensities. Besides, it is their responsibility to provide sex education in a very diplomatic manner trying to drive home that although sex is enjoyable, it is primarily meant for procreation and not for recreation.

Active 'Seeking System Circuit (SSC)' during Teenage

During teenage, the teen brain's 'Seeking System Circuit (SSC)' becomes auto-active. In the pre-historic days, SSC had served the principal purpose of 'Exploration, Experimentation and Learning (EEL)' while embarking upon the hunter-gatherer role. Now that, in the modern society, the teens are well-provided and protected by their parents and caregivers, there is a tendency in many to use EEP in the sexual context. While, in the West, it is a 'done' thing, in our society it is done in the private, behind the eyes of the parents and elders; if not, then it attracts the teenager to porn sites. SMART leading parents ought to be conscious and vigilant about these natural phenomena. Such abilities come from our brain's 'Anterior Cingulate Cortex (ACC)' whose function is to detect ERRORS—any deviation from normal and standards. For developing this power, if you're a parent, you should use the Brain Tool (BT) of 'Change Detection' which is the 1st step in the 'Change Management (CM)' process.

Secondly, to be a SMART leading parent, you should think out strategies for keeping your teenage kid meaningfully busy so that when he (no gender bias) is free from academics, he should indulge in some pursuit related to his DREAM, his VISION. You remember ARKA's case. His DREAM is to become an ace automobile designer. I, as his Mentor, help his parents to ensure that in his free time, he prepares sketches of new types of automobiles (Arka is a talented artist), watches TV programmes and searches the internet to collect data on automobiles besides compiling newspaper and magazine cuttings on autos. I, on my own, introduced him through WhatsApp an acquaintance of mine D.K. Joshi of Ghaziabad who had is automobile engineering internship in Maruti plant at Manesar. I motivated his father to take him on a Sunday to an automobile repair workshop on Kasba bypass in Kolkata in the vicinity of where they live. He got introduced to the Sardarji-owner of the shop and the overtly-impressed Sardar asked Arka to drop in anytime he liked and spend time with him and his technical staff.

All this is not to allow the teenage boy's brain's 'Default Mode Network (DMN)' to become active. DMN is our idle brain's Devil's workshop. When our brain is not engaged in any task ['Task Mode Network (TMN)], it wanders with useless people-related negative thoughts regarding the past or the future. It had a meaningful purpose, in the pre-historic days, for effective hunting-gathering team-building and team-functioning, but now it has a most unproductive role particularly during teenage unless one is trained to use it purposefully. So, one of SMART leading parent's essential lookout would be to ensure that the teenager's brain's DMN compartment does not get engaged with digital games, porn watching and similar other unproductive pursuits.

Changes are Opportunities

Do you not believe that every darkness has a silver lining? Therefore, do not look at a sudden crisis like the COVID-19 Lockdown just as a 'Threat' as most people have done. Think coolly and deeply to identify some totally new 'Opportunities'—some welcome 'changes', under such suddenly altered circumstances, which you would have never dreamt of earlier.

How I always stimulate my brain's circuits to prepare myself for any un-forethought drastic change! I keep a bottle containing a money plant on the window seal near my study table. The bottle is an old tomato ketchup bottle—7 to 8 inches tall. The neck of the bottle is a 'Threat' for the plant's natural growth and development. It no doubt looks like an insurmountable constraint. Yet, how the plant with its own botanical intelligence takes the 'Opportunity' of the window seal utilising its firm support to grow its multiple roots for extending itself horizontally.

I had cut the branch of a decorative plant from my front portico plant-bed and immersed it in water in a medium-sized coffee mug. My cutting it off from the main plant was not regarded as a 'Threat' by the cut branch as within the next 4–5 days, it started growing ROOTs from the stem taking the mug space filled with water as an 'Opportunity'.

I clean up the dry leaves from the backyard of my house with the help of a broomstick and watch the big money plants—how they find alternative routes if I block the way they were growing. Sir Jagadish Chandra Bose who had discovered life in plants and had devised Crescograph—an instrument for measuring plant growth would have written a couple of scientific articles on the observations I make with a different purpose. My purpose is to observe the botanical phenomena to sharpen my own 'Brain Tool (BT)' on 'Change Management (CM)' by feeling deeply inside me how these plants cope with change using their environmental intelligence.

The 2S-5M Formula for Practical Application of 'Change Management (CM)'

Among quite a few of the positive facets of the Lockdown era, a major one is that it provides you with ample 'Opportunity' to familiarise yourself and your pre-teen and teenage kids with 'BT (CM)'. I've developed a 2S-5M formula for CM's practical application. There are seven factors to be considered, starting with an S ('Space'—Ether/Aakash/Param Brahma, of which you're just a part and this 'Space' includes the man-made 'Time' factor also which you and I follow as 'Objective Time') and ending with another S ('Self'—that is 'You'—the inner 'Self'—Jivatman, enveloped by the 'Pancha Kosha' proposed in the Taittiriya Upanishad). Between these two subtle S's are 5 gross M's—all materialistic factors: 'Materials', 'Machines', 'Methods', 'Money' and 'Men'.

In this article, I will dwell on 'Space' only and its relationship with 'Self'—Yourself.

Your Working Life Space: Your Career

My concept of 'Space' here is your entire 'Working Life Space'—your 'Career'. Naturally here by 'Space', I mean the 'Time' factor. At the earliest opportunity, you have to play the role of a SMART leading parent and make time to plan your teenage kid's career. Impress upon him (no gender bias) that every morning he gets on his platter 86,400 units of 'Opportunity'. [24 hours × 60 minutes × 60 seconds = 86,400 seconds and each second is potent with some opportunity—one second gone means one unit of opportunity lost.] Thus, from the teenage himself, one must be groomed not to waste any time (that is, opportunity). In order to achieve this, the teenager must discover his PASSION—in other words his DREAM. The next is to identify from which realm the DREAM is being generated; in other words, wherefrom the DRIVE (the motivating force) is coming. I've had a fair amount of studies on the Western concepts of motivation, performance, personality (including the well-known Maslow's Hierarchy of Human Needs and the more recent Daniel Pink's attractive book called *DRIVE*) but nowhere have I found a convincing basis for my perception of DRIVE than our Vedic concept of Pancha Kosha which had been documented in the Taittiriya Upanishad (a part of Krishna Yajur Veda) written in 6th Century B.C.

The Pancha Kosha proposes that your 'Pure Self' is enveloped by five sheaths (= koshas) of which the gross one is the visible, palpable layer—'Annamaya Kosha (AK)' representing all your materialistic needs, beginning with food and water, moving into clothes, shelter, sex and all objects of pleasure for which you feel you have been brought to this world. So, if any teenager's 'Passion Quotient' or DREAM is to do something with any object of materialistic desire or hedonistic lifestyle, then his DRIVE is coming from AK. An example (I had shared it earlier also but it is such a perfect case study in the truest sense that I am tempted to share it again). A young school boy in Jaipur Rajasthan was crazy about bakery and confectionery products. He would simply love them for breakfast, tiffin and high tea. His DRIVE came from the AK and he nurtured a DREAM to be a bakery chef. Naturally, the DOMAIN ('Domain' is the broad field where you would get the opportunity for realising or materialising your DREAM) would be the hotel and restaurant industry or big elite clubs which have their own bakery products. He was full of positive vibe, studied hard, did well in exams, got admitted into a Hotel and Hospitality Management course, completed it with a rank in the finals, got campus-picked for a 5-star hotel for its Bakery Division, did so well that he got a promotion with special increments within a year, was picked up as the Chief Bakery Chef for a smaller patisserie in Bhopal on a much higher salary and more attractive terms. I am in regular touch with him in Bhopal in India and his dad in Saudi Arabia; both are very happy; no complaints.

Space will not permit me to go into the details of the other Koshas and their related DRIVES, DREAMS and DOMAINS. But what I'd like to highlight here that unless you or your teenage kid is placed on a 'Treadmill' which keeps you and him on your toes to study deeply your subject by using your 'Vijnanamaya Kosha (VK)' which represents your intelligence, cause-and-effect relating analytical ability and, on top of it, triggers your 'Anandamaya Kosha (Ank)' from time to time to create, innovate, invent, discover, get intuitions and insights to offer improvements to old ideas, concepts and products, approaches and strategies you will not be able survive in today's highly competitive and combative market environment.

A Case Study

My friend and research colleague Michael Braudy of New York, USA had a DREAM to be a violinist. The DRIVE came from his 'Monomaya Kosha (MK)' which represents 'Emotions'. He came to India as a disciple of Pt. VG Jog but soon discovered that unless he uses his VK and AnK, he would be nowhere. We met at that juncture and worked together on therapeutic music. It clicked. He went to South India, worked with a lady who is a medical doctor and a top Veena player. Together they produced CDs and DVDs on therapeutic music which were hits. Now Michael practices music therapy and has become popular in the US health and fitness circuit. Most interestingly, Michael has not been jobless during Lockdown as many of you have been. He is very much in demand, in radio and TV channels especially for cheering up people and de-stress them with his music for stress management. So, your teenage kid's career planning should be such that, even during any such crises and critical circumstances, he will not be idling.

BRAIN TOOL 6 Humour

'Key' Points: *Positive and Negative Brain Tools (BTs); The 'Anger' and 'Fear' Families'; Bharat Muni's Nava Rasa; Humour; A Case Study; My Different Experiences with Humour; A Child's First Expression: A Smile; Endorphin: The Humour Molecule; Benefits of Humour; Question.*

Positive and Negative Brain Tools

The cognitive part of your brain would catch it immediately when I point out that there are positive Brain Tools (BT) as well as negative Brain Tools (BT) just the same way as your hand tools have positive as well as negative applications. With a hammer, you can drive a nail (+ve), you can also break someone's head (–ve) with the same hammer to defend yourself. In the same note, two most common negative BTs that Mother Nature did install in every reptile, bird and mammal are 'fight (anger/aggression)' and 'flight (fear/anxiety/depression)' which through my 'Neuro-management (NM)' lessons, I recommend people to tone down. My approach, you ought to find novel and interesting. How and why? I perceive 'Anger' and 'Fear' as two opposite-natured families inside our brain's cobwebbed network.

The 'Anger' and 'Fear' Families

Using a five-point scale of 'low' to 'high', my 'Anger' family comprises: irritability, anger, annoyance, rage and aggression (physical violence/assault); whereas the 'Fear' family follows: gaze avoidance, communication avoidance, reluctance to show up, absenteeism, and disappearance (running away). The anger chemical released is 'adrenaline' (also known as 'epinephrine') and the fear chemical is 'cortisol'—the source for both are your adrenal glands; the level of these also follow the corresponding 'low' to 'high' order. My 'Neuro-management (NM)' prescription is to stop your 'Anger' at the 1st stage of 'irritability' and your 'Fear' at the 1st stage of 'gaze avoidance'. I was invited to conduct a few short and effective workshops on this, many years ago, in Bangladesh.

Bharata Muni's Nava Rasa

'Anger' and 'Fear/Anxiety' belong to our toolkit of 'Emotions'. In ancient times, the Indian sage Bharata had come up with his concept of 'Nava Rasas' (9 emotions) each having its characteristic facial and bodily expressions which are demonstrated in Indian classical dance styles. In the modern West, Paul Ekman, professor emeritus at UCLA, USA had done a worldwide research on emotions and their accompanying facial expressions and according to him and his co-researchers, there are 6 (six) common facial expressions representing: 5 (five) negative—Anger, Disgust, Fear, Sadness and Surprise and only 1 (one) positive—Happiness. Happiness is represented by a smiling face—a face depicting satisfaction, gratification, satiation and contentment. Bharata Muni had described it as 'Hasya Rasa'—Humour.

Humour

'Humour', thus, is a very powerful positive Brain Tool (BT), that we have, installed in our brains. Why positive: because it has many health benefits as it exercises your lungs and abdomen, it strengthens your immune system, it multiplies the killer cells in your blood; it helps you to come close to people and develop bonded relationships; and, it releases the happiness chemical 'Endorphin (E)' from your brain's pituitary glands which serves as your internally generated stress manager.

'Humour', thus, has a healing power. It gives you confidence. It works on your Root Chakra (Muladhar) and makes you feel grounded and stable. The Root Chakra, located at the base of the spine, is associated with the following functions or behavioural characteristics essential for an individual's existence: survival, security, safety, physicality (physical identity and aspects of self), basic needs (food, sleep, a roof over the head for protection from rough weather, self-preservation), foundation for living our lives.

Teenage is the period of a kid's life when he (no gender bias) must get 'Grounded' by attending to the nurture of the Root Chakra. This is an area where SMART leading parents need to lay thrust. Endorphin (E) is an essential brain chemical to be generated in the teen brain for this purpose. Taking regular physical fitness exercises (simple freehand stretching-bending or yoga) would be a suitable one but for many teens it becomes difficult to stick to a routine exercise regime. Eating dark chocolate is also a means but chocolate contains sugar which may turn to be addictive. To my mind, 'Humour' would find a universal application here. This is the reason why pre-teens become addicted to watching cartoons and reading funny stories and comics as such habits help to maintain a balanced level of E in their brains.

A Case Study

My pen would not stop unless I share the case study of Bipul Mandal who hails from an interior village in Bankura. Very poor in background, his father was involved in political activities and did farming on a mini scale. Bipul finished his HS, got his car driving licence at the age of 18, took a train and landed at Howrah. He had stopped at a small stationer's shop to buy a packet of biscuits as he was starving. Bipul might not have a fat wallet but he had the Brain Tool (BT) of HUMOUR. His conversation was so witty that he soon won the heart of the shop owner Das Babu. Das was a bachelor and he owned an ancestral house in Howrah city where he lived alone. Highly impressed by Bipul's sense of humour, he nurtured his Root Chakra and helped him to get GROUNDED.

He not only offered him to stay with him in his house, but also arranged a job for him in his friend's office. This was 10 years ago. Within this period, Bipul has completed his graduation, got confirmation and a few promotions in his office because of his BT-H and is a happy man today with a steady supply of Endorphin in his brain. He is also a constant source for supply of Endorphin to others, whosoever comes in contact with him. The BT (H) provides him with a cutting edge.

If you are used to put up a serious façade, do you realise that most of your physical and mental imbalances are because you hardly use your 'Brain Tool (BT)'—6: Humour? Don't be unkind to your kids, lead them SMARTLY—let them giggle, smile, laugh and, by doing so, enjoy the benefits of 'Endorphin (E).

My Different Experiences with Humour

My student days in UK were full of fun, frolic and humour! Britons have the highest sense of 'Humour' in the whole world and, as humour is contagious, I was always riding the rollercoaster of 'Wit' and 'Pun'. Mornings and afternoons at the Faculty Club (where research scholars could also join with the teaching staff) during tea breaks, you were considered a moron if you hadn't broken into laughter when Prof. Hugh Sutherland cracked his typical highland jokes in Gaelic language. Prof. Sutherland was a gifted joke-pot! So was Tim Jackson, a Physiology lecturer. Lunchtime ambience was hilarious at the Glasgow University Union. Humour in Britain did not have any colour bar. Post-evening time spent at my hall of residence, The Great Western Hotel was also full of joy amidst British, Indian, Pakistani, Bangladeshi, Nepalese, Sri Lankan, Thai, Malaysian, African, Canadian and Australian students. My brain used to have such a good level of 'Endorphin (E)' all the time that I never even suffered from common cough and cold, leave aside flu or diarrhoea, living in the damp, cold, windy city of Glasgow where the Sun God hardly made His appearance in public.

Back in my home base at Calcutta, when I joined an American company as a senior executive, the first thing that struck me was the dull atmosphere because people hardly laughed. Everybody, I found, was wearing a mask as they were all scared of the MD and CEO. However, I was lucky to be close to an English architect Trevor Wall who was like a tiny island of humour in an ocean of glumness. Since he used to stay on my way to the office, I made it a point to pick him up and drop him back every day. During the 40 minutes that we spent together, I earned my 'Endorphin (E)' for the whole day and evening.

During the weekend, when I started teaching medical doctors doing their post-graduates at the University College of Medicine, Calcutta University, I found nobody ever smiled. My co-faculty

Professor Bose asked an MS (Orthopaedics) student to get out of the class because he had violated the conduct code and laughed. I started missing something at both my workplaces—at the corporate as well as at the academic. I broke that culture when I set up my own research team and, believe me or not, we excelled within a very short while so much that in 8 (eight) years' time, me and my research colleagues had more than 40 scientific papers published in peer-reviewed journals overseas [You will find all of those documented in 'ResearchGate'—the website for top scientists].

Today, 'Humour' is being used for pain management. There has been an outstanding research in Hong Kong on this. Every kid should be trained in the benefits and applications of the 'Brain Tool (BT)': Humour (H) right from the teenage and that is a prime responsibility of SMART leading parents.

A Child's First Expression: A Smile

A newly born child's first expression with its mother is exchange of smile. If the mother smiles, the infant also smiles; 'Endorphin (E)' is released in its brain to make him feel secure. Children smile and laugh about 300 to 400 times a day whereas typical adults manage a miserable 15 to 20 and those who feel 'Un-grounded' and insecure, hardly smile.

Endorphin: The Humour Molecule

'Endorphins' are the body's natural opiates. Exercising releases E, leading to a feeling of happiness, even euphoria. Nevertheless, exercise is not the only thing, smiling, eating certain foods which contain chillies, an even gossiping can also do the trick. There are many ways to harness our natural 'Endorphins (E)' to help life's problems melt away.

Find some more reasons to smile and laugh. It is an everyday immediate way to give yourself an 'E' rush. 'E' relieves stress and has many other physical and emotional benefits. Sharing a joke with friends or finding something genuinely funny is the best way to make the most of laughter. Go for a deep, belly laugh that takes over your whole body. Smile, but make sure it's a real one. True smiles, called *Duchene* smiles, result in the production of

'E' giving your mood a boost. A *Duchene* smile is one that engages your entire face, including your eyes. It's almost impossible to fake, and it only happens when you are really feeling happy. A smile that engages just your mouth and not your eyes, does not have the same beneficial effects. To boost your mood with a smile, try looking at pictures that make you smile, or talk to a person who makes you happy.

The level of 'E' in the human body varies from person to person. People who have lower levels of 'E' may be more likely to have depression or fibromyalgia (propensity for body ache and migraine), but more research is needed in this area. Scientists use 'Positron Emission Tomography (PET)' scans to view brains both before and after exercise. They are expected to find an increase in the release of 'E' after exercise. But, while exercising, you must stretch or bend to an extent that it becomes a little painful.

Benefits of Humour

The physical benefits of 'Humour' are: It lowers blood pressure; boosts immune system; improves brain functioning and protects the heart; increases lung capacity; strengthens abdominal muscles; causes reduction in the stress hormones Cortisol and Adrenaline (or Epinephrine); increases energy and can help us perform activities we may otherwise avoid.

Following a humorous encounter, natural killer cell activity increases for as long as 12 hours, bringing about beneficial health outcomes, the use of 'Humour' consistently results in improvements in pain thresholds. Pain management together with 'Humour' was found to be more effective than pain management alone. Qualitative findings have also supported the effectiveness of 'Humour' in patient care.

Question: If you're asked to adorn an interview board for selection of the most eligible candidate for an executive's post, would you select an academically brilliant young man with a serious and glum face or a not-a-ranker but someone who kept smiling throughout the interview and did not break down when you tried to bowl him out?

BRAIN TOOL 7

Belief

'Key' Points: *The Beer Marathon; The Iceberg Mind; A Covid 19 Battle Winner; Impact of Positive and Negative Feedback; Two Case Studies; Two Kinds of Attention; Three More Case Studies; Beliefs Control Biology; The Example of Tiger Woods; Nurturing Beliefs.*

The Beer Marathon

Annual Beer Marathon is a big event in Germany, I had heard but had never attended; only saw it on the TV. So, when I came to know that every year, the Glasgow University Students' Union used to host a Beer Marathon where students from other leading Scottish universities—St. Andrews, Edinburgh, Heriot-Watt, Aberdeen, Dundee, Strathclyde and Stirling would participate, I made it a point to be present as a spectator. It was amazing to see how many pints of beer the contestants

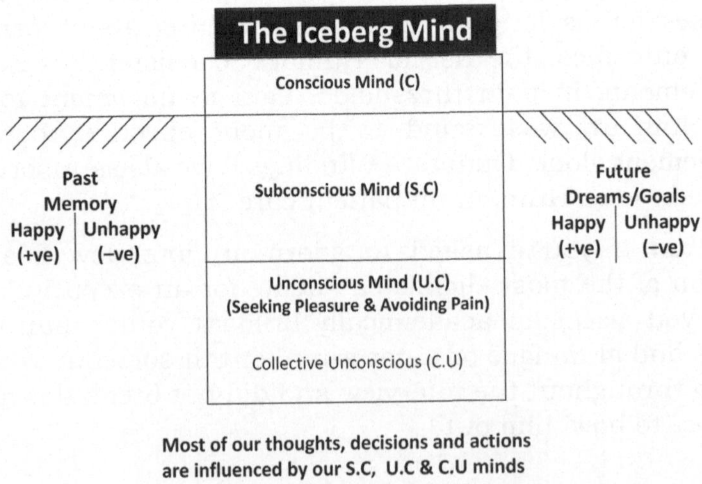

Fig. 6: The Iceberg Mind

would drink without passing out. When I attended it for the 1st time, I asked the champion Bill Crawford how could he manage without getting drunk or sick. He had simply said: 'BELIEF that I shall stay steady and fit.' At that time, I was just getting introduced to Freud's classical model of the Iceberg Mind and it took me no time to relate the 'Belief' concept to this model.

While I am writing this piece, I am operating from my 'Conscious Mind (CM)'—the TIP of the iceberg, if the whole mind is compared to an iceberg. I am consciously deciding what to write, how much to write, where to stop and so on. When you read it, you are also using your CM. However, what I am writing about—the Glasgow University Annual Beer Marathon, I am not imagining it; I am going deep into my 'Sub-Conscious Mind (SCM)'—my mind's memory storage and retrieving the data from there. Right from the moment of conception and zygote formation, memories of all that happens in the External Environment (physical, chemical, psychological, social)—both happy (+ve) and unhappy (–ve)—all are stored in the SCM. Stimuli which are repeated get imprinted and form our 'Beliefs (B)'.

If, in your environment, there have been continuous comments about you: "You're a good boy. You will go to the top" that turns out to be a positive input, gets impregnated into your SCM and motivates you subconsciously to succeed by influencing your every conscious thought and every conscious action. Although your long-term memory storage is the 'Hippocampus (H)' part of your paleo-mammalian mid-brain, each body and brain cell of yours has its own specialised, relevant memory. When in a marriage party in India, a teenager invitee challenges his peers in Gulab Jamun competition, he is getting hidden support from each of his relevant cells (in his Gut Brain) where his past experiences of winning and achievements are stored in the form of a 'Belief' that 'He Will Win'.

A Covid 19 Battle Winner

Times of India, Calcutta edition of 20th May 2020 carried a news item on its page 4: "82-yr-old wins nCOV battle after 24-day stay in hospital". It struck me immediately as the photo accompanying the news was that of my friend and close neighbour Tapan Mitra. My house is 10 Clarke Street and Tapan's is No. 7. Tapan was a good scholar: B.Com (Hons.) from St. Xavier's College, Chartered-Cost and Management Accountant and had 2 MBA degrees—one from the McGill Business School, Canada and the other from the International Management Institute (IMI), Geneva, Switzerland.

When he was studying in IMI Geneva in 1979, I had gone to a few places on a lecture tour of UK and Europe and had made presentations in Geneva including at the WHO, ILO and IMI. I had spent a whole day with him there also. He retired as the MD of Indian Aluminium Ltd. when the Canadian ALCAN group sold it to the A.V. Birla Group's HINDALCO. He was non-executive chairman of Haldia Petrochemicals Ltd. followed by being the Chairman of the Tripura State Planning Board.

Tapan was ailing for quite some time with underlying lung and heart conditions, hypertension and diabetes. Admitted to Fortis Hospital with severe COPD conditions, Mitra tested Covid positive and was in the isolation ward initially. He developed a secondary bacterial infection and was on ventilator for seven days. When interviewed by the press, he said: "I had a horrible journey, but my positive memories kept me going. I constantly kept my mind engaged with good thoughts." If I use my 'Neuro-management (NM)' language, Mr Mitra did not allow his brain's 'Default Mode Network (DMN)' to be active which would have made him stressful as DMN sometimes plays the role of being our brain's devil's workshop. Now, 'Consciously', Mr Mitra used to retrieve his positive memories, but most active in his 'Subconscious' was the 'Belief' that "nothing can take me away....I'll be all right." 'Belief' is thus a 'Brain Tool (BT)' which resides in the thick 'Sub-Conscious' part of our mind.

Impact of Positive and Negative Feedback

I have already mentioned a little while ago that positive feedback arising from the environment about your personality, intelligence and capabilities will crystallize as +ve 'Beliefs' which will support you, work in your favour. It will just be the other way round if you always receive –ve stimulus inputs going into your SCM that "You are hopeless; you're good for nothing; your future is bleak" and so on. I will now share two such case studies.

Two Case Studies

Bichitra Bera was an intelligent boy, good in studies but constitutionally too thin and sickly. He did not enjoy good health but being brainy, could complete his B.Tech in Electronic Engineering. It started off when he was in Class VII, at the onset of teenage. Once he had jaundice which took a long time to get cured. From then on, he used to get messages from all around: "You are too sickly! You'll never regain and become healthy and fit." His father would criticise his small eating habit and compare him with his cousins and class friends. His mother would continually say: "I've so much problem with you. I do not know how would you cope with your academic load in higher classes and in college." And, she used to feed him health drinks and two spoonful of Chawanaprash every day. Still Bichitra's health did not improve. He remained emotional and emaciated. In the 'Subconscious' part of his mind, he had crystallized a 'Belief': "I would never improve. I will never be healthy and fit."

It is not that Bichitra was born with faulty genes which never let him grow. Our total energy is expended in two channels: for 'Survival' or 'Protection' and 'Growth'. His negative 'Belief' was draining out so much of his energy for making him survive, live and protect from serious health hazards that very little energy was left to be spent for his 'Growth' and 'Development'.

I had come across the case of another boy Mukesh Yadav from Bihar. When he was approaching his teens, a few days of acute diarrhoea had made him lose a lot of weight and look awkward—bony and skinny. His stomach would never regain its normal demeanour. He suffered from indigestion, flatulence, irregular bowel movement and irritable bowels syndrome. People in his environment (his widowed mom Juthika, his uncle Raghav and aunt Malati- all) started commenting negatively the essence of which was 'Mukesh will never be healthy and fit'. They spent thousands on his treatment but there was no improvement. He was even wrongly diagnosed as a TB patient and treatment started and continued accordingly. The underlying source of his illness was the negative 'Belief' that had crystallized in his 'Subconscious'. Ultimately, a Calcutta doctor cured him with simple medicine. He actually counselled him which reversed his 'Belief'—turned the negative one into positive: "Who said I will not be OK? I am not a 'gone' case! I will certainly get cured and become healthy and fit". Mukesh, after 4 (four) years, is in much better health and disposition now.

Our lives are not determined by our genes, but by our responses to the environmental signals that propel life. Environmental signals select, modify, and regulate gene activity. Our genes express or repress themselves being guided by our environment. So, what kind of environment a kid is getting to grow up—especially in the teenage, is a much more important factor than 'Gene Only'.

Two Kinds of Attention

There are two kinds of 'Attention' that a growing teenage kid can get from his (no gender bias) environment: 'Positive' ('You're good', 'You're healthy', 'You'll recover', 'You'll win') and 'Negative' ('You're bad', 'You're hopeless', 'You're good for nothing', 'You'll never be healthy and fit', 'You'll never recover', 'You'll lose'. Well-deserved 'Positive Attention' will make him confident and give him a solid base for success. Biased 'Negative Attention' will make him diffident and give him a flimsy grounding.

Two More Case Studies

Simple cases but complex implications. I will share two more case studies, which are really striking.

About 10 years ago, my phone rang. It was Sreya Sarkar, a Marketing Executive of a big oil company. She had attended one of my corporate workshops and was desperately seeking my help. What was the problem? Her teenage son, Soumya, studying in a good English medium school in South Calcutta had not been attending school for the last few days and not studying at home either. He was only drawing sketches after sketches the whole day. He was very good in drawing. Sreya's husband Mukur (who is a freelance Russian translator), Sreya and Soumya came to my Winning Child clinic. I asked Sreya and Mukur to sit in the other room and started talking to Soumya privately. I took his drawing book and started looking at it! Wow! What fantastic sketches—but all of different kinds of snakes; nothing else! "What is your DREAM?" "Sir, I want to be a herpetologist (herpetology is the branch of zoology concerned with the study of reptiles).” “Can you give me a short introductory talk on herpetology?” “Of course, Sir!” And he started talking smartly with full confidence pouring out data that I had never known about. Then he opened up: “Sir I have stopped going to school and studying at home as my mother particularly does not want me to be a herpetologist because she nurtures a BELIEF that such creatures whom I want to study are dangerous and inauspicious. And, my father is indifferent—neither here nor there!” I called Sreya and Mukur and told them not to shatter Soumya’s DREAM with their ‘Belief’. I told them that I can make him attend school and study at home if they did not impose their plan on him based on their ‘Belief’ (that herpetology is a bad career choice, and engineering, general science, physiology, psychology or medicine are good career choices). I emphasized that if they did not agree, I simply could not motivate their son to resume his academic study schedule. The parents agreed most reluctantly and went back.

After 3 days, I got a call from Sreya speaking with a beaming smile (which I couldn’t see): “Sir, your medicine has worked. Soumya has started attending school and studying at home.” The same boy completed his M.Sc. in Zoology from Calcutta University, took his Ph.D. in herpetology and currently doing his post-doc in an Ivy League university in USA.

Sreenivasa Rao was the Calcutta-based Regional Manager of a 2-wheeler company. Married to Madhuri for the long 12 years, they were childless. There were apparently no gynaecological issues, but during one of her home visits to Guntur, Andhra Pradesh, Madhuri had met a tantric in the train who had told her that much though they may try, she will be unable to bear a child. Madhuri was travelling alone in AC 2-tier and this Tamil tantric was her co-passenger on his way to Chennai. Throughout the journey, what the tantric said was ringing like a ringtone into Madhuri’s ears travelling deep into her SCM crystallizing into a –ve ‘Belief’ circuit. Sreeni met me at a workshop which I was conducting for the 2-wheeler industry at the Hotel Oberoi Grand, Calcutta and, knowing my background enquired whether there would be any technique in Brain Science for reversal of the ‘Belief’—turning the –ve into +ve. I was just studying the emerging science of ‘Neuroplasticity’ then which establishes that brain circuits are not rigid and fixed—they can be altered by means of 'Rewiring'. It took me six months and a two-hour session per week to convert the –ve into a positive 'Belief' in Madhuri's SCM. She conceived and after the scheduled period of pregnancy, delivered a healthy male child. Throughout her pregnancy, of course, we had to use Music Therapy for stress management. Madhuri's Music Therapy was based on Telugu old melodies which she loved and, amongst those, the bulk was chosen from Illaya Raja, the talented South Indian composer.

Beliefs Control Biology

'Beliefs' control 'Biology'. Power of the mind is superior to the power of chemicals and the scalpel. The latter two are invasive while the former is non-invasive. Dr. Bruce Moseley of the Baylor School of Medicine, USA, performed a fake knee surgery to cure the osteoarthritis of Tim Perez and cured him entirely on the basis of the fact that Tim nurtured a 'Belief' that he will be cured. In Tim's own words: "In this world anything is possible when you put your mind to it. I know that your mind can work miracles." Thoughts—the mind's energy, directly influence how the physical brain controls the body's physiology. Thought 'energy' can activate or inhibit the cell's function-producing proteins via the mechanics of constructive and destructive interference. If you spend your brain's energy negatively, the outcome would be negative; and vice versa.

The Example of Tiger Woods

A wonderful example of the effectiveness of conscious parenting is superstar golfer Tiger Woods. Although his father was not an accomplished golfer, he made every effort to immerse Tiger in an environment that was rich with opportunities to develop and enhance the mindset, skills, attitudes, and focus of a master golfer. No doubt, Tiger's success is also intimately connected with the Buddhist philosophy that his mother contributed. "Indeed, genes are important—but the importance is only realised through the influence of conscious parenting and the richness of opportunities provided by the environment."

Nurturing Beliefs

Taking cue from Tiger Woods' case, how his father had parented him during his teenage, I would suggest that if you want to qualify as a SMART PARENT, nurture five 'Beliefs' regarding your teenage kid (change the reasons inside brackets according to what suit best and are most appropriate in your case):

- My teenage kid is the BEST among his peers (he is best looking in my opinion);
- My teenage kid will ALWAYS WIN (in table tennis which he plays very well);
- My teenage kid will GROW SQUARELY (my friends and relations already regard him as a rounded personality);
- My teenage kid is HEALTHY and FIT (although he is a little overweight, his fitness is beyond any doubt as he is prompt action-oriented and does not procrastinate);
- My teenage kid is COOL and STEADY (he does not lose his poise if things do not work out the way he desires.

BRAIN TOOL 8

Attachment

'Key' Points: *What is 'Attachment'; Biological and Social Imperatives: the Role of 'Attachment'; A Case Study; Stress During Pregnancy; Attachment and Dependence: Physical Aspects; Attachment and Dependence: Brain Functional Aspects; Attachment is Instinctive Up to a Stage; A Few Live Cases; Attachment Models Inside our Minds; A Concrete Case; Distant Attachment; Different Slots for Different Attachment Models; Attachment with a Motive; A Case of Detachment; Drive for Attachment; The Case of Your Teenage Kid; The Soul Theory; Spiritual Progress; A Teenage Kid's Kosha Attachment; Ego-laid Souls Having Low to Mediocre Consciousness; Ego-laid Souls Having Higher Consciousness; My Kosha Attachment; A Real-life Case Study on a Teenager's Career Planning.*

What is 'Attachment'

Lecture gallery, Jadavpur University, 1957—young Prof. Amartya Sen's first lecture on Economics. I was in first year Engineering. Two things struck me. The first one, the name of Adam Smith—the founder of Economics and that he was the professor of moral philosophy at the University of Glasgow, Scotland, went straight into the deep layers of my 'Sub-Conscious Mind (SCM)' and got precipitated there. The second one was wavering between my 'Conscious Mind (CM)' and SCM. It was Prof. Sen's statement: "The basic premise of Economics is that man is a rational animal". This basic premise has now been challenged as two new branches of Economics have evolved over the last few years: 'Behavioural Economics' and, more recently, 'Neuro-economics' which propagate the truth that man is a social and emotional animal. That means all human beings share a common 'Brain Tool (BT)' and that is 'Attachment'—the emotional need to get 'Attached' to others.

Biological and Social Imperatives: The Role of 'Attachment'

If I am allowed to use my 'Neuro-management (NM)' language, I would say that the hard fact or reality is that we, humans, are brought to this planet to fulfil two imperatives: 1: Biological Imperatives (BI): survival and replication or reproduction; and, 2: Social Imperatives (SI): getting bonded to others in order to get support for the fulfilment of BI. So, together, it is BSI.

'Attachment' has a Link with Both BI and SI

The foetus inside the pregnant woman is not only 'Attached' to, but also totally 'Dependent' on her. Foetus-Womb Owner fit or match is best achieved when the Womb-owner wants the child with her whole heart and soul as the neuro-chemical for 'Attachment'—'Oxytocin (O)' is released in full force inside the Womb-owner's as well as the foetus's developing brain. This is the beginning of bonding.

A Case Study

One case study now. Amal Saikia, an Assamese student of mine and his wife Poly dropped in with their three-month old baby girl. The baby was born premature, frail and underweight, Amal said. When Poly got pregnant, she did not want the child (no 'O' was released—'O' is also responsible for producing breast milk in abundance), she wanted to go for an abortion but Amal's parents and Amal himself did not allow it; so, she carried and delivered the child most unwillingly. "Sir, will the 'O'-deprived child be 'Unattached'?" was Amal's question. I said: "That is not the point, for healthy physical and mental growth of the child, 'Attachment' between the mother and the child is essential." "Has the breast milk production been normal?" I asked Poly: "No Sir!" She answered.

"Now the point is: if you want the child to live and grow healthy both physically and mentally, the strategy would be of one kind; and, if you're not interested in the child, she would live because she won't starve in a business executive's household, but would remain emaciated and ailing—one illness after another because lack of 'Attachment' during the growing years will shatter the growing girl's immune system."

Poly responded immediately: "Sir, looking at the child's innocent eyes, face and smile, I've begun to love her. So, please give me some tips as to how to deal with her so that both of us generate enough 'O' and get 'Attached'."

"Amal, you also have an equally important role to play now in generating the male counterpart of 'O'—'Vasopressin (V)'." I continued: "So, if both of you help to produce adequate quantity of 'Attachment' molecules, the child's growth will be OK! You've come to me at the right time." Poly and Amal followed my tips religiously and came out of the danger zone in just about a year's time.

Stress during Pregnancy

Another most important point for Foetus-Womb Owner perfect fit, is that the Womb Owner must not suffer from STRESS during pregnancy because the stress hormone 'Cortisol (C)' produced from the adrenal glands located on the top of the kidney, will eat up 'O' and the child may be born with some problem, as you will note in the following two cases.

Rohit Srivastava attended my workshop for a Tata Group company in its Tata Centre, Chowringhee corporate office. The young IT executive, 28-year-old, suffered from occasional epileptic seizures and no neurologist in Calcutta nor at the Tata Steel hospital, Jamshedpur, could diagnose the root cause. When he sought my advice, I asked him to check with her mom if she was suffering from acute stress during pregnancy. The next day he confirmed that his father was away on a project outside their home base and his mother was alone with the dominating mother-in-law who used to torture her mentally. To cope with the stress, Rohit's mother got habituated to drinking black coffee not less than 10 to 12 cups per day. And, the impact of caffeine was the epileptic child.

Mohana Roy dropped into my Winning Child clinic with her husband Dipak and the 3-year-old son Jeet. Her problem was

Jeet's hyperactivity. Jeet was physically restless, mentally too. They had admitted him into a regular pre-school but within the first few days the lady principal asked them to take him from there and put him into a special school. Mohana and Dipak used to work in the same office, they liked each other and finally got married. But she faced resistance from the in-laws because she and Dipak belonged to different castes. She became a prey to her in-laws' insulting comments and, in the midst of all this, she became pregnant; and, the result was the birth of an ADHD-afflicted child.

So, when Srimoyi Sarkar, an IT Manager in Tata Consultancy Services, approached me with a question: "Sir, I am a few weeks pregnant and my husband has just flown to USA for a 3-year long assignment. I'm feeling a little insecure in my personal life. What should I do?" I responded straight away: "Either take leave without pay or, if that is not granted, resign and go to join your husband in USA to ensure a normal healthy child." Srimoyi's application for leave was sanctioned and she left for the US.

And, the most interesting facts that are coming to light over the last few years that during pregnancy, the 'Gut Health' of the Womb Owner is extremely important for normal healthy growth of the foetus. For sound 'Gut Health', the trillions of microbes inside her 'Gut Brain' must remain in peace, must be happy and undisturbed so that they can carry out their duties and responsibilities without any destructive interference.

Attachment and Dependence: Physical Aspects

'Attachment' and 'Dependence' go hand in hand for the foetus with the Womb-Owner—pre-birth, post-birth for the newly born and for the growing child up to its stepping into the teenage with the mother. Why only with the mother and not with the father? Because of a few reasons the most important ones being: firstly, according to ancient Tantric texts, a wandering soul enters into the 'Pineal Gland (PG)' of the foetus's brain when the foetus's gender is also determined—whether it will be a female or a male child; secondly, all the mitochondria (the energy generators) inside the child's cells are inherited from the mother; thirdly, the baby being delivered normally by pulling it out through the vaginal passage is bathed in the 'Love' and 'Attachment' molecule

'Oxytocin (O)'; and, fourthly, during normal delivery the child collects all its gut microbes from the mother's vaginal passage.

[In Caesarean section delivery, the last two developments do not take place making the newly born vulnerable to physical and mental health problems later in life.]

Attachment and Dependence: Brain Functional Aspects

The 'Attachment-Dependence' factor is also corroborated by the growing child's brain wave pattern. From birth up to 2 years, the infant displays a 'delta' brain wave (0+ to 4 hertz) which we get during deep, sound, dreamless sleep [the little one must get an absolutely peaceful, stress-free environment for the growth of 'neurons (= brain cells)' and the neural network development]; 2 to 6 years, the child displays a 'theta' brain wave (4 to 7 hertz) equivalent to light sleep—the 'dreaming' state which constitutes the period for trying out the effectiveness of the cell-to-cell webwork; and, 6 to 12 years, the growing kid displays an 'alpha' brain wave (7 to 14 hertz) which is the 'creative' state of the brain which manifests itself in various creative and exploratory activities that the pre-teen child engages in. 14 to 25 hertz—which is conscious wakefulness, represented by the 'beta' wave dawns only at teenage.

Attachment is Instinctive Up to a Stage

Up to this stage, mother-child 'Attachment' is logical. If you study pre-history, this was invariable as there was nothing called customary marriage. Plain and simple physical attraction made a young couple sleep together and by the time the woman showed signs of pregnancy, the biological father of the foetus might have left that forest in search of other terrains providing opportunities for better hunting-gathering. So, 'Attachment' certainly deserves a place in the front row of 'Brain Tools (BT)' because it is instinctive. But why I have brought up this issue because, again in pre-historic times, the teenager used to get 'Detached', breaking into pieces the chain of 'Attachment' with his (no gender bias) mother as by now he has become responsible for fulfilment of his own 'Biological Imperatives (BI)' of 'Survival and Replication'—the woman who had given him birth has no role to play anymore. He enjoys 'Independence'. This system possibly still prevails in primitive tribal societies.

It is not happening in the society which we call civilised and enlightened where formal 'Attachments' like marriages constitute the social norm.

A Few Live Cases

Me and my team members were conducting a two-day workshop based on my best-seller book *Live Happily, Work Happily* for top level managers of The Indian Oil Corpn. Ltd. The day the workshop ended, I got a call from Barun Chatterjee, a Sr. General Manager. Barun, his wife Ruma and son Sudip came to meet me with a serious problem. Sudip, the only child of the Chatterjees has been with his parents all along studying in good schools and performing well at all levels. For his computer science education, he had taken admission in a college in Bengaluru.

Within just two weeks of his being away from home, he took to drugs and now, just within three months, he has become so much of an addict that he has developed some neurological disorders. Reason for his drug habit: inability to cope with the stress of 'Detachment' from his mother. The Chatterjees never realised that Sudip became so much dependent on his mother like a leg handicapped depends on his crutches. But in the case of the leg handicapped, it is only physical dependence which is understandable. In Sudip's case, it was emotional. He felt insecure if he could not see his mother for a day, so he got adapted to drown himself in a drug. I advised him to be admitted into a Detoxification and Drug Rehabilitation Centre first.

I can cite quite a few examples where teenage boys and girls who are sent off to distant places for education have got 'Attached' to nicotine, alcohol or narcotics or even to plain and simple junk food. Rimjhim was one such teenage girl who, on admission into a residential school in the outskirts of Kolkata, became a drug addict for not being able to withstand the anxiety of separation from her divorcee mother to whom she was most strongly 'Attached'.

Sometimes, the mother does not allow the child to grow from the level of boy/girlhood into adolescence. Swapan, a 15-year old Class X student is not allowed by her mother to sleep alone lest he got scared of ghosts. Romen, a 23-year old B.Tech in electronics still sleeps with his mother as the mother feels he would not have sound sleep if he slept alone. Lolita, a Class XII student still sleeps in between her parents although she has a room to herself. She misses her mother while at school during breaks in between classes and insists that the mother comes in the family car to pick her up after school.

During the period 2005 to 2009, we conducted several workshops in the five thermal power stations of the West Bengal Power Development Corporation Limited (WBPDCL): at Bandel, Kolaghat, Santaldih, Bakreswar and Sagardighi. Some of the workshops were attended by the GETs (Graduate Engineering Trainees) who included some of the best boys from Jadavpur University, IIT—Kharagpur and BE College—Shibpore. Many of them used to tell me that despite getting job offers from BHEL, L&T, General Electric, NTPC, Asea Brown Boveri and the like, they chose WBPDCL because every weekend, failing once in 2 or 3 weeks, they could visit their homes and spend a day with their parents, especially the mother. So strong was the power of the BT-8: 'Attachment'.

Don't you see that 'Attachment' which is an essential 'Brain Tool (BT)' for healthy physical and mental growth and development for a growing child becomes a deterrent for the child's career success after the teenage? SMART Leading parents must remember it and take steps at the appropriate time to help teenagers to get adapted to 'Detachment' without suffering from separation anxiety.

Attachment Models Inside our Minds

We create 'Attachment (A)' models inside our minds and when we meet someone for the first time, we try to tally with the most appropriate or most relevant 'A' models stored in our 'Sub-Conscious Mind (SCM)'. It is an interesting function of the 'Mirror Neurons (MN)' which become most active in the brain of a growing child continuing up to the end of the teenage, because they help us to click photos of others' behaviours so that we can comfortably fulfil our 'Biological and Social Imperatives (BSI)'. Mind you, based on my 'Neuro-management (NM)' research in

India, I have redefined the age range for teenage: for males: 13 to 28 = 15 years; and, for females: 12/13 to 22/23 = 10 years. The main job of MN is to click a photo or image of the person in front of you and to mimic him to develop closeness or 'Attachment (A)' so that the person accepts you and gets 'Attached' to you. The entire process is an unconscious reflex—it is 'Instinctive'. So, when our stored 'A' model does not match with that of the person we meet, we start suffering from 'stress'. The 'stress' may be expressed through an 'away' or 'avoidance' response leading to external conflicts or may be suppressed leading to inner turmoil.

A Concrete Case

I had a very friendly, nurturing and understanding mother like what a mother figure should be. We shared many common talents: writing poems and stories, singing songs, and playing the piano; excellent handwriting (as people would say); and shared many common interests as well as likes and dislikes. So, my MNs had sculpted a 'Mother Attachment Model (MAM)' and it got stored inside my SCM. I used to be close to my 'Jethima' (Dad's elder brother's wife) and my Mashimas or Mousis (mother's sisters including the top singer Kabir Suman's mom) and their 'Attachment' models tallied with my MAM almost 85 to 90%.

So, now as a human scientist, I took it as a standard one in my circle of kinship. Therefore, my expectation was—any lady that I will meet playing the motherly or aunt-like role would tally with the stored MAM that I have in my 'Sub-Conscious'. But, Good God! It did not tally with the AM that I confronted after my marriage. My mother-in-law (whom I expected to be a similar soul) was extremely assertive. Outcome: I started having an inner stress which I tolerated with great effort as me and my newly married wife Utpala left for London only a fortnight after our marriage. I sighed my breath of relief when her figure disappeared far away as me and Utpala went into the security enclosure at the old Dum Dum airport. But, when we finally returned after a year and a half, there was no change in my mom-in-law's 'Attachment' model. I repressed my stress which resulted in my over-addiction to nicotine (most stupidly, I'd taken to pipe smoking like a Scotsman while in Scotland). My wife Utpala, who had got habituated to her mom's AM would certainly have found a difference between her and my mother's MAM. We have never touched this most sensitive issue ever.

Distant Attachment

Although I had a little 'Distant Attachment' relationship with my LL.B (London), Barrister-at-Law father, I had a lot of empathy for him he being a throat cancer survivor. Here also, my father's 'Attachment' image did not tally with that of my father-in-law. Although he was the no. 2 of the South Eastern Railway in Garden Reach—a very senior member of the Indian Railway Service (IRS), he was a deeply religious orthodox brahmin from a conservative Bengali semi-urban family.

Luckily, both my parents were SMART and they counselled me on how to adjust with different 'Attachment Styles' at my in-laws' end, without entering into any conflict.

Different Slots for Different Attachment Models

As we grow up, we put the 'Attachment Models' into different slots:

- In the Family and Amongst Friends: Close Attachment; Distant Attachment; Half-way (neither 'Close' nor 'Distant').
- In the Neighbourhood and at the Workplace: Formal Attachment; Informal Attachment.

Attachment with a Motive

Attachment could be just emotional or it could be with a motive as it was in the case that I am sharing with you. The setting of this case was in Hyderabad. I had come to know about it when me and my team members had gone there to conduct workshops for Hindustan Cables Ltd. and Electronics Corporation of India Ltd.

A teenage girl Srilata Naidu came from a middle-class joint family sharing the same house where Srilata, her parents and grandmother had to live in just one small room with no attached toilet. She did not have any dream about her career, her only DREAM was to live in a big house having 2–3 big rooms with attached baths, and a separate kitchen with a pantry. Her father, who was an engineer employed in the state government took housing loan and purchased a small flat in the outskirts of the city.

Srilata was not happy as it had only one room, one drawing-cum-dining space, one common bath room and a small kitchen. She was space hungry. She finally located a boy Shivashakti Rao in her college, two years senior to her who came from an aristocratic Telugu family and owned a big house in a posh locality. She set her eyes on him and devised strategies for getting 'Attached' to with the motive of marrying him. The boy was too naïve to detect her game plan; so, he was caught in the net and finally they got married. She shifted to the big three-storeyed house and had a rush of all happiness chemicals inside her brain.

This is an example of 'Attachment' with a motive. It is common in the workplace circles where subordinates grease the boss's palms to get his favour.

A Case of Detachment

There is an interesting case of 'Detachment' also. Thin and lean, Nobendu Bose studying in St. Xavier's College, Kolkata was going strong and steady with his classmate Lipika Dhar who was slim and pretty. She had done a few modelling assignments for Bengali and Hindi magazines and was in demand. Their 'Close Attachment' was obvious from their frequent togetherness. Suddenly, after a period of nine months, Lipika was found to move with a Sikh boy—very tall, athletic and handsome, Ranjit Singh. This is a case of simple DETACHMENT, just like it happens in the case of separation or divorce after marriage.

Drive for Attachment

Life begins with a DRIVE for 'Attachment'. A sperm manages to get 'Attached' to (fused with) an egg inside the egg-owner's womb. The egg is fertilised and a blob is formed which grows into a tissue bundle that has life but no personality. 49 days (7 weeks) after conception, a 'Soul' (a quantum physics phenomenon—with its typical vibrations which human eyes are not capable to see) enters into the 'Pineal Gland (PG)' of the zygote's brain.

The 'Soul' was wandering in 'Space' looking for a matching womb, where its personality can get 'Attached' to the womb-owner who will provide a hassle-free environment, pre- and post-natal and during the growing years. Soul's motive is thus for 'Attachment' for mutual growth—its own as well as of the womb-owner.

So, the Soul's search is for a womb which fits in with its 'Mother Attachment Model (MAM)'. The aim is advancement and progress of the level of consciousness of both the mother and the child; Nature's plan is to benefit each other. And, normally according to the 'Past Life Theory', any wandering Soul searches for the womb of a female with whom (the Soul has no sex, no gender) it was in 'Soul-mate' or 'Soul-buddy' (very intimate/close) relationship in an earlier life. So, the Soul may enter into its previous life's mother's, or sister's, or daughter's womb and the like (I hope you get it what I mean).

The Case of Your

Teenage Kid

Now, if you, my reader, are a parent, let us take your teenage kid's case. Whatever similarity you find in his (no gender bias) behaviour and conduct—most of it comprises what he has copied with the auto-help of his 'Mirror Neurons (MRs)' from you and your spouse—colloquial vocabulary, language use, body language (postures and gestures) and the like. I got confirmation of this when I had the opportunity to conduct some studies on these aspects for three Calcutta-based renowned NGOs. The question they had put to me was, that, despite teaching and training Calcutta slum and railway platform (both Howrah and Sealdah) children (age group: 11/12 to 19/20 years) and keeping them in hostels with good facilities, why there was no change in their behaviour and conduct although academically they were progressing. The answer was simple, these teenage children had copied the external behaviour and communication from their parents where the mothers worked as part-time maids and fathers were rickshaw-pullers, taxi-bus-auto-private car drivers who used abusive slangs and negative body language.

Whatever it may be in the external façade, your teenage kid's DREAM, DRIVE and DOMAIN (my 3D approach to effective career choice) will depend upon his Soul as the Soul has chosen a womb in this birth which will help it to fulfil its unfulfilled desires, to complete the work which it could not in any of its recent previous births.

The Soul Theory

I had some idea of this Soul Theory, but had doubt about reincarnation. I had started reading Dr. Brian Weiss's book *Many Lives Many Masters* just out of curiosity when it had hit the *New York Times* best-seller list more than once but had put it aside after glancing half way through as it still didn't get a place in the BELIEF domain of my brain.

I got convinced only when Mr. RS (name disguised) the top honcho of a Tata group company told me that his incurable long-lasting low back pain got cured as he took a couple of 'Past Life Therapy (PLT)' sessions with a specialist during a recent business trip to Germany. I listened to him with apt attention, asked him probing questions which he answered to my full satisfaction holding my hand to convert me from disbelief into 'Belief'. The therapist had also told him a lot about the 'Soulmates' and 'Soul-buddies'. The therapist said that RS had moved fast to occupy the topmost management chair at such a young age (only 42 years) as his Soul could find an ideally matching womb of his mother who, in the last birth, was his elder sister and both were soulmates or soul-buddies. There was thus a perfect fit between the womb-owner and the soul who had been wondering with an unfulfilled DREAM of his last life. Mr. RS, the therapist told him, could not reach the top of his career in his last life and died of an untimely cardiac arrest with the unfulfilled desire to reach the top in his immediate past earlier life.

The wandering soul which is not liberated (who has neither discovered his 'True Passion'—the purpose of his life nor has fulfilled that purpose) is in great pain. It suffers as it is desperate to find a suitable womb not later than 7 weeks after it left the body of its previous birth. The circulation of the Soul in the birth-death-rebirth cycle is usually between or amongst the soulmates or soul-buddies. Until such a mate or buddy is found the Soul, in desperation, may enter into an unmatching womb and continue to suffer because of mismatch in vibrations (each

Soul has its own characteristic vibration which is almost the same as that of his soulmate or soul-buddy).

It keeps a vigil and track of a 'Soulmate' who is getting ready for conception. The moment it can detect that conception has taken place, it prepares to leave and enter the pineal gland of the zygote in the soulmate's womb at the end of the 7th week after conception. But what would it do to its present body? It, in most cases, sows the seed of a disease to attract a wandering soul whose container-body had suffered from the same disease but died untimely with the unfulfilled desire to live for some more time bearing the trials and tribulations of the same disease but enjoying the air, water and resources of the Planet Earth. Or, it desperately leaves the body causing sudden unexpected death of the individual.

Spiritual Progress

Spiritual progress means progress and advancement in the level of consciousness. From plain and simple living to eat, drink and be merry (mere reptilian and paleo-mammalian) to eating to live (higher order of neo-mammalian or neo-cortical) existence.

The Soul enters the bundle of flesh and blood—the zygote through its pineal gland, which looks like a pine cone, unpaired, and described as the Third Eye in a few religions including Hinduism. The Soul is the subtle body—'sukshma sharira'; it enters into the gross bundle of tissue—the zygote—the 'sthula sharira' which will take the shape of the 'Annamaya Kosha (AK)'—visible, palpable. The Soul, in an ideal case, will get distributed into the 'Pranamaya Kosha (PK)', 'Monomaya Kosha (MK)', 'Vijnanamaya Kosha (VK)' and 'Anandamaya Kosha (AnK)' equally as the gross body grows (as it had happened in my case). Otherwise, the Soul (subtle energy) will manifest in any one (including AK for those who are materialistically inclined and promote a hedonistic lifestyle), any two or any three of the 'Koshas'.

I have definitely progressed spiritually in my lifetime. My mother had also progressed spiritually which was proven when she boldly faced the challenge that cropped up when my father was diagnosed with throat cancer. Because of her strong spiritual radiation, my father underwent laryngectomy—and thereafter not only survived cancer but pursued a very active working career and social life. He lived for another 20 years post retirement from service and died not of a relapsed carcinogenic condition but entirely due to old age.

A Teenage Kid's Kosha Attachment

Here, I will talk about a teenage kid's 'Kosha Attachment'.

Let me first clear the perception regarding Soul as it is purely a matter of 'Belief', the entity being invisible and non-palpable to our limited senses. Some of us human scientists, who are trying to integrate modern neuro-sciences with the scientific doctrines documented in the Vedas-Upanishads and other religious scriptures, try to correlate things to provide a morphic form to such so-called abstract philosophical concepts.

We know of the Universal Soul which is the beyond-doubt 'Cosmic Energy'. It has its own vibrations. A yogi meditates to synchronize the vibrations of his own body and brain cells, and also the vibrations of the wandering soul which had entered the pineal gland of the zygote in the pregnant mother's womb, the vibrations of the cosmos. This harmony produces eternal BLISS.

All living creatures have their own characteristic vibrations of the whole body, of the different systems and organs, and of the constituent elements. In human males, the sperm has its own Soul which is responsible for its livingness. In the same way, in human females, the ovum has its own Soul profile. The physical quality of the fertilised egg depends upon the quality of these two Souls when they get fused with each other—deciding upon the health and fitness factors of the zygote. So, we have just now met two Souls—those of the father and the mother. However, these two create the physical body and the physical brain—the tissues. Now, at the appropriate or opportune time (although I had mentioned 49 days or 7 weeks in my earlier writings, there is a controversy regarding this in different major religious scriptures like the Upanishads, the Quran, the Bible and so on), the 3rd SOUL enters the zygote's brain. This 3rd Soul (which apparently has a mind) is one which had left a dying body recently and was evaluating its good and bad deeds of the immediate one or two past lives and trying to identify specifically what would be most appropriate DREAM and DRIVE for the new life. The 3rd Soul thus has an individual Ego—it is Ego-laid. By Soul (S), I will mean this Ego-laid Soul from now on.

Ego-laid Souls (S) Having Low to Mediocre Consciousness

In Souls (S) having a low to mediocre consciousness, we get 3 types:

1. Desire(s) for rebirth is triggered by the DRIVE for worldly or material things which could not be fulfilled in the immediate past earlier lives: related to the Gross Body (sthula sharira)—'Annamaya Kosha (AK)'; such people's DREAMs will also be materialistic.
2. There was a physical or mental health or fitness problem, for which, the individual had to suffer a lot and die in great pain and distress—so now there is a desire to be reborn and take extra care of the physical, neurological, or mental health or chose a health-care or healing related profession: DRIVEs and DREAMs are related to the 2nd sheath which is the 1st layer of the Subtle Body (sukhsma sharira)—'Pranamaya Kosha (PK)'.
3. There was a strong desire for any emotional relationship or 'Attachment' model, but it did not materialise in one-to-one, one-to-two, one-to-a few, or one-to-many situations: DRIVEs and DREAMs related to the 3rd sheath which is the 2nd layer of the Subtle Body (sukhsma sharira)—'Monomaya Kosha (MK)'. This includes the 'Entertainment' DOMAIN: poem, story, novel, drama writing, music, dancing, film-making, acting, painting, sculpting, model or image-making.

Ego-laid Souls (S) Having Higher Consciousness

In Souls (S) having a higher consciousness (who have already moved through 1, 2 and 3 above in the same or in earlier lives):

1. A desire to undertake deep study of anything (may be literature, art, music, dance, drama, science, medicine, philosophy, film-making) and develop 'Mastery' (practising for minimum

10,000 hours: refer to Malcolm Gladwell's fascinating book *The Outliers*, New York: Little, Brown and Company, 2008): related to the 4th sheath which is the 3rd layer of the Subtle Body (sukhsma sharira)—'Vijnanamaya Kosha (VK)' [which in my Neuro-management (NM) theory, represents the Left side of the Neo-cortex in right-handed persons].

2. A burning desire to Create, Invent, Innovate, Discover, Pioneer, Change-make to give back to the society what Mother Earth has given you by bringing you to this beautiful planet—to 'Add Value' to what already exists—'Ananadamaya Kosha (AnK)' [which according to my Neuro-management (NM) theory, represents a 'hemi-sync' situation—integrating the powers of the left and right—both sides of the neo-cortex. At this level, you get 'Intuitions' and 'Insights'].

Interestingly, whatever may be the level of consciousness, this 3rd Soul(S) which has come from outside the sperm and the ovum and made the zygote its home for one lifetime is not PURE like the cosmic soul—it is contaminated by some desire. So, such Souls would be called 'Egoistic' (I have already described it as 'Ego-laid' where Ego is represented by the desire).

By observing the teenage kid, a Smart leading parent ought to find out his Kosha Attachment and, accordingly, guide him.

My Kosha Attachments

If you're a SMART leading parent, you will keep yourself alert about the activities of your kid as he steps into his (no gender bias) pre-teen years to identify his level of consciousness and his Ego-laid Soul's Kosha Attachment. Thinking in retrospect, now I think this was what my mother did. She used to play orchestrated music on the gramophone and I used to start dancing rhythmically using my own choreography. I used to give tune to my school text poems. So, she could feel a seed of 'creativity' in me. I could not sketch, draw or paint so well that it would be regarded as one of my special attributes; so, she encouraged me to write poems as I had an excellent sense of rhythm. My poems wore my signature; readers could feel they were 'Unique' and 'Different'. [Manifestation of 'Anandamaya

Kosha (AnK)]. As I grew into my teens, I started going deep into English and Bengali languages and literature [Manifestation of the 'Vijnanamaya Kosha (VK)'– so much so that I stood 1st in both in School Final in the West Bengal Board in 1955 (15 years age) and again 1st in both the subjects amongst all the Intermediate level students of Calcutta University in 1957 (16-1/2 years). Throughout my life, now I feel, I had much stronger VK and AnK Kosha Attachment having a just-enough relationship with AK, PK and MK.

A Real-life Case Study on a Teenager's Career Planning

I will present here a real-life case study on how to take a cue from my 'Kosha Attachment' principle to prepare a teenager's career plan.

Arka Ghosh Chaudhury (Date of birth: 3rd September 2005), who is based at Kolkata, used to play with toy cars during his pre-teen years. But almost all pre-teen boys from middle class families play with toy cars. The more aggressive types, of course, play with toy guns and pistols. But there were three striking differences that Arka displayed compared to other toy car kids. The 1st difference: he used to get hold of his father's hand tools (screw driver etc.) and open up those toys to see what was inside—like a medical student trying to learn the innards by dissecting a cadaver in the anatomy class. The 2nd difference: he would borrow his father's smartphone outside office hours and search the internet for data on automobiles. The 3rd difference: he would watch on the TV, Discovery, National Geographic or any other educational programmes on automobiles—what are the different kinds of automobiles, how are they designed and manufactured, how many models are available in each make or brand, what are the facilities available, what are the prices etc. Automobile means Motion, Speed and Energy and Motion, Speed and Energy are all related to the 'Pranamaya Kosha (PK)', if I take the help of the 'Pancha Kosha (PK)'concept of the Taittiriya Upanishad for personality analysis. It shows that his DRIVE came from the 'PK'.

From around 24th February 2018, I started mentoring him and, finding his area of interest, we together decided that his DREAM should be to become an 'Automobile Designer' (and not just an 'Automobile Engineer'), the broad DOMAIN being 'Automobile'. 'Designer' because he possessed the artistic skill of sketching and drawing using pencil, sketch pens, even water colours. He is really good at it.

From his boyhood, Arka had developed an interest in the game of cricket and used to play with friends in school and boys in his locality. His parents thought that learning and practising cricket in the proper manner would not only be good for his health and fitness, but it could also be a career option in future. So, they put him into a reputed cricket coaching centre in 2013 at the age of 8 only. He started doing well in cricket but although it occupied a place in his passion pie, it could never surpass his DREAM for an auto career. Sports and games which are related to physical energy has a direct link with the 'Pranamaya Kosha (PK)'. So that became an added advantage for his brain—matching of DRIVEs from two different channels: physical and mental.

I have already pinpointed and emphasized on DRIVE, DREAM and DOMAIN, the 3 components of my 3-D approach for Career Selection. Coming to the 3rd component DOMAIN, let me tell you that there are 3 ways of generating income. One is 'Employment (E)' where you take up a job and get a compensation for the time, energy and effort that you put in to get some work done. Another is 'Self-Employment (SE)' where you are a freelancer; you set up a shop or an office to provide service in your specialised domain and get compensated for the service rendered. The third one is 'Entrepreneurship (Ent)' where you invest your resources and take the risk of setting up an enterprise to provide products or services in your DREAM DOMAIN. So, now the next step is to make out a 'Plan' as to what 'Actions' are to be taken to reach the 3D Goal.

Arka's ultimate DREAM is to become an 'Entrepreneur' and set up an 'Enterprise' called 'NAD' dealing with 'Neuro Automobile Design' with the aim of making history by doing what has never been done before. NAD would be a company where customers' wishes or dreams would be given special priority. All customers will be getting a chance to select a car body from the present cars (it may be a supercar also) and the price of the car will be ridiculously low as because Arka is going to import cars from the Dubai junkyard and upgrade it according to the customers' wishes. Combining his own designer touch, the ultimate automobile would be a completely new, novel and different one. Arka plans to open this company in Dubai as the largest car auction takes place there, he says. His DREAM is also to have branches of NAD, ultimately as it grew, all over the world.

Arka has worked out his 'Action Plan' as follows:

- *Alternative 1:* Complete Class X; Take Science in HS; Complete Joint Entrance in Engineering; Study Mechanical Engineering to major in Automobile Engineering; After completion, join an automobile company which has a branch in Dubai; Get transferred to Dubai; Work for some years, save some money; Open a start-up Company in Dubai.
- *Alternative 2:* Complete Class X; If he does not get Science, take Commerce; Take admission in a Hotel and Hospitality Management course; After completion, go for a hotel job in Dubai; After earning enough money and building some capital, he will start NAD as well as a cake shop.
- *Alternative 3:* Perform very well in X and XII; Complete B.Com/ BBA with marketing specialisation; Apply for a sales job in the automobile industry (ought to get through in the test and interview because of his thorough knowledge of automobiles); Try to get a transfer in the Company's Dubaibased branch/ showroom or apply for a Sales Executive's job in an automobile company in the Middle-East; Have a frugal life to save money from the high remuneration received and wait for the right chance to open NAD in Dubai and go ahead. The NAD set-up would have a cake-coffee-and-candy shop also.

The whole idea for Career Planning for Teenagers is to have at least three Alternative Plans to reach the 3D-Goal. If Alternative 1 does not work out, the teenager will try out Alternative 2. If that also does not work, then hands will be laid on Alternative 3. Arka's DREAM to be an Automobile Designer is so strong that he has kept the Goal as one but has found out 3 routes to reach it.

Brain Tool 9

Trans-Technicality (TT)

'Key' Points: *Two Memorable Experiences; A Third Case Study; What Is So Special in These Individuals; 'Trans-technicality (TT)' Explained; Ten Case Studies.*

Two Memorable Experiences

It happened 4 (four) years ago, but the memory is still vivid like a video. Me and my team member Pervez Alam were waiting in the lounge of Taj Santa Cruz Hotel in Mumbai; suddenly the elevator stopped and a few people rushed out. In a split second, we were face to face with Sanjeev Kapoor, the celebrity chef. As it was most unexpected, I murmured: "Good morning, Mr. Kapoor!" He was promptly courteous with a genuine smile: "Good morning Sir!" and passed by! What a grace and smartness that radiated from the man.

Popped up on my mental screen another flashback memory—still alive with full details although it had happened more than 20 years ago. It was a film-making event at the BM Birla Heart Research Centre, Kolkata. I was involved in making a film on the King of Cardiac Surgery in India—Dr. Devi Shetty. How he behaved with his clinical team members including junior nurses, instrument technicians and Class IV staff, absolutely egolessly, before, during and after the surgical event, I thought, was really exemplary. Post-op, he came out to meet the family and folks of the patient with full humility and empathy and assured them of the best possible care until his release from the healthcare facility. Again, a living example of grace and smartness. This grace and smartness combined, I call 'Trans-Technicality (TT)'.

Sanjeev Kapoor acquired his hotel management diploma from IHM-Pusa, New Delhi followed by training in a reputed hotel as a 'chef'. That is how he had got his 'Technical (T)' knowledge and skill. Devi Shetty attended medical school at Kasturba Medical College, Mangalore followed by his postgraduate training in general surgery in the same college. Subsequently, he got his Fellowship from the Royal College of Surgeons, England. That was the 'Technical (T)' part of Devi Shetty.

A Third Case Study

Jayanta Mitra and I went to the same school. He was a barrister's son, so was I. So, we were family friends. He was not only good in studies, he sparkled with good manners and behaviour. His younger brother was just the opposite. After school, our paths separated. Subsequently, he went to London for his Bar-at-Law and I went to Glasgow for my post-graduation in Engineering. We lost touch for decades. A few years ago, I went to the Calcutta High Court in connection with a case. The hearing was going on, suddenly there was a murmur in the court room: Jayanta Mitra is coming. And, there he was. The whole court room became silent. Even the Hon'ble Judge stood up to greet him. But Jayanta looked straight into my eyes and walked up to hug me: "How are you Siddhartha? After so many years...what brings the Neuro-management scholar to the Court of Law?" He radiated a grand personality. Jayanta was the Advocate General of Bengal in those days. Even today, he is the most sought after as well as the costliest lawyer in Kolkata. I felt so proud about him and his aura.

What Is So Special in These Individuals

So many hundreds and thousands of boys and girls are attending courses on hotel and hospitality management. So many hundreds and thousands of boys and girls attend medical schools for graduation and post-graduation, go for their clinical internship. So many hundreds and thousands of boys and girls go to law schools—even to London to be called to the Bar. But how many of them emerge as Sanjeev Kapoors, Devi Shettys and Jayanta Mitras? Very few. There is a general 'Belief' in social circles that it is the 'Luck Factor'.

'Trans-technicality (TT)' Explained

As a human scientist, I have spent years on the phenomenon of 'Success' and have come to the conclusion that there is nothing called LUCK. You and I are genetically 99.9 percent identical (between a chimpanzee and a human, the genetic similarity is 98.5 to 99 percent—it has been well proven). Then where is the difference? The difference is how you groom yourself or get 'Mentored' by a 'Life Coach' on 'Trans-technically (TT)'. TT means how you keep yourself healthy and fit (planned balanced diet, planned physical fitness activities, planned sound sleep synchronous with the natural rhythms), how you use your body language positively, how you walk with grace, how you establish and maintain your gaze, how patiently you talk and listen, how promptly you take action and decisions and solve problems, how imaginative-creative-and-innovative you are and how intelligently you handle your own and others' emotions (anger and anxiety management); and, last but not the least, how much you are able to influence and convince others keeping cool and balanced.

The places at the TOP are reserved (like the royal seats in an opera house) for those who are not only efficient in T but also strong in TT. I hope you are now almost clear about my 'Trans-technicality (TT)' concept which is a 'Brain Tool (BT)' indeed. It requires 'Self-Mentoring' or 'Mentoring' by an expert life coach.

If you are a parent and had never imagined that putting your kid into an expensive English medium school, arranging top-class tutors or tutorials for him, getting him coached on-line by spending a lot, arranging high-class digital equipment for him were not adequate for his 'Success' in life, I shall not demean you by saying that you are wrong about the perception of 'Success', may I politely say that you have not behaved like a SMART parent?

Ten Case Studies

My empirical bell curve on the world's human resource population is well-known in corporate circles. It depicts an 80–20 standard distribution. Around 80 percent people in this world are born 'Normal' or 'Ordinary', meaning they are normal in their body, brain and soul—no complaints whatsoever. Having the urge and given the opportunity, they can qualify in any subject and can join any profession and come up to a certain senior (more than middle) level. 10 percent are on the negative side (abnormal or subnormal from birth) and the other 10 percent are on the positive side. The positive 10 percent includes 'Extraordinary' people.

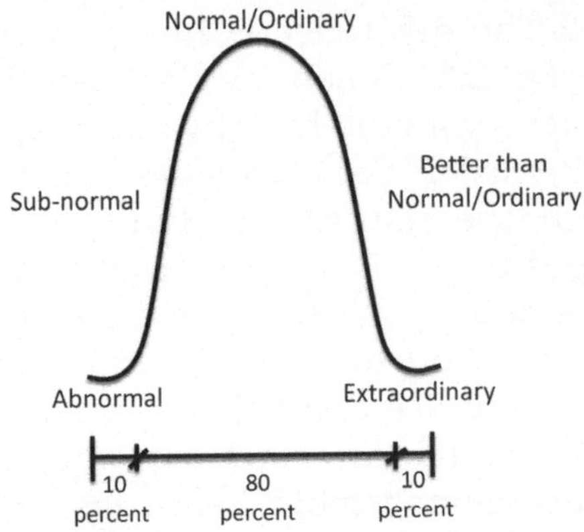

Fig. 7: The Human Resource Bell Curve

Amongst Indians, the 'Extraordinary' category includes the versatiles like Rabindranath Tagore and Satyajit Ray, spiritually advanced few like Ramakrishna Paramhansa, Swami Vivekananda, Rishi Aurobindo and Mahatma Gandhi and Nobel Laureates like C.V. Raman, Amartya Sen and Abhijit Vinayak Banerjee.

The founder father of the giant National Panasonic brand of Japan—Konosuke Matsushita believed that the 'Ordinary' people can be made 'Extraordinary' by guiding them properly. I tend to differ with him as I believe 'Extraordinary' people either ought to be born with 'Extraordinary' potential or, at some stage of their life, there has to be a trigger which kindles the fire in them to 'Excel' and become 'Extraordinary'. However, what I strongly believe is that 'Normal or Ordinary' people can be groomed to become 'Better than Normal' or 'Better than Ordinary' just like medium quality coal can be washed to be upgraded. Washing coal, refining petroleum or beneficiation of iron ore is equivalent to grooming 'Normal' or 'Ordinary' human resource and converting them into a 'Better Than Normal' or 'Better Than Ordinary' grade.

Time is ripe for me to share live case studies of a few 'Normal' or 'Ordinary' people from different walks of life who became 'Better than Normal' or 'Better than Ordinary'. I should not take full credit for their transformation but certainly claim at least 40 percent for 'mentoring' them as they themselves had 60 percent potential in them which qualified them to come under my 'Better than Normal' or 'Better than Ordinary' group. Identities (like names etc.) are being kept under cover for obvious reasons.

Industry: Public Sector: I trained him first when he was a departmental head in a region. He rose to the position of Chairman and Managing Director of Indian Oil Corporation Ltd.—a 'Fortune 500' company.

Industry: Private Sector: I trained him when he was Junior Officer (Accounts) in an Indian business house. He rose to the position of MD in a Birla Company followed by MD in the Emami Group before he retired.

Politics: I trained him when he was Asst. Manager in a large Govt. of India Undertaking. He took my training from his head and heart both. He has been a very senior minister in the WB Govt. cabinet for the last few years.

University Administration: He was mentored by me for his doctoral work in Physiology (Physical Education and Sports Science). He worked in my laboratory for 4 years before he got his Ph.D. He retired after having been the Vice Chancellor of a leading University of West Bengal for a few years. During his tenure, the University could attain new heights.

Medicine: He was mentored by me when he was in charge of the medical and health wing of a Tata group company. I motivated him to complete his MBA in Health Administration. Post-MBA, he joined Woodlands Hospital as Medical Director and later became the Medical Director of Fortis and now Director-Medical Services of the IQ City Narayana Multi-speciality Hospital (Feb. 2019—present).

Surgery: He was being groomed by me for his Ph.D in Orthopaedic Surgery at Calcutta University. Already had a roaring private practice with a busy chamber in Shakespeare Sarani, Kolkata, but unfortunately died prematurely. He stood 1st in his M.S. (Orth).

Bioengineering: I mentored him outright for his Ph.D. in Applied Physics. He worked in my research projects as a 'key' member for 6 years. Retired as the Professor and Head of the School of Life Sciences and Engineering, Jadavpur University. He also had an untimely death, post-retirement, in 2020.

State Educational Administration: He was groomed as a research assistant in my team at the University College of Medicine, Calcutta University. He retired as the Secretary of the Board of Secondary Education, Govt. of West Bengal.

International Management Consultancy: A young engineer from IIT-Delhi whom I had mentored immediately after his graduation during his post-graduate training in a British Company in Calcutta rose to and retired from the position of Chairman, MD and CEO of a top-ranking International Management Consultancy having worldwide operations.

Music: He was mentored for some time by me on music and its impact on the brain, pursued his research leading to a Ph.D. in music from a leading university. He had been regularly giving his instrumental recitals in UK, Europe and North America apart from being a top-grade artist in Akashvani and Door Darshan which led to his acquiring the title of Pandit. So, he has now Pandit Dr. prefix to his name. My special contribution to his success was motivating him to create music rather than following the routine taught by his gurus.

I am currently in the midst of mentoring and coaching: (i) an accomplished dancer, dance and movement therapist; (ii) 2 (two) skilled neuro-physio-yoga therapists; (iii) a Kriya Yoga practitioner; (iv) a talented entrepreneur; and others.

You may be wondering what is the difference between my mentoring and coaching and the methodology of the leading mentors and coaches of the Western world including the front-runner top coach Marshall Goldsmith, Ph.D. of USA who has written the Foreword of my book 'Conscious Management'. My approach is to help developing the 4 (four) personal resources that you have: your body, brain, mind and soul. I help the mentee to develop a well-coordinated neuro-system and not only a 'Hemi-sync' state which is the expression for the synchronised left and right hemispheres of the brain.

BRAIN TOOL 10

Create Your Own Luck Factor (CYOLF)

'Key' Points: *Self-discovery: The 'Luck Factor'; Ancestral Audit; What Proverbs Say and What A Top Expert Thinks; Dr. Richard Wiseman's Story; What Lucky People Are Like; Four Basic Principles for Generating Good Fortune; Personal SWOT; Track Opportunities and Avoid Threats; Keep Away from; Wrong Expectations; A Very Special Case Study; The Genius (G) in You; Case Studies on 'Genius (G)'; One Genius (G) Is Not Enough; How Do You Track the Genius (G) in You; Your Genius and ROI; ROI: Qualitative; ROI: Quantitative; The 'Genius (G) in You and the 'Responsibility Centre' Concept; The Role of A Pre-teen or A Teenager; 'Responsibility Centre' and Time Management; Bad Luck Could Be Your Good Luck; My Father's Case Was A Turning Point; Tanmay's Case Study; Your Luck Story; Male-Female Mateships; Luck Game: The 2nd Round; The Pregnant Woman's Wish; The Luck Game: The 3rd Round Onwards; A Child's Lifescript; Check Your Luck.*

Self-Discovery: The 'Luck Factor'

My perception of the 'Luck Factor (LF)' was very easy to understand from the scientific point of view. It was like this: I was born as a combination of 'Ganguli' on my father's side and 'Bhattacharya' on my mother's side. Hence, it was obvious that my genome (the complete set of 'genes' carrying the hereditary features, present in me) will be a mix of Ganguli and Bhattacharya genes typical of their respective Hindu 'gotra's– which might have appeared not necessarily from my parents but even from their ancestors by skipping the family trees on both sides.

Although there is still a controversy, the body and brain tissues are inherited from the parents including the colour and texture of the skin, size, shape and colour of the eyes and so on. The hind- and midbrain's inborn circuits are gifts from the mother as those contain functions and reflexes essential for the child's survival, whereas the growing child's interaction with the environment is largely responsible for formation of the forebrain circuits and the role of the environment where and how the child is being brought up is most vital.

The reach of the powers of my body and brain—the capabilities and limitations would be restricted to the Ganguli-Bhattacharya clan genome. There is no possibility of any infiltration of a few Birla or Goenka genes barring exceptions where the third element—the *soul* might have had entered my mother's womb during her conception. [As it had possibly happened in the case of the Bengali industrialist of yesteryears—Sir Rajendra Nath Mukherjee—the founder of the Burn and Co. Ltd., Howrah—the Martin Burn Group of Companies—and the Indian Iron and Steel Co. Ltd., Burnpur and its associated collieries and firebrick plants. None of Mukherjee's ancestors on either side had ever displayed any business acumen whereas he was a giant of an entrepreneur—how can you explain it without the possibility of the *soul factor* being responsible.]

Ancestral Audit

So, in order to identify your 'Luck Factor', please do an 'Ancestral Audit'. Extend it to your next generation—do a similar audit to get an idea of your teenage kid's 'Luck Factor': what 'Strengths' and what 'Weaknesses' has he (no gender bias) inherited, firstly from you and your spouse. Then go over to your parents—your teenage kid's grandparents. Has he inherited any character traits from your parents and your spouse's parents? It will be easy for you to follow my methodology of determining the 'Luck Factor' if I use my own case for illustration.

My 'Strengths' (I will mention only a couple of them): I have inherited my Sanskrit and Bengali language skill and writing talent from my mother and her father (my grandfather Pt. Rajendra Nath Bidyabhushan was a great Sanskrit scholar, a contemporary favourite of Sir Ashutosh Mukherjee, had tutored Atal Bihari Bajpaeyi Ji while heading the Sanskrit Dept. in Varanasi, authored several critiques of Kalidasa, Vedas and Upanishads);

and command over English language and writing skill from my father who had inherited it from his maternal uncles—all of whom were highly accomplished: Sir Atul Chatterjee, ICS (the first Indian High Commissioner in UK whose wife British Lady Gladys, LL.D, Bar-at-Law I had met and spent a weekend with her in London), the next two uncles—one was the Indian representative in UNESCO-Paris and another the Indian representative in ILO-Geneva, and the youngest one Dr. Sisir Chatterjee, MD (Edin.), FRCP (London), FRCP (Edin.), Medical Director of BN Railway who had a Scottish wife and had settled down in St. Andrews, Fife, Scotland—post-retirement, with whom I had spent many weekends during my University of Glasgow days.

I have inherited my entrepreneurial skill from my paternal grand-father [Rai Bahadur M.L. Ganguli who was a renowned contractor on his own, had partnership with his cousins N.B. Ganguli and Co. who had the maintenance contract of the Calcutta Race Course (Royal Calcutta Turf Club) and co-shared the Ganguli Bagan (acres worth of land in Jadavpur)] which made me leave my employment career at the young age of 40 years to start my own enterprise—first in manufacturing along with a friend of mine (I was involved in the start-up years)—then my own body-brain-mind-soul management and development boutique 'Learning Club' which I ran with full gusto for 35 years from 1983 to 2018 conducting workshops all over India and in the neighbouring countries of Nepal, Bhutan and Bangladesh. My oratorial skill has come from both my parents' sides.

My one weakness catches the public eye: I am not a social person—the party type. I mix with people but do not socialise. But this weakness I have turned into an outstanding strength in three ways: if I do attend any social gathering I do not talk much, I observe and listen to people—I study them which has helped me tremendously in my career; if I do not attend any get-together, I utilise that time in my writing and research work; I make it a point to attend celebrations linked with my mental health patients whom I had Mentored to restore normalcy—their birthdays, weddings, wedding anniversaries, their children's rice ceremonies—why you know—I observe how they are behaving—is there any shade of sub-normality still remaining in them, and so on. So, learn to convert your 'Weaknesses' into 'Strengths' wherever possible. Take similar steps for your teenage kid—help him to practice such reversal.

Have you understood what I mean by 'Create Your Own Luck Factor (CYOLF)'? 'Self-discovery' through 'Ancestral Audit' is a fascinating exercise and you can play games on this, if you're a Smart Leading Parent, with your teenage kid(s).

What Proverbs Say and What A Top Expert Thinks

Here, I would like to take you out of my own world to a much wider, expansive world. Let me first open the chest of old proverbs and pick up only three witty ones—the first one is about 'Luck' in general, the second one is about 'Bad Luck' and the third one is related to 'Good Luck'.

'Luck is the Idol of the Idle' —***An English proverb***

'If an unlucky man sold umbrellas, it would stop raining. If he sold candles, the sun would never set. And, if he made coffins, people would stop dying.' —***A Jewish saying***

'Throw a lucky man in the sea and he will come up with a fish in his mouth.' —***An Arab proverb***

Dr. Richard Wiseman's Story

Now, let me expose you to what a top expert thinks about the 'Luck Factor (LF)'. Richard Wiseman, Ph.D. is today the world's topmost researcher on LF. His story is indeed very special. When he was a child, he became fascinated with magic and illusion. In his early teens, he joined the magician's club—'The Magic Circle' in London and by his early twenties he performed several times at the prestigious 'Magic Castle' in Hollywood. Magic prompted Richard to probe into the human mind. As a conjuror, he became very keen on understanding the psychology of people, took a degree in psychology from the University College, London and later a Ph.D. from the University of Edinburgh, Scotland. He then established his own research unit at the University of Hertfordshire in U.K. where he currently holds the Professorship of Public Understanding of Psychology.

Once, he was demonstrating a magic trick in front of an audience as part of a professional speech and was intrigued by a woman who was totally unsurprised that his trick had worked, not because she saw through his sleight-of-hand, but because she considered herself always lucky. Therefore, making the right choice had nothing to do with the way the trick worked, but with her own innate luck. This incident acted as a trigger. Dr. Wiseman decided to investigate the phenomenon of 'Luck' and to conduct an extensive study of what makes some people lucky and others so unlucky. His book *The Luck Factor* (New York: Hyperion, 2003) is the result of that research. HE CONCLUDED THAT YOU CAN CREATE YOUR OWN LUCK FACTOR AND CONTROL YOUR LUCK.

Wiseman reminds us that many of the advancements of modern science and technology resulted from chance and/or accidental discoveries, e.g., penicillin, Velcro, safety glass etc. His research has also shown that those whom unlucky people consider as lucky, their good fortune extends to several areas of their lives—family, work sphere, neighbourhood and locality rather than being confined to just one.

What Lucky People Are Like

Wiseman's studies confirmed that lucky people are friendly yet controlled—they do not get carried away neglecting their main duties or responsibilities. They are most practical and, therefore, they create and maintain a large web of friends and acquaintances. They do not restrict themselves to their own clan and limited circle of relations and friends. They are open-minded and relaxed which makes their antennas most active to detect and grab opportunities.

Four Basic Principles for Generating Good Fortune

According to Wiseman, lucky people generate their own good fortune via 4 (four) basic principles. And, everyone has the opportunity to become luckier by following them:

1. Maximise Your Chances to be Lucky
   - take plunge, don't just think—*act* and *take risk.*
   - do not waste time by thinking—should I or should I not.
   - create a network of people; interact with people using WhatsApp, mobile, Facebook, LinkedIn, Twitter; while on

the way to and from the market, while on morning walk or in the swimming pool, while travelling by bus, train or air.

2. Listen to Your Instincts, Intuitions, Hunches and Gut Feelings
3. Always Expect that You'll Win and Never Lose
   - attract winning molecules driving losing molecules away
   - anxiety at any time disrupts the people's ability to notice the unexpected.
4. Always Look at the Bright Side of things
   - what you are gaining, not what you are losing.

Lucky people are skilled at creating and noticing chance opportunities, make lucky decisions by listening to their intuitions. They are apt at creating self-fulfilling prophesies via positive expectations, and adopt a resilient attitude that transforms 'Bad Luck' into 'Good Luck'.

Personal SWOT

I am enjoying playing this 'Luck Factor (LF)' game with you, my dear readers!! The theme is warming up with different points of view—both in favour and against. I am taking this opportunity to look at the 'LF' from another angle here.

SWOT Analysis is a much-used management tool. In SWOT, 'S' stands for 'Strengths', 'W' for 'Weaknesses', 'O' for 'Opportunities' and 'T' for 'Threats'. In the management context, it is used for analysing the corporate organisation as a whole, or a 'Strategic Business Unit (SBU)', a department, a branch, a product group, or even an individual product. Here, I shall be emphasizing how you can use it to identify what 'strengths' of yours you can readily apply to tap some current 'opportunity' and how would you overcome a 'threat' by reducing a 'weakness' that you have in your personality. In other words, how would you create a 'Good Luck' and stay away from a 'Bad Luck'.

Personal SWOT means, you make a list of your major 'Strengths' or 'Plus Points (PP)' and most critical 'Weaknesses' or 'Minus Points (MP)'. Sometimes, for my own analysis, I would add a special category: my 'Most Unique Points (MUP)' which makes me 'Different' from others. But, how do you identify your 'S' and

'W'?.

Method 1: Make a record of all your 'Achievements' where you got some recognition or appreciation in the form of a reward—formal or informal, where the credit for the achievement was entirely yours. Now, if you analyse each 'Achievement' thoroughly, you will be able to identify the 'Strengths' in your personality which were responsible for the achievement. Sift out the 'Highest Common Strengths' and you get your 'Core Competencies (CC)'.

Now, make a list of your 'Failures (F)' where the failure could be attributable to some 'Weakness' in your personality. Now, make a list of all your 'Weaknesses' and sift out the 'Most Critical Ones' which represent your 'Core Incompetencies (CI)'. Now, segregate the 'Weaknesses' into 'Constraints (C)' and 'Deficiencies (D)'. 'C's are those that are insurmountable—cannot be overcome much though you may try; and 'D's are those that are surmountable—can be overcome by making and implementing an action plan. Don't waste your time over the 'C's. Concentrate on the 'D's.

Method 2: Make an analysis of Others' Feedback regarding you—your parents, elders, teachers, tutors, boss, seniors, colleagues, juniors and so on. Common positive feedback factors are your 'CC' and common negative feedback factors are your 'CI'.

Prepare action plans to add value and provide reinforcement to your 'CC' and reduce (and, if possible, totally eradicate) your 'CI'.

Track Opportunities and Avoid Threats

Keep your antennas open to track 'Opportunities (O)' and grab them before they are lost and avoid or overcome 'Threats (T)' posed by one or a few amongst your CI.

Be obsessed with personal SWOT and develop the uncanny ability to be in the right place at the right time and enjoy more than your fair share of lucky breaks. Do not wait to avail any opportunity that has arisen or to avert any threat that you encounter. Act, Do Not Wait.

Keep Away from Wrong Expectations

Do not be clouded or deluded by wrong expectations! Let me explain what I want to say. India is rich in mineral resources. Coal is one of them. Nevertheless, the properties of coal vary from one region of the country to another. The Salem, Tamil Nadu coal is different from the Nagpur or Bilaspur coal. The Singareni, UP coal is different from the Margarite coal seam coal in Northern Assam. The Ranchi coal is different from the coal mined in Ranigunge.

I being a Bengali brahmin should not expect to possess an inherent industry-start-up acumen like a Marwari [For validation, please read the excellent book *The Marwaris: From Traders to Industrialists* by the American scholar Thomas A. Timberg (New Delhi: Vikas Publishing, 1978, 1st Edition)]. The Marwari-Gujarati (includes Parsis also who had migrated from Iran to India's west coast) type of character trait has its roots in the soils of their native places which were dry and barren unlike the Gangetic plains. Many people from those arid zones had to migrate to UP, Bihar, Assam and Bengal to try their luck.

Migration psychology has its typical features. Migrants remain most vigilant and alert looking for 'opportunities' and 'threats'—which is an essential strength for trading and business career. They observe the local people who are least competitive; complaisant in their native 'comfort zones'—fit only for employment and humdrum self-employment, and nurture a DREAM to overtake them fast with 'display of wealth'. So, they go for expensive flats, big houses, almost one car for each member of the family (possibly copying the North American rich after one or two foreign business trips)—although maintaining their most traditional living style including vegetarianism.

While conducting workshops for Birla companies in Birla Buildings and Industry House in Kolkata, we were served high-class vegetarian lunch in western style by liveried trained English-speaking waiters. And, while conducting a project for a Bangur company, we had to take off our shoes to enter the guest house, first go to the Puja Room to pay respect to Goddess Lakshmi before checking into the guest rooms; and, were served traditional Marwari vegetarian lunch on banana leaves. So, I should be realistic and try to place myself largely in my own community background to identify my 'Strengths' and matching 'Opportunities', and also track 'Threats' typical of its 'Weaknesses'.

Do you realise that your 'Strengths (S)' and 'Weaknesses (W)' constitute your 'Luck Factor (LF)'? Possibly you were vague about your 'LF' as you had never analysed your 'S' and 'W' seriously and that is why you have been stumbling in your life's journey. Now, make a fresh beginning and see if you 'win' or 'lose' in the game.

A Very Special Case Study

In 1979, I had an invitation to chair a session on 'Shift-work and Brain' in the International Conference on Production Research at Amsterdam in The Netherlands. Post-conference, I became the guest-of-honour of a top high-technology multi-national corporation (MNC), headquartered in Europe. One of the MNC board directors took me along with him to their electronic assembly units in different parts of Europe. As a part of my tour, I was taken to the MNC's Central R and D Laboratory. It was indeed a remarkable experience how the MNC's world-class research engineers and scientists were working on the technology of tomorrow including in medical electronics in which I was particularly interested as I was heading at that time the Bioengineering Unit at the University College of Medicine (Goenka Hospital), University of Calcutta purely in an honorary capacity like all medical faculty members of the University.

That day, when I returned to my guest house where I was staying, the European guest house manager who had become quite friendly with me joined me for dinner. He asked me: how did I like the R&D set-up of the MNC which was then the largest of its kind in the world. During our conversation, suddenly he moved close to me and whispered into my ears: "Doctor, do you know what had happened in the same lab quite some years ago?" Then he continued the story, which I will now narrate to you in my own words.

5 (five) post-graduate electronic students (2 girls and 3 boys) from Japan came on a study tour of Europe. They were taken

to the R&D Centre as a matter of routine. All their belongings including notepads and pen-pencils had to be left at the Security Office. But the students had come totally prepared as to what their task would be. For one of them—a male student, the outstanding 'Strength (S)' was his leadership quality (l call him L). L called T whose 'Strength (S)' was 'Technicality'. L told T to prompt technical questions in Japanese to E whose 'Strength (S)' was English-speaking. L told E to translate all Japanese technical questions into English and shoot them to the R & D Centre engineers and scientists. L called the girl student A whose 'Strength (S)' was 'Audio Recording Power'—if she wished and concentrated, she could record every bit of a conversation just with the help of her ears and her brain's copying mechanism—the 'Mirror Neurons (MN)'. L asked her to use this strength to record all the presentation along with the questions and answers coming up during the visit. The girl who was left out was V—she had 'Visual' recording power or 'photographic memory' as her 'Strength (S)' (again, a MN-linked brain power). L told her to take photos of all the circuits and other things which will be shown to them and store those photos inside her brain. When L, T, E, A and V came out of the R and D Centre after a sumptuous lunch at the canteen, they had with them the entire plan of a new product that the MNC was researching on for the last 3 (three) years.

The 5 (five) students came back to Tokyo within a few days' time. The very next day after their arrival, L rang up the MD and CEO of a Tokyo-based high technology giant and introduced himself as a PG student. The MD and CEO thought that the boy was seeking an employment; so, he, in his typical polite manner, asked him to contact the Company's HR dept. But L insisted that he and his four pals should be given an 'Opportunity (O)' to meet him not for the purpose of 'getting' a job but for 'giving' him something. The MD and CEO found it very strange; but, anyway, he gave them an appointment. When they arrived, L asked for some papers and pencils as their belongings had to be left behind in the custody of the Security Office at the main gate. The 5 (five) students reproduced the design of an entirely new product. The MD and CEO was awe-struck and fascinated. His Company was starving for new and novel high-tech products. When he asked where from they had got it, they did not disclose because being the best and most intelligent group of PG electronics students they had already improved upon the original European design so that nobody could catch them for outright copyright infringement. The MD and CEO asked them: "How much payment do you want?" L said: "Nothing. This is our *gift* to our Motherland. We want this 'Made in Japan' product to become the market leaders. So just produce and promote. We want our Japanese flag to fly higher than the flags of our competitors' nations."

What do we learn from this very special case study:

1. Utilise your 'Strengths (S)' to tap 'Opportunities (O)' before you miss them. So, don't waste time in Thinking and Wondering—Just Act and Implement.
2. In a team situation, build up the team work using complementary 'Strengths (S)' of the team members. This is applicable in a family also as well as in a very small work unit.
3. Mother Nature has given us birth in a particular country—a particular nation. That land is our 'Mother'. We must make it a point to give back to our 'Motherland' more than what we have got and taken from her.

Don't you feel now that you've been so much bogged down in your day-to-day routinised living and working, that so many golden 'Opportunities (O)' might have just passed by fast which you could have availed of utilising some of your outstanding 'Strengths (S)' but you could not as you are fitted with antennas which have not been maintained and sharpened properly for how many years that God only knows?

The 'Genius (G)' in You

Hope you remember my Human Resource bell curve. There, you may believe it or not, it is not only the 'Supernormal' or 'Extraordinary' people who are 'Geniuses'. I have the uncanny power to discover a 'Genius' hidden in everyone including you. Every 'Normal' or 'Ordinary' individual has a streak of 'Genius (G)' in him (no gender bias) which provides him with an edge over others in his family, social or work circle. During my growing years, I used to approach my father whose 'Strength (S)' was drafting in English. My elder cousin brothers would also bank on him for English drafting. For drafting in Bengali, we would go to my mother as she was the best amongst all in our family circle. So, in our circle, my dad and mom were regarded as some sort of a 'Genius (G)' in English and Bengali respectively. When I grew up and just embarked upon my teenage, I was considered a 'G' in both English and Bengali drafting and eventually these became my outstanding 'S's.

Every individual thus has one or more hidden 'G' within him. That or those 'G' has or have to be discovered. This exercise is a part of 'Create Your Own Luck Factor (CYOLF)'. But, how do you do it—what method would you adopt—what approach would you take? Let me elaborate. Each of us is endowed with three-fold body and brain powers. The most common are the 'Skills (S)': Body Skills (fit and flexible body, degrees of freedom at the joints, ease of movement as is required in postures, gestures, games, sports, performing yogic asanas, dancing etc.) and Brain Skills (reflexes, memory—long- and short-term). 'S' can be inborn as well as acquired. Acquired 'S' include: cycling, swimming, driving, rowing, sewing, stitching, cooking, singing, playing a musical instrument, using hand tools, running a lathe machine etc. 'Skills', both inborn and acquired, are related to the hind (reptilian) and middle (paleo-mammalian) portions of our brains.

'Intelligences (I)' and 'Talents (T)'—both represent powers of the Brain. For right-handed persons, the 'Intelligences (I)' like planning, programming, preparation of a checklist or 'To Do' list, arithmetical calculations-estimation-measurement, language use (grammar, word power, composition) are all related to the left half of the Neo-mammalian brain or Neo-cortex; whereas 'Talents (T)' which include the power of designing something original or creating something, are related to the same brain's right hemisphere. This Left Brain-Right Brain theory was an outcome of my Brain Guru Dr. Roger Sperry's split-brain surgery work which earned him a Nobel Prize in medicine and physiology in 1981.

Case Studies on Genius (G)

During my growing years, we had a whole time cook in our family. His name was Suren Maity and he was from Midnapore. Surenda was far from literate. His cooking 'Skill (S)' was superb; nobody else could beat him. That was a streak of 'Genius (G)' in him. He used to 'plan' the menu himself, make a purchase 'Budget' and ask for the money from my mom. Planning, estimating and budgeting are inter-related 'Intelligences (I)'. Occasionally, he will ask for some extra money to purchase some special items for cooking a special dish which was his own brainchild. Such creative streak would be regarded as a 'Talent (T)'. So, he had not just one but multiple streaks of 'Genius (G)' in him. Just imagine! A rural rustic, with no education, made himself indispensable in our household because of 3 (three) distinctly different streaks of G – in S, I and T.

During the period 1990 to 2008, in my own family household, we had a part-time cook Shyamali Roy. She had good enough cooking 'Skill (S)' but whenever my wife Utpala would be away to my daughter's place in Mumbai for a few months, I had to chalk out a menu plan because Shyamali simply could not plan. She lacked the 'Intelligence (I)' required for planning. If I would sometimes say: "Shyamali, the same items every week become a little boring, monotonous." She would immediately react: "I do not know anything better. You get a new idea and then tell me what to do and how to do. I will do it." That indicated that she never had any cooking talent. She used to cook most mechanically as that profession was giving her bread and butter; she did not have any passion or love for cooking. In any case, even with only a single G—her cooking skill, she had made a firm footing for herself in our household just because we were all totally dependent on her for our cooked food. If she was absent for a day, we had to manage with sandwiches or order food from a local food joint.

One Genius (G) is Not Enough

Nevertheless, with a single G you cannot go far in life. I will prove it through the same Shyamali's example. As her cooking was getting a little stale for us, we took a decision to try out a new hand and luckily, we got a young man Prabir who was multi-skilled and not very costly. So Shyamali was served a month's notice; and, then she had to leave as Prabir had already joined. We got the information from people who knew her that, even after six months, she could not get a cooking assignment. She had been employed in another household for other types of jobs; that continued but the void created by us was not filled. On the contrary, Suren Maity with multiple G's was picked up by a celebrity (I shall not name him) friend of my father on much better and higher terms than my parents could offer.

How Do You Track the Genius (G) in You

So, there is certainly a 'Genius (G)' inside you. Quite easy to find. Is there anything 'Unique' in you? Is there some task (s) for which others in your circle (family or workplace) are dependent on you; if you are not available it (those) remain (s) undone? There may be more than one also. You only have to recognise it or those and apply in practice 'consciously' as that or those constitute your 'Good Luck Factor'.

Your 'Genius (G)' and ROI

You might have discovered your G, double G, or multiple G with a little nudge that you got from me a little while ago. But have you worked out the ROI of those?

What is ROI? ROI is the 'Return on Investment'. What are the 'Takes' or 'Gets' for or from the 'Investment' of your G. A common example from the teenage crowd. Pratik Mallik is a 2nd year hotel management student in a premier hospitality institute of Kolkata. While at home, Pratik plays the guitar and sings popular songs for three to four hours every day. Venue: his attic; audience: his pet dog Julie. Playing the guitar and singing songs composed by others are 'Skills (S)'—which constitute his G. What does Pratik get as his ROI—in exchange of the time, energy, effort 'invested' by him in the activities? He does not calculate as it has never occurred to him that it can be and has to be calculated to ensure that he is a 'Neuro-Managed (NM)' person. How can it occur as this approach is fresh from the oven—I am cooking it according to my 'Neuro-Management (NM)' recipe.

Do not get a culture shock! Read on with a cool brain. Every morning we get on the platter 86,400 units of 'Opportunity (O)' [24 hours × 60 minutes × 60 seconds = 86,400 seconds and each second may bear or bring some 'O'.] So, we have to learn to calculate the 'Return (R)' we get by 'Investing' our effortful 'Time'.

ROI: Qualitative

ROI may be 'qualitative' or 'quantitative'. The satisfaction, the enjoyment, that Pratik gets every day by spending around 3 (three) hours playing the guitar and singing along is 'qualitative'—it cannot be calculated arithmetically. Nevertheless, it can be expressed in terms of 'Neuro-Management (NM)'!! Pratik gets his supply of 'motivational' neuro-chemical 'Dopamine (D)' and 'mood balancing/feel good' neuro-chemical 'Serotonin (S)' from that experience.

Most interestingly, 'S' is produced 90% and 'D' 50% in our digestive organs belonging to the 'Gut Brain' ('Enteric Nervous System') when we eat our favourite food items. If Pratik would not have played the guitar and sang along, 'Ghrelin'—the hunger hormone would have been produced in his gastrointestinal tract, especially the stomach and he would have turned greedy and consumed junk food like a glutton—which precisely was his habit when he did not pick up the musical hobby. Now, he can go without breakfast if he practices music for an hour in the morning after his wash.

As a matter fact, there is another case which I handled. Ramen Roy, a 23-year B.Tech in Electronics and Communication Engineering was addicted to video films which he would watch 3 (three) to 4 (four) hours every day to get his supply (without his conscious participation) of D and S. Whenever, his smartphone would conk off and sent for repair, he would eat up all the biscuits—whatever would be available at home and face rough weather from his mom and his older sister—as his GI tract and stomach would have been bathed by the hunger hormone Ghrelin. I did not tell you about Ramen's 'G'. He analyses every film—its directional-cinematographic-editing qualities, audience impact, box office success or failure features with some special 'Intelligence (I)'. His boyhood DREAM was to be a film-maker.

ROI: Quantitative

I have talked so far about the 'qualitative' ROI. Pratik is doing hotel management and Ramen has already completed his B.Tech degree—what for? To earn 'quantitative' ROI—money—CASH. When they take up a job or go for self-employment or set up an enterprise, most of their waking hours will be spent in obtaining the 'quantitative' ROI and they will be suffering from 'qualitative' ROI deprivation or deficiency unless (note this please), of course, they get into their DREAM occupations for which they had a DRIVE (= strong passion and motivation) from within. And, I can predict their future health (both physical as well as mental) conditions right from now. Why, you know? Pratik's teenage DREAM was to be a musician. But his mother nudged him to go for hotel management as it has glamour and good money. Intelligent boy, he could clear the entrance test and got admitted. When I asked him about his future, he said that he plans to go to a Dubai hotel, save enough money for 5 (five) years by spending less maintaining frugality and, then, get back to India to start his own music studio. Ramen has left two jobs already. He did qualify in Kolkata Metro Railway Project written test, but did not go for the interview and viva-voce. Reason: He cannot stay without watching a video film. Both boys are intelligent, academically did well all along but the problem is elsewhere—in their G-ROI dilemma.

Do you feel (put your hand on your chest) you get your supply of 'qualitative' ROI: 'Dopamine (D)' and 'Serotonin (S)' [these are the two main neuro-chemicals cross-connected with motivation, mood and the digestive system as in the pre-historic times, there were no choice of profession or occupation—which can be counted in thousands now—it was only hunting, gathering fruits and vegetables and having sex—like it still is in today's many tribal societies] from your main occupation which is giving you your 'quantitative' ROI?

The 'Genius (G)' in You and the 'Responsibility Centre (RC)' Concept

From 'Return on Investment (ROI)' let me hold your hand and introduce you to the 'Responsibility Centre (RC)' concept. 'RC' is from the domain of Economics and Finance. However, I have modified it to suit my purpose.

[How do I know about this? For quite some time, I used to write a regular column in The Management Accountant—the monthly journal of the Institute of Cost and Works Accountants of India. I used to be a commissioned writer in the journals of The Institute of Chartered Accountants of India, The Institute of Company Secretaries of India, a centre page writer in Business Standard and a columnist in Business World, Commerce, Capital, Economic and Political Weekly.]

In a group situation, every member of a group is regarded as a 'Responsibility Centre (RC)'. Like in your family, if you are the earning member, then you are an 'Income Centre (IC)' [In Business Management, it is called a 'Revenue Centre (RC)']. If your spouse is also earning, then both of you are 'Income Centres (IC)'. Your spouse may not be employed, she may be a freelancer or self-employed or may run a small business like a Xerox shop, or she may have some rental income from a property she owns or has inherited from her parents' side, or may have income from stocks, shares, mutual fund and bank deposits; or, she provides private tuition, or makes and sells soft toys. The whole idea is to have both husband and wife as earning members—so that both are 'Income Centres'. Both are using their 'Geniuses (G)'—single, double or multiple and earning ROI—quantitative and, may be also, qualitative.

What is the opposite of 'Income'? It is 'Expenditure' or 'Cost'. So, the opposite of 'Income Centre (IC)' is 'Cost Centre (CC)'. The concept of 'CC' is applicable when the member of the unit is not having any 'Cash Income', but has an 'Economic Role'. How? By performing work activities for which the unit had to engage someone else by making payment for his services. So, instead of incurring 'Costs', she is 'Saving' some costs and adding to the cash surplus of the family—so I designate her—the homemaker, the housewife, in the dignified role of a 'Profit Centre (PC)' as that surplus or profit or saving can be 'Invested' to earn an 'Return on Investment (ROI)'. And, even if she is not performing any physical activity (thereby saving the labour cost), if she 'Manages' everything so well that she plans, prepares budgets, reviews the actuals with the budgeted figures, puts her foot down to curtail costs and generates savings for investment, she uses 3Gs—Skills, Intelligences and Talents (SIT). Effective managers are all mixtures of SITs. So, a homemaker who has such efficiency is no less than an Effective Manager.

The Role of a Pre-teen or a Teenager

What is the role of a pre-teen or teenage member of the family? Should he (no gender bias) remain happy by limiting himself to the role of a 'Cost Centre (CC)' only? Certainly not! But he may not be mature enough to identify an alternative purposeful role. It is the responsibility of the Smart leading parents to train him to develop into a 'Profit Centre (PC)' by cutting costs following frugal habits and lifestyle. He should be trained to prepare a daily shopping budget for household provisions and ensure that the budget is not exceeded; on the contrary, some money (whatever may be the quantity) is saved from the budgeted amount and it is saved in a piggy bank. Similarly, while going for picnics or on annual holidays or for festival shopping, the budgeting responsibility should be entrusted to the teenage kid.

Now, get exposed to some painful reality! If you are very good in sketching, drawing, painting and spending a lot of your waking time in that kind of pursuit you are earning your qualitative ROI but no quantitative ROI. Naturally, your family would regard you as a 'Cost Centre (CC)' as your investment of time, energy, effort is not leading to any 'Economic Return'. You are getting an 'Emotional Return' only. Try to convert that 'Skill' or 'Talent' into an economic activity so that you live with honour and dignity in your family unit. If a teenage member of your family has sketching, drawing and painting talent, help him to plan his life in such way that the career that he chooses has some significant place for artistic inputs as I have done in my TMP (Teen Mentoring Project) for Arka (automobile design), for Prarthana and Trisha (fashion design), for Sanchayan (comedy film-making) and for Tryambak (human sciences—robotics).

'Responsibility Centre' and Time Management

The 'RC' concept I integrate with 'Time Management'. You must identify your 'Time Wasters'—where you are 'wasting' your time thus functioning as a 'Cost Centre (CC)'. If you allow your 'Time' to be 'Killed' by somebody else then also you are no better than a 'CC'. And, finally allowing your' Time' to be 'Stolen' where you have no control like in the case of a traffic jam, delayed flight or cancellation of a train you are not utilising your 'G' effectively.

Always be ready with Alternatives as I have taught you in Career Planning.

Are you getting a culture shock? Don't you think that if you measure and quantify everything then it loses its charm? Because those who do not live their lives by applying such 'Neuro-economics' or 'Neuro-finance' principles, when they reach their middle age they start suffering from mid-age blues when they compare where they are with their contemporaries who have risen much higher may not be in terms of wealth but in terms of contribution towards socio-economic progress which is our basic responsibility as humans.

'Bad Luck' Could Be Your 'Good Luck'

A 'De-abled' (I avoid the undignified terms 'disabled' and 'handi-capped' unless these are unavoidable) member in the family! Not a liability or a burden or, rather, a 'Bad Luck' for you—on the contrary, learn to treat this as 'Good Luck' for you and regard him (no gender bias) as an 'Asset' as he is giving you the 'Opportunity' to be his 'Care-giver' or 'Service-provider'. Plus, probe to discover his 'Abled' (not 'De-abled') Skills, Intelligences and Talents—in other words, his GENIUS (es) (G) which can then be turned by your encouragement into 'Assets' for the society. No 'Human Resource (HR)' should go to waste. It is your responsibility as a parent to turn every HR in your family into an 'Asset'—a 'Human Capital (HC)'. That is what 'Mentoring' is. So, every parent has a 'Mentoring' role. And, you should be open to learn from anyone even your own spouse, or your child.

My Father's Case Was A Turning Point

My father Monoj Ganguli became speech-de-abled when I was in my teens—in 2nd year engineering (1958) in Jadavpur University. A continually choked voice led to lot of investigations including a biopsy and he was detected with laryngeal cancer. A young surgeon, highly qualified and fresh from USA, UK and France Dr. Ranesh Chakrabarty (elder brother of the famous Indologist Prof. Gayatri Chakrabarty Spivak of Columbia University—who stood 1st all along right from her school-leaving board level up to MA in Calcutta University) performed laryngectomy on my dad at the SSKM hospital.

I being the elder son and very close to my mother, she whispered into my years: "Babul (my home name)—this is 'Good Luck' for me (I was awe-struck) because this is an 'Opportunity' that has come to me for giving 'Selfless Service'. All these years, and more so when I was studying in India and your father was studying in England, I was very 'Selfish'. I wanted to steal all the attention of my in-laws, I wanted to come 1st in my class in college. It worked—I became the apple of the eye of my in-laws, I bagged the Calcutta University gold medals having topped in both Intermediate and Bachelor's Honours....but I now feel I was self-oriented like everyone else in the society. I now want to take a 180-degree turn—from one pole to the opposite pole—from 'Selfishness' to 'Selflessness'".

My late mother's voice still rings into my ears as if she is there—sitting in front of me. And, she gave totally selfless service so much so that my dad lived as a cancer-survivor for another 35 years. Since he was the first laryngectomy case in Calcutta, mom got an artificial larynx (with a spare as a standby) from USA with batteries imported from UK every year with a special import licence, trained him in artificial speaking, made him go back to active life to the Calcutta High Court and to give moral support to other throat cancer victims in public forums and privately at home. She became my role model in this respect.

Tanmay's Case Study

In 1968, when, at the instance of Prof. A.K. Basu, Dean-Faculty of Medicine and Prof. K.S. Bose, Head of Orthopaedics, Calcutta University, I joined the Calcutta University College of Medicine in a purely honorary capacity, I received a letter by post (we had to rely on the land phone and Posts and Telegraphs Department in those days) penned in most immature teenage handwriting. 14-year-old Tanmay Chakrabarty from Agartala, Tripura!! Whether we can fit him with artificial legs which we had just started making with World Bank funds as the Below-Knee (BK) portions of both his legs had been missing from birth. But he had no funds to buy the air tickets, nor had he any place to stay in Calcutta.

It was an 'Opportunity' for me and my wife Utpala to provide 'Selfless Service'—and, of course, for Tanmay too. We purchased his air ticket, brought him from the Calcutta Airport in our car, kept him with our family, fitted him with artificial legs, trained him to walk in phases for one long year and then sent him back home. While he stayed with us at our home, I discovered his 'Talent' in painting, bought him all the materials to start his painting career.

After a year, when we went to Agartala on a follow-up visit, we were appalled at the abject poverty of the family (his father was a priest—brahmin pujari) but were happy that Tanmay had started earning by selling his paintings and giving painting lessons to kids. The tragic facts, however, were: Tanmay's elder brother went to Russia on a scholarship, completed his Ph.D. in mechanical engineering, came as a lecturer in IIT-Kanpur, was indifferent to his family, and was devoting his spare time in locating opportunities for immigration to USA—complete SELF-orientation.

A Point for you to ponder: Have you ever looked at your 'Bad Luck' as your 'Good Luck'—'Opportunity' to provide 'Selfless Service', 'Opportunity' for 'Volunteering'?

[Brain research has shown 'Selfless Service' and 'Volunteering' auto-releases four positive brain chemicals—EDSO (Endorphin, Dopamine, Serotonin and Oxytocin) inside your brain. It releases Melatonin also and gives you sound, dreamless, undisturbed sleep.]

Your Luck Story

Your 'Luck Story' is something untold, unheard, unwritten, unread and unknown to the medics and the midwifes who delivered you from your mother's womb as they all were and are still concerned with the 'Gross Body' ('Sthula Sarira') which is visible and palpable—readily available for physical and physiological measurements and investigations. The real story reveals itself only to those who try to study the 'Subtle Body' ('Sukshma Sarira') and the 'Causal Body' ('Karana Sarira').

[Conceptualisations present in 'Your Luck Story' are entirely mine. May not tally with your existing knowledge-linked perceptions based on other sources. I am exposing you to my thoughts just to nudge you to consider that the issue can be looked at from other angles too.]

The 21st century, for me, started with a 'Big Bang' when I embarked on my 'Dream Child'('Swapna Santan') research project. I set off on this exploration being cornered with a few prickly questions, which never bother obstetricians, nurses, paediatricians, psychologists or other human scientists. For instance, some people—both male and female are crude looking, coarse and rude in their behaviour; whereas some people are generally OK—nothing to complain, nor there is anything to write home about; and, some people are very fine featured and refined in their conduct, humble and polite in their communication by nature. These, if you may note, have their corresponding counterparts in the Vedic Sciences—in respectively the 'Rakhshasa', 'Nara or Manushya' and 'Deva' 'Gana's (meaning 'phenotypes' in the language of modern genetics). And, why every child is not complete in all respects in its four components: the tissues of the body and the brain, the mind (the circuits—particularly in the upper forebrain or neo-cortex), and, of course, the 'Soul'. I had presumed at that juncture that one perhaps has to go back to the 'Foreplay', 'Consummation' and 'Conception' phases of the *Birth Science*.

When my Bengali treatise on the subject started getting serialised in the leading Bengali health magazine *Suswastha*, there was a big sensation in the reader circles. As if somebody had tossed a pebble into a still pond and ripples had started getting generated. Every day, I will get six to seven phone calls for a period of two long years before it got published in book form and got sold in thousands. Subsequently, however, over the last fifteen years I have gone sea-deep into the male-female relationships.

Male-Female Mateships

I classify male-female mateships (for brevity, I call close intimate 'love', 'live in' or 'married' relationships by this name) into: (i) 'play-mates' (both were neighbours or classmates in school—fell for each other and finally got married—all happiness chemicals continue to be released—EDSOM: 'Endorphin', 'Dopamine', 'Serotonin', 'Oxytocin' and 'Melatonin'); (ii) 'bodymates' (either love or negotiated marriage but the bonding element is attraction for each other's body: only 'Dopamine' is released in anticipation or visualisation of or on actual physical body contact as in DATING);

(iii) 'heartmates' (either love or negotiated marriage but the bonding is emotional: primarily a lot of 'Oxytocin' is released—followed by 'Dopamine' and 'Serotonin'); (iv) 'mindmates' (either love or negotiated marriage but the bonding is on an intellectual plane—'Dopamine' and 'Serotonin' are released followed by 'Oxytocin'); and, (v) 'soulmates' (either love or negotiated marriage but the bonding is on the highest spiritual plane—all EDSOM are released).

If the playmates continue to remain on the 'playmate' relationship plane, then during consummation, their sperms and ova start playing like little kids inside the female's womb and conception never takes place naturally much though they may desire and try as the childhood relationship continues to remain in the 'Subtle Body' ('Sukshma Sarira'); and, does not come to the 'Gross Body' ('Sthula Sarira') plane unless they undergo a special attitudinal intervention which is available in my 'Neuro-management' Brain Toolkit and I call it 'Dream Personality Analysis'. In the 'bodymate' relationship, as years go by, bodies get old and stale so the quality of the sperms and ova also get inferior in their properties and if fertilisation takes place, the quality of the foetus suffers. [I have handled a case where despite the wife being present the husband seeks access to a new woman every week; otherwise, he turns violent—an obsession—in modern society we call it perversion, but in prehistoric hunter-gatherer society it was quite common.]

'Heartmate' relationship may suffer when children come as, then the prime actor of this bonding—'Oxytocin', gets diluted and distributed to all the loved ones so the input for the husband and the wife reduces—they start looking for 'Oxytocin' sources elsewhere—so friends become equally important. Now, as for the 'mindmate' relationship, the intellect or the mind, which is available in the neo-cortex, may lose its efficiency and power due to lack of use beyond middle age, so the relationship may suffer if both the husband and the wife do not continue productive and meaningful use of their forebrain by indulging in intellectual or creative pursuits even at an old age. The reason is simple. All our body and brain cells follow a golden rule: "Use me or lose me". Lack of use leads to atrophy of body and brain cells both. 'Soulmateship' never gets obsolete or stale but soulmates who exist on the spiritual plane do not have any interest to come down to body mateship ever [Example: Sri Ramakrishna Paramhansa and Sri Sri Saradamani.]

So, your 'Luck' has been decided by:

- *Number One:* at what age and under what kind of 'mateship' consciousness you had been conceived.
- *Number Two:* are you a child of 'Lust' (just to get physically satisfied the couple went for sex, and the pregnancy was unplanned, accidental) or a child of 'Love' (emotionally the couple are tightly connected with each other and possibly it was a planned pregnancy).

  Now try to imagine the prehistoric hunter-gatherer society scenario. Most children were kids of 'Lust' as it was just for the sake of pleasure that sex took place. So, it reflected on the product—the child—his looks, his conduct, his behaviour. The more the relationship moved from 'heartmateship' upwards, the more well-proportioned would be the body, the more refined would be the features and fixtures and the more sober and polite would be the communication and behaviour.
- *Number Three:* the zygote that was created as a result of fertilisation, what kind of 'Soul' entered into it. So now comes the mother's role in determining your 'Luck' profile. What kind of child she had desired to have?

Luck Game—The 2nd Round

With the sperm of the man getting firmly fused with the egg of the woman, the first round of the Luck Game is over. The quality of the outcome would depend upon the kind of 'mateship'. The compatibility-incompatibility between the sperm and the egg is also a critical factor here. If the sperm has an inherent propensity to play a 'I win, you lose' game with the ovum and the latter is overpowered by the sperm for some reason (for instance, one rare reason that I have come across in my scientific research career is that the woman has put the man on a very high pedestal—simply adores and worships him next to God, having a 'You win, I lose'-flavoured surrendering attitude, then the child may have a propensity to become 'psychotic' or 'schizophrenic'—some authentic research work has been done in UK and USA). On the contrary, if the woman tries to control and dominate the man—has a much stronger personality having an unchangeable 'I win you lose' attitude, then the child that will come has a strong possibility of becoming a victim of 'Autism Spectrum Disorder (ASD)'.

The best combination is the 'You win, I also win' attitude for both involved in the 'mateship'. Invariably it leads to a child of 'Love'. Here, by 'attitude' I mean what thoughts had filled their minds when the game was being played between the two—the 'Pair'.

Now, the 2nd round of the game is a solo game where only the woman is involved—the 'mother-to-be' of the child. This round is played for 49 (forty-nine) days, that is, 7 (seven) weeks. What does she think of the pregnancy: it may be an unplanned one but is it welcome or not? If it is not welcome and she wants to terminate or abort it, is she being prevented by the environment? Does it mean that she is carrying it unwillingly [which will mean the love or bonding molecule 'Oxytocin (O)' will not be released from her brain's 'Pituitary Gland']. This will have the same effect as any other kind of stress that a pregnant lady may suffer from the root causes being: daughter-in-law- mother-in-law conflict; mama's boy husband taking mother's side; absentee husband (including husband being away to a different location for long); frequently touring husband; despite husband being present he has no time to supply Oxytocin to the wife through his conduct and communication; working woman—self-employed or entrepreneur and cannot take time off from work.... etc. Stress hormone 'Cortisol' will be released continuously and the outcome may be a 'subnormal' child—such as a victim of ADD (Attention Deficit Disorder) or ADHD (Attention Deficit Hyperactivity Disorder).

Not, let us assume, the mother-to-be has no such problem. Planned or unplanned, she is most happy becoming pregnant. Now what kind of a child she wants—that would be the guiding factor in inviting a specific 'Soul' from the 'Soul-land' (to put it lightly).

At the moment of death of a person, his body and brain—the hard tissues stop functioning. The mind which is nothing but the huge conglomerate of brain circuits also become dysfunctional. But the 'Atman' (the 'Soul') of the person which is a kind of ENERGY (cannot be seen with our eyes) leaves the gross body ('sthula sarira') of the individual.

The 'Soul' leaves with its memories, experiences and propensities in the external environment. It thus has its typical profile which is entirely and exclusively its own. The main thing that bothers this wandering 'Soul' now is its unfulfilled desires, ambitions and aspirations in its previous life and the goals that could not be reached, the tasks that could not be accomplished, the work assignment which could not be completed in the immediate past life.

The 'Soul' is hungry for the happiness chemicals: E (Endorphin), D (Dopamine), S (Serotonin), O (Oxytocin) and M (Melatonin) that it could not get as much as it had desired in its last life. It could be the hunger for only one, or any two, or any three, or any four or all the five chemicals. The 'Soul' is looking for a 'Womb'—a mother who personally and whose environment would provide it with the opportunity for satiation of such hunger.

The Pregnant Woman's Wish

Now what kind of a child (leave the gender factor aside for this discussion) the pregnant woman desires would depend upon her *consciousness*. Here I would take the help of the Pancha Kosha Theory of the Taittiriya Upanishad.

If she is very worldly and of grossly materialistic type—guided by the 'Annamaya Kosha (AK)' propensities and wants the child to be of the same profile—very worldly type, materially successful, she will attract a 'Soul' which has a burning earthly and materialistic desire. If she is guided by the 'Pranamaya Kosha (PK)'—health, fitness, vitality, bursting with energy, she would want a child having the same type of personality and, therefore invite a 'Soul' who is looking for that kind of an opportunity. If the woman is friendly sociable, loves human company, she will nurture the profile of a dreamchild of this type. And this is the domain of the 'Monomaya Kosha (MK)'—the sheath representing emotions and feelings. So, a MK-hungry 'Soul' will arrive.

In terms of the ancient Vedic concept of 'Triguna', the first type AK is 'Tamasik', the next two PK and MK are 'Rajasik'. The highest and the purest type—'Sattwik' is manifested in the 'Vijnanamaya Kosha (VK)'—the Kosha representing logic and intelligence; and in the 'Anandamaya Kosha (AnK)'—creativity, innovation, invention, discovery, insight, higher forms of intuition (not plain and simple 'gut feelings'). 'Sattwik' mothers are not just pious or ritualistically religious. The pious and ritualistically religious mothers are—not seeking the truth, but running after selfish interests of her family—food, clothes, shelter, wealth, advancement in prestige and status and so on. 'Sattwik' mothers are spiritual who are seekers of truth and who long for universal well-being, growth and advancement who pray for having children who would contribute towards socio-cultural-economic development. So, they would invite such rare 'Souls'. Most interestingly, if they do not get such rare 'Souls' to enter their wombs, whatever quality they get, they will accept and endeavour lifelong for their serious upliftment.

At the end of the 7th week of pregnancy, the 'Soul' will enter the 'Pineal Gland (PG)' inside the woman's brain and the 3rd round of the 'Luck Game' will begin.

Luck Game: The 3rd Round Onwards

The 7th week onwards, more critical than the physical health of the mother-to-be, is her mental health—her brain state. This is the time when to restrict her 'Default Mode Network (DMN)' to be active, she should listen to music that she enjoys. But the music has to be of slow, soft, instrumental type—neither loud nor fast beats. String instruments like sitar, sarod, santoor, mandolin and guitar light classical and melodious tunes are suggested during wakefulness and flute recitals at sleeping time during day as well as night.

Brain's DMN which used to play a very important role as a strategic planning tool (by recapitulating the hazards encountered in the past to plan precautionary measures to safeguard against future threats, if any) during prehistoric times in the hunter-gatherer society, has now become a deterrent towards mental focus after languages were discovered and the language function occupied large portions of our neo-mammalian brain or neo-cortex. Now if your brain is not occupied in any 'Task Mode Network'—on some specific assignment, then the DMN gets engaged with negative thoughts about the past and the future which serve as meaningless stressors.

2.5 million years ago, at the dawn of the human evolution, the forest-dwelling women were no better than baby-making machines—guided entirely by their womanly (not maternal or motherly) instincts to protect the fertilised womb. Even after delivery, the female will instinctively protect the offspring and ensure its survival and unaffected growth until it can handle itself independently. It followed the same pattern as in the case of a dog, cat, tiger, monkey or chimpanzee—purely 'creaturely' behaviour (not 'motherly').

With the coming of the linguistic society, the baby-making machine was elevated to the role of a care-giver. Then, with the installation of the custom of marriage and living in families, the parental roles emerged. However, in the god-fearing primitive society, it was the mother who would pray for her offspring's well-being. As civilisation came and settled, mothers continued to pray for their children—not only for their physical well-being, but material well-being was also added—that they should never be deprived of food, clothes and shelter ('Annamaya' and 'Pranamaya' Koshas—AK and PK). Most mothers, even today, pray for the same 'Good Luck'; some may add material wealth—a well-developed, thick 'Annamaya Kosha (AK)'. A few sometimes add social wealth ('Monomaya Kosha'—MK)—excellent bonding with relations and friends. This is my 'Social Imperative (SI)' added to the 'Biological Imperatives (BI)' of survival and replication to complete BSI. A few mothers long for her child's knowledge wealth or wisdom ('Vijnanamaya Kosha' or VK). A rare one or two may pray for their kids' 'Self-realisation' ('Anandamaya Kosha' or 'AnK').

A Child's Life-Script

So, a child's 'Life-script' writing by its mother begins during the 3rd round of the LUCK GAME. In any case, all these mothers are selfish in a way. After all, they belong to the human species which represents a sophisticated variety of 2 (two)-legged tailless animal. All these thoughts vibrate inside the 'Default

Mode Network' (DMN)' of the pregnant woman's brain and those vibration molecules reach the foetus inside her womb trying to work out the embryonic software. A highly pure and spiritual lady having no carnal needs has no prayer to offer. Such a virgin was Mary in whose womb Jesus Christ just appeared from nothing—without any courtship and consummation, the conception took place.

After expiry of the term of pregnancy, when the delivery date arrives, if the delivery is a normal one, then a few things work in favour of the newborn: Number one: while it is brought out of the vaginal passage it is bathed in the love and trust molecule 'Oxytocin (O); Number two: while coming out it collects healthy microbial organisms from the mother's vaginal passage and the adjoining anal area—this helps the infant to start a healthy microbial colony inside its 'Enteric Nervous System (ENS)'. On the contrary, if for the sake of comfort and convenience, the pregnant woman makes a deal with the gynaecologist or the obstetrician takes the decision to go for a Caesarean (C)-section, both the gains become losses as there is neither any contact with 'O' nor there is any collection of healthy gut microbes—instead the infant may collect infectious bacteria from the hospital linens or nurses' gloved hands. Number three: the other normal thing is the infant must cry spontaneously when it sees the light of day. In embryological state the alveoli in the lungs of the newborn baby are filled with fluids. At the moment of birth, the respiratory system must become active. It needs to exchange air from the atmosphere. Crying lustily or in desperation is the one and only mechanism to make this happen; so, it is a must. If it does not cry, the obstetrician gives it a gentle pat on the back or tickle under the toe.

Therefore, if you are a parent, whether your teenage kid has got a hedonistic-materialistic luck ('Annamaya Kosha'—AK), a physically active-energetic luck ('Pranamaya Kosha'—PK), a friendly sociable emotional luck ('Monomaya Kosha' – MK), an intellectual-intelligent-analytical luck ('Vijnanamaya Kosha'–VK) or a creative-innovative-inventive-pioneering luck ('Anandamaya Kosha' – AnK)—all depended upon the kid's biological mother's mindset before, during and after pregnancy—what kind of wish waves she was transmitting silently in the environment. If she was humdrum and did not have any such wave of thoughts and feelings inside her mind, then the child will also, in all probability, be humdrum like most of the kids scattered around us in the society.

I will end the 'Luck Game' here and shift to 'Check Your Luck' in my next outpourings lest the baby making and grooming sport becomes too technical and boring for you.

Check Your Luck

Location: Santaldih Thermal Power Station in the interior terrain of Purulia—a backward district of West Bengal. Period: some time during 2009 or 2010. As you come out of the guest house in broad daylight you might be surrounded by macaque monkeys as they live in the forests nearby. And, if you are wearing something red, even have a red handkerchief in hand, they will attack you. They dislike red as they cannot differentiate between blood and anything else of red colour.

My workshop was over. I was mentoring the participants one-to-one. It was Deputy General Manager (DGM) Sandipan Banerjee's turn. The first thing he said that: "I feel I can earn and do much better". Sandipan was talking about his ROI vis-à-vis his GENIUS (G). "My position will also be much better with a higher designation—may be 'Vice President' and enhanced responsibility"…….he went on saying. "I'm talking about Jindal Power or Adani Power or Tata Power. But I can't figure out whether it will be Good or Bad Luck for me if I change."

I said: "Get a pad and a pen. I'll teach you the 'Luck Check' technique that I have developed in 'Neuro-management (NM)'."

On the left-hand side, write down the alternative choices that you have. On the right-hand side, put 3 columns: Col. I – Plus Points (PP); Col. II – Minus Points (MP); Col. III – Most Interesting Points (MIP) which should highlight any unique feature of the Alternative.

So, the Alternatives would be:

Alternative 1

If I continue to remain
in my present job

Alternative 2

If I change over to
Jindal Power

Alternative 3

If I change over to
Tata Power.

You can make a very rough analysis or go for a very thorough one. In order to go into the details, you have to use both hemispheres of your brain—Left as well as Right. Left has the power of intelligence, analysis, probing in detail; whereas the Right has the power of imagination and visualisation. Try to evaluate on the following factors: technical gain or loss; managerial gain or loss; economic gain or loss; emotional (whether your family will like or not the change of place, culture etc.) gain or loss; social (friends-relations) gain/loss; environmental gain or loss; any other.

Finally, you rank order the three choices: First you reject one outright which has Maximum MP, No MIP and Minimum PP. Rank 1 would be: Maximum PP, Minimum MP and Maximum MIP.

Sandipan Banerjee came to meet me at the guest house the same evening. "Sir, your LUCK CHECK technique is really fantastic!!! I've been suffering from doubt and dilemma for the last six months after I got offers from both Jindal and Tata Powers. I was totally confused as to what should I do. Your 'Luck Check' has solved the problem. I'm going to finalise with Tata Powers. Thank you so much Sir!" Sandipan looked and sounded really relieved and grateful.

A Smart parent would use the same 'Luck Check' technique for checking his teenage kid's 'Career Luck' by choosing three alternative career options and doing the PP-MP-MIP analysis for each to select the one offering the 'Best of Luck'.

Brain Tool 11

Emotional Intelligence (EI)

'Key' Points: *Heart Facts; The Heart Neurons and the Heart-Brain Axis; Heart Feelings (HF); 'Emotional Intelligence (EI)'; The 5P Formula; Father of 'Emotional Intelligence' and 'Emotional Quotient'; Impulse Management and Empathy; Tips for Developing 'Emotional Intelligence (EI)'; 'Disagreeing Agreeably (DA)'; The 'Sandwich Technique (ST)'; External Stimulus Reception at Brain's Two Different Levels; 'Sandwich Technique (ST)': An Application; An Insight into the Developing Teenage Brain; Importance of 'Hands-In' Learning; The SCARF Model.*

Heart Facts

Heart is a physiological wonder!! Dr. Christiaan Barnard (1922–2001), South African heart surgeon performed world's first heart transplantation surgery (replacement of a defective heart by a good working heart from a donor) on 3rd December 1967 and his feat received round-the-world publicity. I was studying in UK then and I saw it live on BBC TV.

Dr. Michael DeBakey (1908–2008) of the Baylor College of Medicine, Houston, Texas, pioneered the development of an artificial heart and was the first to use an external heart pump successfully in a patient. Dr. Denton Cooley (1920–2016) performed the first implantation of a total artificial heart on a human in 1970 as no donor heart was immediately available for transplantation. In 1997, Dr. Dhani Ram Baruah was the first to transplant in Assam, India, a pig's heart into a 32-year old man who survived for 7 (seven) days. A renowned cardiac surgeon, trained in UK, he was jailed for 40 (forty) days (as animal-to-man organ transplantation was illegal) and then released on bail.

The Heart Neurons and the Heart-Brain Axis

What all these pioneers possibly did not know that because heart beats represent 'Unstruck Sound', the Yogic Chakra located at the heart level is known in Yogic Sciences as the 'ANAHATA CHAKRA'—'anahata' meaning 'unstruck'. Besides, what was perhaps an obscure knowledge to them is now fully established that there is rich intrinsic innervation of the heart that includes the cardiac ganglions, collectively termed 'ganglionic plexus'. The heart has 40,000 sensory 'neurons' (= brain cells) sending information to the brain. The heart, through the 'heart-brain axis' is connected to the brain's 'Anterior Cingulate Cortex (ACC)', 'Pre-Frontal Cortex (PFC)' and 'Amygdala' and other areas involved in autonomic control.

The heart influences the brain a lot more than we had thought earlier. The 'neurons' inside the heart send more information to the brain daily via the nervous system connections and via the hormones created within the heart. They transmit to the brain biomechanical information through blood pressure waves. The heart has an electromagnetic field, called the 'cardiac energy field' (which is 5,000 times more powerful than the brain's) and an electrical field which is 60 (sixty) times greater than the activities of the brain. This field, measured by electronic means, can be detected several feet away from the body. The cardiac energy field is modulated by different emotional states. This field may transmit information that can be received by others.

Heart Feelings (HF)

When you rode your bike for the first time, your heart started beating faster. When your pet died, your heart crashed. Heart is thus not just a blood circulating pump; it is also responsible for our emotional experiences. 'Heart Feelings (HF)' thus are the emotional feelings that come spontaneously from an individual's heart.

Emotional Intelligence (EI)

However, instead of HF being regarded as a 'Brain Tool (BT)', you have to develop 'Emotional Intelligence (EI)' as a BT. EI, therefore, is the special ability that you have to develop in you to appreciate the feelings of others that you are dealing with and responding in a way that there is an unconscious vibe of liking for you in the other person and he starts trusting you—possibly ending up in a well-bonded relationship.

The 5P Formula

For developing a good bit of EI, follow my 5P formula in practice while interacting with others: one-to-one, one-to-two, one-to-a few, and one-to-a-group:

> 'P' for 'Pleasant' (maintain a happy, smiling face); 'P' for 'Polite' (make it a point to behave and communicate politely—be conscious to avoid rudeness); 'P' for 'Pro-active' (do not be impulsive and reactive, think before you respond); 'P' for 'Purposeful' (meet, interact and talk to people but do not get carried away; don't forget your tasks and priorities); 'P' for 'Passionate' (passionately believe in what you say; do not have two faces—do not behave hypocritically).

Once you have tried 5P out and found that it works, pass it on to your teenage kid whose brain is undergoing a social exposure tending to become independent and free from the parental protection. He (no gender bias) should pick it up seriously to avoid people-related problems that he may encounter while embarking on a career.

Do you understand that EI and its formula 5P that I have developed means 'Egolessness' which really indicates feeling from the heart?

Father of 'Emotional Intelligence' and 'Emotional Quotient'

You take a stock of people who were academically brilliant in the school-college-university days and of others who were better than the mediocre but socially apt and successful in their personal relationships. In life's journey, the 2nd category generally overtakes the 1st category you will find. At least I have found so. Intellectual ability or your 'Intelligence Quotient (IQ)' is not enough, on its own, to achieve success and to be happy in life. Yes, IQ can help a teenager to get into a good college or university, but it is your 'Emotional Quotient (EQ)' that will help him (no gender bias) to manage his negative emotions (like anger, fear, sadness, surprise, disgust and horror) so that he is not carried away by impulses that flood his teen brain every day. The entire credit for coining the terms 'Emotional Intelligence (EI)' and 'Emotional Quotient (EQ)' ought to go to the science journalist and best-selling author psychologist Daniel Goleman, PhD (1946 born) of USA.

Back to emotions!! 'Infatuation' or short-lived attraction is another very common negative emotion that is a time- and focus-killer for many a teenager. Palas Pramanik was academically brilliant always getting high ranks at school level. He went to a boys' school all along up to senior secondary. As a fresher in a co-ed college, he became a star-gazer and fell for a pretty girl—Bipasha Mandal. It was sheer infatuation—a short-lived splash of 'Dopamine (D)'—that he did not realise. He had a high IQ but a very low EQ as he could not manage his impulsive emotions. Teenage is the time when kids have got to be exposed to the EQ concept by Smart leading parents or mentors. Palas came from a broken family with his mom and pop mutually separated (not divorced) and neither of them were capable of pointing out to him that he must control himself. His 'Good Luck' was that he happens to be under the tutelage of an excellent Mentor who put up in front of him the pros and cons of such a relationship and could dissuade him to get back to his academics with the help of the just-sown seed of EQ inside his brain. Should I or should I not? What would be my gains and losses? He was taught the 'Luck Check' technique to evaluate the PP-MP-MIP of his going steady with Bipasha vis-à-vis dropping her altogether.

Tips for Developing 'Emotional Intelligence (EI)'

Emotional Intelligence (EI) and Emotional Quotient (EQ) both have to be built into the teenage brain every day by SMART parenting or mentoring. How?? I am providing a few tips below with a request to you to pass the whole set on to a teenage member of the family:

1. *Impulse Management*

Take a pause before you 'leap', as your 'leap' is guided by an 'impulse'. Impulsiveness is emotionally a most unintelligent trait. Some experts like Prof. Daniel J. Siegel, MD of UCLA call it 'hyper rational thinking' where the gains overshadow the losses or the risks, although the teenager knows that risks are involved. Typical impulsive teenage behaviours are: driving the dad's 2-wheeler or 4-wheeler without much training or practice (I still vividly remember when my younger brother Tota was 16, one morning he disappeared with the family car and driver and before we could figure out that they were not there, a phone call came to my father that his son has met with an accident—Tota had driven the car straight into the front garden of a house crashing the entrance gate); jumping into or out of a running bus or train (a very common occurrence every day at every railway station in India); crossing the rail track instead of using the footbridge (a regular affair).

There is a tremendous drive for 'Reward' ['Dopamine' (D)] in the teen brain because the reward circuits are getting hardwired. The teenage kid in prehistoric times had to have his 'Seeking System Circuit (SSC)' to be active manifesting into behaviours representing 'Exploration, Experimentation, Learning (EEL)'. EEL should produce the desirable outcome of the acts of hunting and gathering, the anticipation of which will produce 'D' and, further on, achievement—more 'D'. Here 'Emotional Intelligence (EI)' and 'Emotional Quotient (EQ)' would prompt the teenager to delay his gratification by inhibiting the strong desire for instantaneous or immediate gratification.

2. *Empathy for Parents*

A teenager is neither a kid nor an adult. So, he will tend to shuttle away from adults and mix more with his peers and be influenced and guided more by them. EI and EQ are musts for him to appreciate the parents' point of view. Parents and family elders may scold, discipline, take a teenage kid to task but what for—so that he walks on the right path, behaves properly—not irrationally. In the prehistoric times, teens getting disconnected from the tribal cluster was not uncommon. That is not desirable in modern times; teens need to be active and responsible members of the family. Smart parenting means to dissuade them from developing the bad habit of staying at home but digitally engaged, disconnected from the family.

Do you realise how far-reaching is the arm of 'Emotional Intelligence (EI)' which our educationists have never thought of including in the high school curricula? Until that is done, it is the Smart leading parents' responsibility to give it a prominent place in the mentoring curricula at home [In the US, Daniel Goleman has been kept busy, for more than a decade now, by a few leading universities on projects as to how EI and EQ can be practically taught at the school level.]

Disagreeing Agreeably (DA)

A teenage kid indulges in 'hyperrationality' which makes him 'Disagree Disagreeably (DD)'. By DD, I mean arguing without thinking about the consequences; he throws his 'Disagreement' right on your face. DD is a very common occurrence—why only in teenagers—in the case of many adults too who have the bad habit of making snap negative responses. As a SMART parent, you have to make the teenage kid to move to the broader consideration called 'gist thinking'—considering the larger context of the decision—making him aware of how the 'Receiver' of the message will take it. You mentor him to use the technique of 'Disagreeing Agreeably (DA)'. DA is: you firmly agree with the other person's 2 or 3 points which are acceptable to you, but then show your 'disagreement' with 2 more points. But this 'disagreement' should not be direct—by making a snap statement like "On the following points, I do not agree with you". Instead you put the ball in his court this way: "Don't you think on the other two points one could have a different point of view? In other words, there could be diverse opinions on those—wouldn't you think so?" When you put your disagreement not flatly on his face but in the form of a query for his consideration, he will take it as a question and start thinking as the 'Stimulus (S)' in the form of a question is received at his brain's upper floor by the 'Pre-frontal Cortex (PFC)'.

The 'Sandwich Technique (ST)'

A little modification of this disagreement style is what I call the 'Sandwich Technique (ST)'. In 'ST', first you are putting a +ve point (your agreement) and then you are bringing a –ve point (your disagreement) in a most tactful way; and, finally you top it up in a way which pleases him and makes him happy.

External Stimulus Reception at Brain's Two Different Levels

Any stimulus coming from the external environment by way of a message communicated by someone can be received by your brain at two (2) different levels. The first one is most common in teenagers as well as many adults with an immature forebrain and, that is, at the 'Limbic System (LS)' which is the most active and sensitive emotional centre located in your mid-brain or paleo-mammalian complex. If this stimulus is not liked by your LS and regarded as a 'threat' to your EGO (= Self-esteem), the immediate response would be Freeze (zero-response) or Fight (anger/aggression) or Flight (anxiety/fear/panic). The second one is at the level of the PFC in your Neo-cortex the function of which is to apply intelligence to analyse, to reason out why is it so. This is what 'Emotional Intelligence (EI)' is and the handy strategy to be used is the 'Sandwich Technique'.

'Sandwich Technique (ST)': An Application

How the teenage kid would use his EI to apply 'Sandwich Technique' when the parent says: "I think you have got digitally addicted. You're playing games, watching movies, listening to music, browsing the internet frequently. You must stop all this nonsense."?

When Arka's (whom I am mentoring for the last 2 years) mom Malabika who is a working lady and stays away from home from 9 am to 6 pm, charged Arka like this, Arka handled it more than perfectly: "Mom, You're absolutely right when you say I play video games. See I've kept a record (Arka shows his Timesheet where he keeps a record of his time-task activities)—I played games for 2 hours and watched a comedy movie for 1 hour, but look at this... I browsed the internet in connection with my studies for 2 hours, the rest of the time I studied with full concentration and was doing the Maths tasks which my Maths tutor had given me. Don't you think I—a grown-up boy now, ought to have some freedom to spend my time on digital devices on extra-curriculars? Mom, you're a very sensible person. I think you'll not disagree with me. I would never take advantage and misuse the freedom that you've given me." Arka's mom Malabika was so spellbound with Arka's pleading, that she had no words to express.

An Insight into the Developing Teenage Brain

The cortex, as it gets formatted and stabilised, helps the teenager to be conscious, to think clearly about things, to assess a situation realistically. The front part of the cortex is called the 'executive region'. It is the 'Master Control Centre (MCC)' that coordinates and balances the whole brain and the body. This portion continues to grow in the whole of childhood and during the pre-school years. But during the teens, the changes that take place in this region are really dramatic. The cortex has an integrated role—it oversees much of what happens throughout the brain and even in the nervous system of the body as a whole.

What are the signs that the brain's master control centre—the 'Pre-frontal Cortex (PFC)' is not mature enough? Hyper rationality, impulsive behaviour and emotional stupidity. It takes up to minimum 25 (twenty-five) years for a teenager to develop a mature PFC. PFC maturity can be accelerated by taking part in sports and games including swimming, wrestling, martial arts and jogging.

For some teenagers, teenage is the period for intense social engagement with peers. During the lockdown period, those who are intensely peer and social engagement type like Shamin who is in 2nd year college have been having a most boring time as there was no opportunity for meeting friends face to face and in person. The more social exposure the teenager has, the better will be his EQ. Since girls are more friendly than boys, they would be expected to have higher EI and higher EQs.

Some teenagers have relatively more active 'Error Detection Circuits (EDC)' in their brains' 'Anterior Cingulate Cortices' which makes them fall a prey to the 'Disagreeing Disagreeably (DD)' habit. What could be the root cause? One school believes that the mother during pregnancy was suffering from acute morning sickness and nausea, having been sensitive to trivial irregularities. Teenagers with active EDCs, have difficulty in developing EI and EQ. But, one remedy for them would be—to provide more and more social exposure.

Importance of 'Hands-In' Learning

Much of what happens in families and in schools and undergraduate colleges, and even on the Internet and with the social media, pulls our focus of attention to the outer world. Think of how much time many of us spend on smartphones, iPads, and other devices absorbing an endless stream of information—mostly hard data. In many teenagers who have and are growing up with the digital technology, e-mailing, chatting via text and surfing the Net are just a regular part of life. And while there are a lot of great contacts we can make through social media that enhance friendships and social connections in general, the danger is that we fail to pay attention to other aspects of our lives. Hours and days can go by without extending our mind's arm into the mind itself to just be with our inner life, the life of our own mind. You are more than familiar with the concept of 'hands-on' learning, what I am meaning here is 'hands-in' learning. Such learning is possible only by extending your mind's hand into the subconscious part of your mind and start probing.

I am imagining you are a parent having a teenage kid. To be a SMART parent, you have to go for the 'hands-in' exploration and ask yourself questions such as:

- Why does my teenage kid behave with me in that fashion;
- Is it because our paths are not meeting somewhere;
- Is it that what he likes I dislike and vice versa;
- Can I identify some common interests which will bring us closer to each other;
- Why couldn't I tell him that I disliked the way he behaved with me;
- Should I gain by being straightforward or by being tactful;
- Did he react intensely to my point of view because the soothing circuits of his 'Pre-frontal Cortex (PFC)' (in neuroscience known as 'inhibitory fibres') are still under construction?

Once you are able to find authentic answers to such questions, you will find that you are gradually becoming empathetic towards him instead of being aversive. Because by posing such questions to your inner self using the 'hands-in' approach, you have tinkled the logical-analytical part of your brain—the 'Prefrontal Cortex (PFC)'.

The SCARF Model

Every individual's brain, without exception, seeks pleasure and avoids pain; the variation may be just a matter of a few degrees. Emotionally intelligent people chant this principle like a *mantra* so that they can practice it consciously in their behaviour not to hurt or antagonise others, ever, through their communication.

My work station, you can easily imagine, how it would be for a busy scientist. I work with two laptops on my desk. From time to time I check on my smartphone which also has a place on the table. There are books and papers all over the place. In one corner of the room, my Secretary sits with his desktop and smartphone. Another desktop is waiting to be used by another team member when he joins.

Surama Roy, a psychologist, had made an appointment with me. She dropped in right on dot but made a snap comment: "Sir, your chamber is so disorganised and untidy. Once I start getting mentored by you, I'll organise everything here and make it clean and tidy." She didn't realise that she had hit my brain's need for STATUS ('S' of the SCARF model which is the theme of this piece). Spontaneously, my response was: "Surama, I'm very much tied up with my different projects. I'll let you know from when I can take you on." I said good bye to her with an artificial smile on my face. Her visit was soon followed by another psychologist's. This time it was Chanda Sen. The moment she entered my office, she exclaimed: "Wow! I really can feel that I am in a top scientist's study. How fabulous is your work environment! I myself feel losing my sense of time and space here!". Chanda fulfilled my brain's STATUS need; so, I told her spontaneously: "Thank you Chanda! I'm glad that you like and get motivated in this environment. Fine! Can we start on our project right from today—just now? Are you ready?" The STATUS need is your brain's need to 'Feel Important'.

Ratish Banerjee, a neuro-therapist, being mentored by me had promised to send me the mobile number of a friend of his, who was interested in talking to me. When I sent him a WhatsApp message enquiring about the status, he just replied: "Sending....." and left at that making things 'Uncertain'. CERTAINTY is another critical need of our brain. Many a times, when we are in doubt we ask: "Are you sure.....?" We want to be 'Certain'. If we know something is coming by such and such date and time, our brain starts getting a rush of the anticipatory reward brain chemical 'Dopamine (D)' and releases the stress-relieving neuro-chemical 'Endorphin (E)'.

A teenager's brain is hungry for AUTONOMY. If for everything the parents try to dictate and control the teenage kid, he gets fed up and either becomes too argumentative or starts avoiding them. If you are a Smart parent, you have to be conscious about this need in your teenage kid and loosen the reins in situations where little or no risks are involved. With 'Autonomy', the brain has spontaneous endogenous supply of the happiness brain chemicals: 'Endorphin (E)', 'Dopamine (D)', 'Serotonin (S)' and Oxytocin (O)'.

Our brain, barring in exceptional cases, hates 'Isolation' and 'Rejection'. It longs for the opposite—RELATEDNESS which, when achieved, releases the love and trust molecule 'Oxytocin (O)' from the brain's pituitary gland. This need is strong in the teen brain for relationship-building with peers.

'Relatedness' is expressed through friendly handshake (conveying a 'You win—I also win' attitude). There are two other styles of handshake which do not represent such 'Win-Win' attitude. Those are: handshakes with a very firm, strong, overpowering grip ('I win, you lose') and just 'touch and go' handshake ('I feel I will lose and you will win if I become friendly') representing an 'avoidance' or an 'away' response as we find in surgeons and string instrument players who are extremely conscious about their fingers. Apart from handshake, 'Relatedness' is expressed through hugging, holding and lightly pressing the hand and patting softly on the back. All these gestures have twin implications: neurochemical and neuro-electrical. These gestures will lead to the release of the love-trust-bonding molecule 'Oxytocin (O)' inside the brain of both the giver and the receiver. And, it will add electrical energy to the 'Aura' of the receiver. [What is this 'Aura'? Like every living creature, we humans are also enveloped by an oscillating energy field which cannot be seen with our eyes but its photo can be taken by Kirlian camera. If I bring the Pancha Kosha concept, then such gestures add 'Emotional Energy (EE)' to your 'Monomaya Kosha (MK)' and inflates it with motivation].

The teen brain is very sensitive regarding any discrimination on any ground—be it religious, caste, community, skin colour or socio-economic background. A teenager simply cannot stand any 'Unfair' criticism. He will either flair up [aggressive hormone 'Adrenaline (A)' will rush out from his adrenal glands] and voice his dissatisfaction or supress the hurt feeling [stress hormone 'Cortisol (C)' will be released] which may adversely affect his physical or mental health eventually. He likes 'Fair' treatment—FAIRNESS.

In the social context, there are two types of responses: 'Towards' meaning coming close; and 'Away' means moving away as threat is anticipated. If the entire SCARF model is fulfilled then the response is 'Toward'; otherwise, lack in any of the components leads to 'Away'.

This excellent model for practising 'Emotional Intelligence (EI)' was first proposed by David Rock, Ph.D. who has authored several books and provides coaching on 'Neuro-leadership'.

What are you wondering about now—to apply the whole SCARF together or use it piece by piece? I'd recommend you go piece by piece, at least when Mentoring your teenage kids. Let them start with STATUS. How? When they meet elders—kins or family friends they must respect their higher STATUS by bowing down a little to say: "Hello Sir/Hello Madam!". That will be a good start.

BRAIN TOOL 12

Communication For Influencing (CFI)

'Key' Points: *Influencing Others: A Great Power; The Root Chakra (Muladhar)—Throat Chakra (Visuddha) Axis; Communication For Influencing (CFI) Is the Key for Getting Grounded; The Significance of 'Grooming'; The 'Orchestrated Communication (OC)' Formula K-P-S-L; The Golden Communication Formula; A Case Study; Communication 'Non-Achievement' and 'Achievement' Cycles; Transmitter (T) and Receiver (R) Formulas;' Standard' and 'Non-standard' People; Tailor-made Communication; 'People-profiling (PP)' and 'Tailor-making Communication (TMC)'; A Case Study; A Smart Parenting Application.*

Influencing Others: A Great Power

People do communicate but very few can *influence* others through their communication. *Influencing* means: convincing, making people accept without doubt, motivating, making others understand very clearly in the very first go; breaking the resistance and making entry deep inside the mind's positive reward centre. If you have said something but the other person does not agree with you, it is your failure; you have not used 'Communication For Influencing (CFI)'. CFI is a 'science' as well as an 'art'. Science where you are using the right word, phrase or clause; making the correct composition and pronunciation; using the correct grammar. But focusing only on the 'science' of communication may not help you to 'influence' others.

'Influencing' also requires the 'art'—loaded with 'Emotional Intelligence (EI)'—who are you speaking to, what frame of mind he has when you are speaking to him (no gender bias)—what kind of mood he is into, when and where the communication is taking place, what is his status compared to yours, what are his likes and dislikes, what is his value system.....so on and so forth. Some people are 'Born Influencers'; but those who are not can be 'made' into effective 'influencers' with practice [whether 10,000 hours of practice according to the best-selling author of *Outliers*—Malcolm Gladwell (New York: Little, Brown and Company, 2011) will apply in this case, I have no clue.]

This perception of CFI, I developed by reading hundreds of books, articles and scientific papers written by communication experts from the West. I sat at the feet of my management guru the legendary Peter Drucker with whom I spent a good part of a whole week at the World Management Congress in 1978 where he was the keynote speaker and I was the Rapporteur; he taught me CFI with great love and care. I attended special courses by Father John Thom—the famous communication aficionado of Loyola University, USA. Only, when I started integrating the Western neuro-scientific concepts and techniques with those developed by ancient Indian sages, I was awe-struck.

The Root Chakra (Muladhar)-Throat (Visuddha) Chakra Axis

The tantric-yogic sciences were developed by the Rishis and Munis who had no scientific laboratory, they could not dissect cadavers to learn anatomy and physiology. They could use only their brain's 'Third Eye' to scan through the external tissues and visualise the inner parts, neural networks and working of the organs and systems. They came up with the concept of 'Chakras'—the bundle of nerves—expressed as 'plexuses' in Western anatomy. These 'Chakras' are vibrating centres which receive energy inputs from cosmos—the universal energy centre and give out energy to the external environment. In short, they function as energy input-output centres.

There are seven principal 'Chakras' which are located right from the top of the head—the Crown Chakra (Sahasrar); moving downwards: the Third Eye Chakra (Ajna), the Throat Chakra (Visuddha or Visuddhi), the Heart Chakra (Anahata), the Solar Plexus (Manipura), the Sacral Chakra (Swadhisthana) and the last of all—the Root Chakra (Muladhara).

The creators of Tantric-Yogic Sciences had highlighted the importance of the Muladhara (Root Chakra)—Visuddha/Visuddhi

(Throat Chakra) axis. What does that mean? The main energetic contribution of the Throat Chakra is in 'Communication' in the oral mode using a language. The significance of the Root Chakra is to be 'rooted' firmly into the ground. In Yogic language, I express it as being 'Grounded'. A plant or a tree which does not have a deep and firm root will get easily uprooted. I have in my backyard two mango and two jackfruit trees firmly rooted and grounded. The Amphan cyclone failed to uproot them. But 90 percent of the trees in the sprawling mango orchard near Mandir Bazar, Lakshmikantapur, 24 Pgs. (South) belonging to my student Anil Kayal and his family got uprooted.

In pre-historic, pre-language society, hunter-gatherer tribesmen used to communicate between themselves using only their postures, gestures and vocal modulations. But as the environmental scenarios changed, the prehistoric humans also were compelled to develop language as the main medium of communication. Robin Dunbar of Oxford University, UK has done pioneering research on the origin of language-based communication and has documented it in his best-selling book: *Grooming, Gossip and the Evolution of Language;* London: faber and faber, 1996.

Communication For Influencing (CFI) is the Key for Getting Grounded

While communicating orally, if we take out or mask the 'verbal (linguistic)' mode, one's expressions become limited to his emotions only which can be expressed with postures, gestures and vocal modulations or intonations. I had kept a deaf and dumb youth (23/24 years of age) with my family and did research on him. His communication was extremely limited and far from CFI. I was very patient being a scientist-observer but he got so restless after three months that he suddenly started showing the signs of cutting the paddy and left with his brother-in-law to work in the field where CFI won't be necessary.

Coming back to the Chakras, unless your 'Throat Chakra' is very effective in CFI, your 'Root Chakra' will be weak. You might have difficulty to have a solid, sound base for success in life. You may not feel confident, and, as I would express it, 'Grounded', although you may be very resourceful otherwise. You will fumble, falter and stumble in life's long journey.

Orchestrated Communication (OC)

'Communication For Influencing (CFI)' as an inborn skill is rare. For the bulk of the population, it has to be acquired. Still many youngsters continue to be CFI-deficient as most of the parents lay thrust on academic attainment and not on CFI development. CFI deficiency, which affects the Root Chakra (Muladhar) thus making the individual diffident, mentally confused and unstable in decisions, is most likely to affect the other chakras on the way to the Throat Chakra (Visuddha)—that is, the Sacral Chakra (Swadhisthan), the Solar Plexus (Manipura), and the Heart Chakra (Anahata).

I have come across the following CFI-deficient cases in youngsters of late:

> Tarun Chanda, Howrah; Nurul Islam and his wife, Fatima Bibi, West Burdwan; Rahul Singh, Bhagalpur, Bihar; Shreya Chatterjee, Kolkata; Tamal Karmakar, Kolkata; Rajesh Rout, Bhubaneswar, Odisha. They are all: cold, frigid (lack of libido) [Sacral Chakra—Swadhisthan problem]; constipated, tends to suffer from 'Irritable Bowels Syndrome (IBS)'[Sacral and Solar Plexus—Swadhisthan and Manipura problem]; emotionally unexpressive, hard-hearted [Heart Chakra—Anahata problem]; some (not all) have thyroid issues [Throat Chakra—Visuddha problem as the glands associated with this Chakra are the Thyroids.] I have just cited these examples for no other reason than to validate my emphasis on CFI as a 'Brain Tool (BT)' for development.

The Significance of 'Grooming'

Robin Dunbar's classical research says it all started with 'Grooming'—how a monkey provides 'Grooming' (the practice of brushing and cleaning the coat with fingers) to another monkey—it can be mutual also. 'Grooming' produces 'Endorphin (E)'—the endogenous stress relieving chemical (like the pain-reliever 'Morphine') inside the brains of both the groomer and the groomed. It also releases 'Oxytocin (O)'—the trust and bonded relationship-building neurochemical. Since it is an enjoyable practice, it becomes a regular habit between monkeys and other varieties of the primate species—orangutans, baboons, macaques, bonobos and chimpanzees.

This 'Grooming' eventually evolved into 'Gossips' (casual, informal chats) with different types of tonal fluctuations and voice modulations—finally leading to the development of 'Language'. Language can thus be used positively in a conscious, planned way to generate happiness chemicals in the Receiver—who receives the message from the Transmitter, who speaks. When the Receiver is convinced or he accepts—agrees with the message without any note of dissent, the Transmitter also has release of happiness chemicals: 'Endorphin (E)', 'Dopamine (D)', 'Serotonin (S)' and 'Oxytocin (O)' inside his brain. This is thus a case of 'Communication For Influencing (CFI)'.

The 'Orchestrated Communication (OC)' Formula K-P-S-L

In any inter-personal communication event, there are 2 (two) roles: one is that of the 'Transmitter (T)' [sometimes, 'T' is also described as 'Sender (S)'] who is at the giving end and at the receiving end there is the 'Receiver (R)'. 'T' transmits or sends a 'Message (M)'. So, the flow diagram is: T...>.....M...>......R.

Now, for CFI, I have developed an 'Orchestrated Communication (OC)' formula K-P-S-L.

K Kinesics	P Proxemics	S Sonics	L Linguistics
• Health • Fitness • Gait (style of walking) • Postures • Gestures	• Inter-personal Distance	• Sound/ Voice - Soft - Strong - Steady - Sonorous	Language - Short message - Slow speaking speed - Words: Sweet Simple Specific Superlative(+ve) • Right Positioning • Use of motivation/ mood-boosters (like humour)

Fig. 8: The 'Orchestrated Communication (OC)' Formula K-P-S-L

'K' stands for 'Kinesics' meaning: postures (whole body movements like standing, sitting, walking, running) and gestures (movement of body parts like that of hands and legs). While standing or sitting, positive postures would be with erect spine but not held stiffly—must be quite relaxed; the body should not move, unconsciously, forward-backward or side to side which are signs of discomfort and diffidence. Walking should be at a moderate pace, neither too fast nor too slow. Talking about hand and finger movements, baton-chopping-cutting-blow-fist signals should be avoided; instead smooth, easy flowing, graceful movements should be consciously incorporated.

'P' stands for 'Proxemics' which deals with inter-personal distance. When two persons are standing and talking to each other face to face, a distance of 1 ft. (30 cm) to 1.5 ft. (45 cm) is acceptable between the two—neither more, nor less. Only in the case of hugging or embracing, the two can come closer. While sitting across a table, one should not lean too much towards the other person—in that case, it will be an encroachment into the other's personal territory. However, leaning forward (not too much though), closing the gap between the two is a 'toward' response meaning the mental gap is being bridged—some kind of an understanding is being developed. Moving away from the other person means, for some reason, a mental gap or distance has been created. When sitting on a long sofa or bench together, unless it is impossible, again a social distance has to be maintained. One leg on top of the other or squatting on the chair should not feature in any formal event.

'S' stands for 'Sonics' which means the sound of the voice. Voice should be soft ('ga-ma-pa' in the 'sa-re-ga-ma-pa-dha-ni' saptaswar scale of the Indian classical music). Negatives are: 'sa-re'—which is commanding, dominating, overpowering—and 'dha-ni': quarrelsome, argumentative—nagging and manipulating. Voice should be strong, exuberating confidence and steady, - not fluctuating too much. Voice should be sonorous and melodious.

'L' stands for 'Linguistics'. Words and phrases should be 'Simple'—easy to understand—technical jargons should be avoided. Words should be 'Sweet' (like: please, thank you, I'm much obliged, I'm grateful; so nice/kind of you etc.), 'Specific' (expression should be direct and to-the-point and not expressed in a round-about way); and Superlative Positive—as expressed in words like: fantastic, great, awesome, extraordinary, disputable, unparalleled, marvellous, most fascinating. Choice of words, phrases and clauses should be consciously done. Composition and use of grammar should be error-free.

The Golden Communication Formula

In my twenties, as I turned into an 'Income Centre (IC)' or 'Revenue Centre (RC)', my bread-and-butter started coming from the corporate sector. First, simple 2 slices of bread sandwiched with butter as I joined an American company in Calcutta; the butter was replaced by marmalade as I changed to a British company from the American one; then when I joined the prestigious Calcutta Management Association as its CEO, the marmalade disappeared, instead delicious cheese paste took its place; thereafter as I entered an Indo-German company as its Managing Director, the cheese got mixed with freshly boiled chicken. Finally, when I became an entrepreneur and set up my own body-brain-mind-soul management and development boutique, the sandwich was replaced by cheese burger. As my workshops and services 'flourished', the cheeseburger became chicken burger; and very soon turned into double-decker cheese and chicken burger which I enjoyed for 35 years.

I had been thick with the Indian corporate sector and got glimpses of the corporate and government sectors in Bangladesh, Nepal and Bhutan. I was over exposed to the communication culture in the government, business and industry in this part of the world. Before I introduce you to the theme formula of this Brain Tool, let me give you one weird communication case study.

A Case Study

In an Indian big business house, the final interview was taking place for the position of a Vice President which is equivalent to a General Manager's post in the public sector. The interviewer, the Director (HR), opens the dialogue by saying: "Mr. X, we're most happy to offer you the post. Now, select the furniture you would like to have in your office (variety of office furniture were displayed on the big TV screen mounted on the wall—the Director had the remote in his hand.) Now, what should be the colour scheme of your office...what kind of curtains, lamp shades and air-conditioners would you love....and what digital devices you'd dream to have?" Mr. X's Dopamine-level inside the brain was rising...he was getting happier and happier.

Finally, the Director clicked the remote and on the TV screen there were photos of seven pretty women. Now he said: "This is the final question. Which one amongst these you would like to have as your private secretary?" Mr. X was speechless with pleasure. "OK! On this, you can reflect and tell me later." Now the Director opens his drawer and takes out a sheet of paper and says: "Mr. X, You have got from us all that you had desired—exactly to your specification. Now, take this paper and read the contents. These are the things we want from you. We'll give you 6 months' time. If you fail to give us what we want from you, we will ask you to submit your resignation letter. We do not believe in a sacking culture. We're a zero-sack company." Mr. X was stunned. What a give-and-take style of communication. Mr. X was my student so he just paused for a little while and thought: "What style of communication is this? Can it qualify as Dr. Ganguli's CFI?" Now let me come to our current agenda!!

I had already introduced you to the two roles in any communication event. The 'Transmitter (T)' (some refer to it as 'Sender' or 'S'—I prefer to stick to 'T') who sends a 'Message (M)' to the 'Receiver (R)'. For the practice of 'Communication For Influencing (CFI)' one has to do effective 'Message Management (MM)'. For 'MM', I have developed a few formulas, one of which I will introduce in this article.

P-L-E-A-S-E

It is the 'Golden Communication Formula' PLEASE. In PLEASE, 'P' stands for 'Start positively to provide happiness' (just saying 'Good Morning' or 'Good Afternoon' or 'Good Evening' is not enough—you've to be an 'Influencer'; so, say, for example: 'This dress suits you ideally' or 'What a beautiful salt-and-pepper hairstyle you have!'); 'L' stands for 'Listen attentively without any interruption'—you must not lose patience and interrupt when somebody is speaking—that is very bad manners—let him finish what he wants to say, only then you barge in by saying: 'If you have finished, may I just say something?'—and throughout the conversation, you maintain a sustained positive eye contact.

'E' stands for 'Empathize'. I have highlighted the importance of 'Empathy' while talking about 'Emotional Intelligence (EI)'. You get so much absorbed into what the other person is saying—you forget who you are, where the conversation is taking place at what time of the day or evening—as if you have got out of your shoes and entered into T's—and having the same feeling as him. Your 'Mirror Neurons (MN)' support you to display empathy.

'A' stands for "Your message should be 'Attractive.'" You must be able to attract the attention of the 'Receiver (R)'—what you say ought to be so interesting in content as well as in presentation.

'S' stands for 10-S. Your 'Message' should be 'Short' (even a 'Long' sentence should be broken into small parts); the 'Speaking Speed' should be 'Slow'—100 to 120 words/minute—neither too fast nor too slow; your 'Voice' should be Soft, Strong, Steady and Sonorous (= melodious). Your 'Words' should be: Sweet, Simple, Specific and Superlative (positive) (e.g., awesome, fantastic, unbelievable, marvellous etc.)!

'E' stands for 'End positively to provide happiness'. How do you do it? You say: "These 3-4 minutes that we have conversed, it has not only been a learning experience for me. I have picked up something totally new which I don't suppose I knew earlier. It has been a remarkable lesson for me. I don't know how to express my gratitude".

Communication 'Non-Achievement' and 'Achievement' Cycles

Before you start expressing yourself, your brain remains busy with 'Self-talk' or 'Mind-chatter'. If you doubt your CFI ability—your capacity for 'Influencing' the other person, there will be a Negative Self-talk going on inside your brain. It will get reflected in your body language; you will lose your confidence and your expression will be negative—your voice will be weak, you may fumble and falter, you may not be able to complete your message. What impression will it have on the Receiver 'R': definitely not positive. His dissatisfaction would be visible in his body language and audible in his spoken words. So, you've placed yourself in a 'Non-achievement Cycle'.

You will never be able to come out of it unless you start with a Positive Self-talk. Once you have planned and prepared yourself properly well in advance, you will be 'grounded' and will have confidence. It will show up in your body language, tone of the voice and choice of words, phrases and clauses. Your positivity will impress the 'Receiver (R)' and he will be prepared to listen to your whole story or presentation without cutting you off abruptly in the middle. You have managed to place yourself this time in the 'Communication Achievement Cycle'.

Transmitter (T) and Receiver (R) Formulas

In one-to-one communication, 'Transmitter (T)' is the 'Sender (S)'. He (no gender bias) is the speaker in oral communication and writer in written communication. E-mail, text messaging, WhatsApp messaging, sending a write-up in the pdf format are all different types of written communication; and, in the digital era, the use of such communication has increased manifold more than what used to be in the pre-digital age. Hence, the importance of correct spelling, grammar and composition has correspondingly increased.

Irrespective of whether it is in the 'oral' or in the 'written' form, the 'Transmitter (T)' must ensure to follow the 'T' formula 'TAG' where:

'T' Means: Translating Your Ideas into a 'Meaningful/Purposeful' Message

Let me elaborate. As I had pointed out earlier, every event of communication has a purpose like: passing an information, or trying to motivate or influence, or promoting a product or a service. So, the first question you must ask yourself is: WHY are you communicating—what is the 'purpose' of this event of communication.

The next question that you must ask yourself is: WHO is the 'Receiver (R)'—what is your relationship with him—what is your status vis-à-vis his—what are his 'likes' and 'dislikes' [you remember the SCARF model of 'Emotional Intelligence (EI)']—what are his 'strengths' and 'weaknesses'—does he have any unique feature that makes him different from others.

Then comes WHEN/AT WHAT TIME of the day the communication is taking place? This is an important factor as morning time up to forenoon is ideal for complex communication because, after a good night's sleep, our mind generally remains fresh. As the day rolls by, our brain becomes so much cluttered that our thinking becomes shallow—we cannot handle anything complex in the afternoon and evening (unless you take a minimum one-hour nap before evening) and, of course, at night (there are exceptions though).

Now, WHERE is the communication taking place? In T's territory he feels confident and strong; whereas in R's territory it happens the other way round. Sometimes, it is wiser to choose a neutral territory, like a café, a restaurant, or a club.

'A' in the 'TAG' formula means: Attracting Attention. For this, power point presentations, sketches, drawings, graphics, slides, video films, models, samples, prototypes have gained importance in corporate communication. [In the early 1990's, me and my team members were engaged by Mahindra and Mahindra (M&M) Automotive Division to conduct a countrywide dealer development project where in every workshop, at my instance, a M&M vehicle was brought and kept at the venue so that I can give the dealers' sales and service personnel a hands-on experience!]

'G' stands for: Getting a 'Feedback' response from the 'Receiver (R)'. If 'T' does not get either a positive or a negative feedback from 'R', his communication is not complete. It becomes a one-way communication just like when you are reading a book or an article or a scientific paper (and you cannot interact with the author—your questions and comments remain with you) or watching a video or a movie. In any case, the loop between 'T' and 'R' has to be closed to make the communication 'effective'. A 'Feedback' from 'R' to 'T' closes it. But, if 'R' does not give you any feedback, then you close it by a 'Check-back' loop by asking: "Am I clear or not?" if the 'R' is your peer or junior. If 'R' is your senior your 'Check-back' style would be: either, "Sir, have I been able to make myself clear?" or "Shall I repeat the message Sir, in case I went too fast?"

Now, it is my turn to share my 'Receiver (R)' formula with you. The 'R' formula is 'EAR'.

In the 'EAR' formula, 'E' stands for: Establishing and sustaining positive eye contact throughout the period of interaction. As long as you are talking—receiving a 'Message (M)' from 'T', you must not avoid eye contact with him; on the contrary, you must maintain or sustain positive eye contact which is equivalent to personal touch. It will provide 'T' with a feeling of trust.

'A' stands for: Attending to the message with whole-hearted concentration. This will serve twin purposes. Number one, making 'T' feel important since your attention is sincere and earnest. Number two: if you are fully attentive, you will receive the whole message in full so you will be better prepared to ask questions and offer justified comments.

'R' stands for Responding to the Message 'M' with a most appropriate feedback. Even if you have not agreed (fully or partly), give your feedback in a tactful manner using the 'Disagreeing Agreeably (DA)' strategy expressed through the SANDWICH technique.

'Standard' and 'Non-standard' People

There are two types of human bodies: 'standard' and 'non-standard'. 'Standard' bodies have no problem with 'ready-made' or 'ready-to-wear' garments, which are easily and abundantly available in garment stores in different 'standard' sizes. 'Ready-made' or 'ready-to-wear' garments do not fit 'non-standard' bodies which are either too short or too tall in height—or either too thin and lean, bony and skinny or too fat, plump or obese in their body shapes. 'Non-standard' bodies include 'apple' and 'pear'-shaped figures also. For such 'non-standard' people, you need 'tailor-made' or 'made-to-measure' clothes.

In the same note, for people having 'standard' minds there is no problem with 'standard' communication, but for people with

Fig. 9: Human Beings: 'Standard' and 'Non-standard'

'non-standard' minds (meaning those who suffer from some complex or are highly egoistic in nature), you need 'tailor-made' or 'made-to-measure' communication.

Thus, where 'R' is someone with a 'kink' in the mind—not very simple and straight, but still has to be won over, 'T' must study him thoroughly and collect as much data as possible on his 'Likes' and 'Dislikes' as well as 'Strengths (or Plus Points)', 'Weaknesses (Minus Points)' and 'Any Other Unique Features' using my LLF formula where. 'L' = Looking around for 'Displays' and 'Details' ['Displays' would include an artificial fitting, fixture or an accessory such as a ring or any other piece of jewellery, or a tie, a watch, a smartphone or a tattoo—'Details' are natural like a beauty spot or a salt-and-pepper hairstyle]

The second 'L' stands for: Listening attentively without any interruption; and 'F' stands for: Feeling (empathy). You ought to keep in mind such data while composing the 'Message (M)' to be transmitted and while listening to your 'R''s responses. In a way, you are 'Tailor-making' the communication to 'Influence' that particular person.

Have you now understood why some time you fail to convince someone although your message had been based on solid logic?

People Profiling (PP) and Tailor Making Communication (TMC)

In difficult cases, for CFI management, 'People Profiling (PP)' needs to be done in a very systematic manner for 'Tailor Making Communication (TMC)'.

What is 'TMC'? People who are very difficult to be convinced and influenced have a 'Non-standard Mind' unlike people having a 'Standard Mind' who accept logic and are open to reasoning or get easily convinced or influenced out of empathy and concern for the Transmitter 'T'. So, just like people having 'Non-standard Bodies' cannot readily use ready-made garments as such garments do not fit them—become either too loose or too tight, too long or too short, for people having 'Non-standard' minds, their minds have got to be measured to find out what would appeal to them, accordingly communication has to be tailored to suit their taste [One major factor for having a 'Non-standard' mind could be the person's 'Ego' and the foundation of the 'Ego'—which I describe as 'Ego-base' could be: physical strength, family background, social status, high qualifications, or wide and long experience, knowledge, looks, personal or family wealth etc.]. This I call 'Tailor-made Communication (TMC)'. For 'TMC', you require detailed data about that person, just like for tailoring a suit to fit a non-standard body, you require a few specific measurements.

What is 'PP'? 'PP' is collecting various types of data about the person in question and organising them properly. The various types of data to be collected are:

1. *Hard Data:* Name, Address, E-mail, Mobile, Date of Birth, Qualifications, Experience, Present Occupation, Marital Status, Occupation of the Spouse, Children if any, Hobbies and Pastimes, and so on.
2. *Soft Data:* Likes and Dislikes, Strengths and Weaknesses, Any Other Unique Feature(s) which make him Different from others around.

After you collect all such data, note them down in a 'People Profile Data Book'. And, how would you collect such data? Hard data by asking questions or asking him for his CV; soft data by using the LLF formula, where the first 'L' is 'Looking around for displays (artificial—like a photograph, a jewellery or a tattoo) and details (natural—like a salt-and-pepper hairline, a beauty spot on the face, or the sharp, intelligent features)'; the second 'L' is 'Listening with apt attention without any disruption'; and 'F' is 'Feeling (that is empathy or concern for the person)'.

A Case Study

Now let me share a case study. In the early 90's, I was assigned to do a project in the corporate office of Engineers India Ltd. in New Delhi. Mr. Pranit Chopra was one of the General Managers who were being trained by me. In the next level down below him, were the Deputy General Managers (DGMs). They were three in number. Two of them had excellent relationship with him. They were frequently visiting his chamber, sitting there and chatting. He would also come out of his office and go to the work stations of those two DGMs.

Sarvodaya Seshan, the third DGM was being left out from Chopra's close circle. Neither was he called by the boss to his chamber, nor did the boss come down to him. After my workshop, Seshan selected as his task 'Bridge Building' with his GM Pranit Chopra. He had been asked by me to collect some soft data about Mr. Chopra as hard data were available in the internet HR excel data sheet. Seshan stayed back after office and entered into Chopra's office after he had left at 7 pm. Seshan was looking for displays by way of calendars, framed photos, books and periodicals, clocks and other decorative pieces on display on the desktop and also on the walls. In one corner of the boss's desk, he could find a photo of Baba Ramdev placed on top of copies of Ramdev Ji's books. His job was done. In the evening after the cleaners cleaned up the whole place, Seshan left.

The very next morning when Seshan came in, he went straight into Chopra's office as no one was there and after wishing him good morning, he asked straight away: "Sir, do you know Baba Ramdev?" And, Chopra was overwhelmed and responded quickly: "Know means, I know him very well. It is he who saved my life when I was seriously ill after a trip to our London office." And, he went on and on and on... non-stop telling the entire story. His face, his hands and fingers, his whole body was charged with positive excitement....one could see from his body language. His body leaned forward to close the gap with Seshan and for a moment, the two persons leaning forward towards each other looked like a bridge. From that very day, Seshan started enjoying an excellent relationship with his boss Pranit Chopra.

A Smart Parenting Application

How does a SMART parent use it with his (no gender bias) teenage son? Imagine you are the SMART parent and your teenage son is Avik, studying in Class X. You come back from work, enter into the living room and find Avik watching a Sharukh Khan movie.

Instead of shouting and screaming in disapproval, you quietly and coolly sit down beside Avik, put one hand on his shoulder and ask him: "Sharukh is your favourite actor, no beta?" Prompt comes the reply: "Yes, dad, he is simply great." Avik looks and sounds happy as you are talking in a language that he likes.

"May I sit for a little while and watch the movie with you?" you ask. Avik can't believe his senses; he unconsciously exclaims: "Sure dad! of course!" You continue to watch for a few minutes to make Avik's happiness rise, which you can figure out from his disposition. Now you say: "Tomorrow your terminal exam starts, isn't it?" "Yes dad" Avik agrees. "Don't you worry dad, the movie will be over in another 10 minutes' time and I will get up and get on with my studies right away." "OK!" you say. And, what happens then? Exactly after 10 minutes, Avik gets up and goes straight to his work desk and starts studying uninterruptedly. You've been able to motivate Avik to study without any hassle by building a bridge with him and Sharukh Khan was the material used here. Such is the power of 'Tailor-making Communication (TMC)'. See now, you are getting the hang of 'Communication For Influencing (CFI)'.

Brain Tool 13

Motivation For Good Performance (MFGP)

'Key' Points: *Work and Work Performance; Three Types of Work; Working Personality (WP) and Working Personality Principle (WPP); The Working Personality Principle (WPP) and Teenage Kids; Teenage Kid's Working Personality and Work Menu Matching; A Concrete Example; My Theory of Work; The Fivefold Theory of Work; Brain in Top Gear; A Peep into Bill Gates's Brain; Points to Be Pondered Upon; The ACM Style of Parenting.*

Work and Work Performance

Performance is 'work performance'. 'Good performance' is better than average—70 to 80 percent, whereas 'Peak performance' is 90 to 100 percent. 'Motivation' is the DRIVE—the desire to perform.

Dear Reader, if you are a parent, are you happy about your teenage kid's study habits? Most probably not—just like most other parents are not. At least that is what Monomita told me. Monomita is Sakya's mother and she regularly interacts with mothers of other kids of Sakya's age. The reason is that they do not know anything about—even the first few alphabets of the science of 'Work' and 'Work Performance'. Every activity, every action where you make effort and spend your 'Energy' is 'Work'. So 'Studying' is certainly a type of work. I have spent more than 40 (forty) years researching on different types of work and some of my 'key' findings have been documented in my popular book: *Performance Management: First time Right* (Kolkata: Platinum Publishers, 2008).

Three Types of Work

I have put all types of work for our daily living, working, leisure and entertainment into three broad categories. The first one is:

'Self-Engagement (SE)' where it is the brain of the performer that is engaged in work and nobody else is involved. The second one is: 'People and Social Engagement (PSE)' where the work involves interaction with other people—one-to-one, one-to-two, one-to-a-few and one-to-many. And, the third and the last one is: 'Physical Engagement (PE)' where the work involves largely physical actions such as in manual work and outdoor activities like in games and sports, cultivations and plantations, shop-floor and project sites, door-to-door and field sales.

Working Personality (WP) and Working Personality Principle (WPP)

Now, the interesting thing is this: it is generally observed that every individual is born with a specific 'Working Personality (WP)' which means, every individual can perform all the three types of work but will give 'peak performance' in only one work segment or category, his (no gender bias) inherent, inborn personal resource (body-brain-mind-soul) qualities are such. In some cases, however, some individuals are equally apt in two types of work such as SE and PSE or SE and PE or PSE and PE; and, in very rare cases, one may be equally active in all the three. This is, what I call: the 'Working Personality Principle (WPP)'

The 'Working Personality Principle (WPP)' and Teenage Kids

Now applying this 'Working Personality Principle (WPP)' to teenage kids, you will find that the SE-strong kids would be interested in self-study, digital engagement like watching videos and movies, net surfing, listening to music and written work, where no other person is involved; PSE kids would love to have joint study with one or more peers or will study only when the private tutor comes neglecting self-study and writing practice; PE kids will be more interested in physical activities like going for marketing and shopping, games and sports, roaming with friends; since they are physically very active, it will be relatively difficult for them to 'concentrate' or 'focus' for long. In this context, I would call those parents 'Smart' who would observe the kid's nature, identify his 'Working Personality (WP)' and try to plan his work menu or work diet accordingly.

Teenage Kid's Working Personality and Work Menu Matching

Let us go a little deeper. The first step is to figure out the kid's WP composition: the proportions of SE, PSE and PE. A SE (60) PSE (30) PE (10) kid would avoid physical activities altogether so a Smart parent would be one who would not waste his (no gender bias) time, energy and effort trying to persuade or force such a kid to go for any outdoor family work or any game or sport; instead encourage his working alone habit with some mixture of PSE type of work—studying and or spending time with one or more friends indoors... A PSE (60) PE (30) SE (10) would tend to avoid working or studying alone; would instead like to spend more time with peers and friends for academic work, informal chats as well as sports and games... A PE (60) PSE (30) SE (10) would tend to avoid working and studying alone, would be motivated to do fieldwork outdoors including sports and games.

A parent who would assign tasks to his (no gender bias) kid that do not match or suit his nature, will put the kid under stress and the performance will be much below what may be given by another kid whose WP matches with the work menu.

A kid who has almost equal proportions of SE, PSE, and PE can handle any of the three activities equally well and will do equally well in any of these activities, but to get PEAK PERFORMANCE from him, we have to take advantage of another principle which I will discuss a little later.

A Concrete Example

Let us take one concrete example—that of SAKYA. SAKYA's estimated WP composition is: PE (45), PSE (30) SE (25). How his 24 hours could be divided into work according to his WP to mobilise performance?

- SE: Self-study: Morning—2 hrs.; Afternoon: 2 hrs.; Night: 2 hrs.
- PSE: On-line: 2 hrs.; Tutors: 2 hrs; Mentor: 1 hr; Facebook: 0.5 hr.
- PE: 2 hrs. daily indoor freehand stretching-bending exercise (Three times a week: 4 hrs. each time, outdoor, cricket practice at the coaching centre); Sleep: 8 hrs.; Personal Chores: 2.5 hrs).

My Theory of Work

Your brain is never at rest. When you are at physical rest but awake—may be lying on bed or relaxing on an armchair, your brain will be auto-engaged in its 'Default Mode Network (DMN)' which had some utility in the pre-historic hunter-gatherer society. A tribal would retrieve from his memory his past experiences of 'Opportunities' and 'Threats' and prepare his future plans of action. DMN remains engaged at the present moment with thoughts related to the past and the future. Today, we are not dependent on hunting-gathering for our survival, we are placed in a safe and secure shelter—we do not have to formulate strategies for saving ourselves from attack by predators and other enemy tribes, so common people's DMN (which is freed from such thoughts) gets engaged with thoughts related to earning the livelihood—generating income with own effort and in cooperation with others. There may be variations from these but essentially the trains of thoughts would be self- and people-related.

I can merrily compare you with an automobile. You are at rest but the brain is DMN-engaged in a state analogous to a stationery automobile with its engine running. The moment you get engaged in a 'Task' or 'Work Activity (WA)', your brain gets engaged in a 'Task Mode Network (TMN)' and it has changed its gear. The 'Brain in Top Gear' in my language, means you are engaged in a 'WA' with high concentration and full focus. In ancient times, the yogis had devised mantras and prayers which, when chanted rhythmically and melodically will disengage the brain from its DMN state even when you are not engaged in any 'WA' as such. Even meditation or 'dhyanam' is a TMN brain state.

It is important for anyone, equally so for a teenage kid, to find out ways and means of how can you spend many hours in a day with your brain in a 'Top Gear' state—fully focused with high concentration—driving yourself towards your more important goals, driving away all time-killing distractions. In order to understand this mechanism, you have to hold my hand and enter into the world of the 'Theory of Work' which I have developed through four decades of research.

The Fivefold Theory of Work

For the first stage of understanding I will expose you to the 'Fivefold Theory of Work'. My research studies have revealed that there are five (5) types of 'Work Activities (WA)'. The first three amongst them release positive chemicals and positive electricity inside your brain while the last two generate the opposite—negative molecules and negative oscillations.

Work Activity (WA) 1

It represents something which comes naturally to you, for which neither you need to be trained nor you have to give any special effort.

For example, singing light songs came naturally to me from my primary school days—so did it come to Suman (Kabir Suman now) or his elder brother Mukut—who are my first cousins. The same spontaneous expression came as I began writing poems and essays when I reached my teens. Stage acting also came most easily—I could act in any role without much practice. My acting talent reached its culmination when I acted in the role of King Dushwanta in Kalidas's Shakuntala (English version) at the famous Alhambra Theatre in Glasgow, Scotland. Two of my distant cousins also displayed this WA1 flair in acting and they became accomplished stage and movie actors—Late Anil Chatterjee and Dhritiman Chatterjee.

So, WA 1 are those for which you have a natural flair; coaching or training hones up that skill. Physically, I could never ride a bicycle or play football or class team cricket. But swimming! The very first day when my mom pushed me into the swimming pool in ILSS's Anderson House in the Rabindra Sarobar, Kolkata, Nalin Malik, an Olympian swimmer who later on trained me made a prophecy: "This boy is going to be a swimming champ." And his prophecy came true. Even when I was studying overseas in UK, I represented our University of Glasgow a few times in Inter-University swimming events. WA 1 activities you perform at a fast speed and error-free (zero-defect) as those come naturally and spontaneously to you, without any effort. Your quality of output and productivity are much higher.

Relating these examples to the Pancha Kosha concept, I would say, swimming being a sport is related to 'Pranamaya Kosha (PK)'. For Nalin Malik, he linked his swimming skill to Annamaya Kosha (AK) as AK is related to your bread-and-butter for survival and growth whereas for me it remained at the PK level. For Kabir Suman, Late Anil Chatterjee and Dhritiman Chatterjee—their respective musical and acting talents [which are related to providing entertainment to others—Monomaya Kosha (MK)], they took advantage of their MK talents to earn their livelihood—by linking it to the Annamaya Kosha (AK).

Are you a Smart leading parent? Have you been able to identify what Work Activities come to your teenage kid naturally, spontaneously—for which lay people may make the 'Luck Factor' responsible and say: "He is born with that 'Luck'! He is specially gifted"? Can your teenage kid pursue that WA 1 and make a 'career' out of it—by linking it to the 'Annamaya Kosha (AK)'?

Work Activity (WA) 2

It represents some WA that you enjoy most; so much so that you get creative flashes—you get a rush of the anticipatory reward brain chemical 'Dopamine (D)' at the very thought of it...and when you get engaged in it, you get engrossed...you get totally lost...losing the sense of space (location), time (also date), self (who you are), and your 'Ego'—because of the release of all the happiness chemicals: Endorphin (E), Dopamine (D), Serotonin (S), and Oxytocin (O). The Pituitary and the Pineal Glands are both involved; Pituitary for Endorphin and Oxytocin and Pineal for Serotonin and Melatonin (if you enter into a 'trance'-like brain-state). Dopamine is stored in and released by Dopaminergic neurons which are spread over the brain's 'Reward Circuit' (Substantia Nigra, Ventral Tegmental Area amongst others).

You have penetrated the 'Anandamaya Kosha (AnK)' and have become a receptor of cosmic energy going into your nervous system through the Crown Chakra (Sahasrar). This WA 2 involves some 'Creation', some 'Innovation', some 'Discovery', some 'Invention', some 'Intuition'. Right from ancient times, all the creators have experienced the fruits of WA 2. The magnitude of the Creation could range from a small creative spark like a new tool design and making it for use in prehistoric times to my 'Working Personality Principle (WPP)' in modern times to a huge inferno like discovery of a new forest full of resources for survival in pre-historic times to Tagore's 'Gitanjali' or Einstein's 'Theory of Relativity' which have the power to destroy the old paradigms, concepts and techniques, in modern times.

Please do not mix up WA 2 with WA 1. The latter does not involve creating anything original or discovering something which existed but was not known, whereas the former essentially does. In WA 2, your Soul gets involved whereas in WA 1 it is a way of engaging your body and or brain. So, WA 2, I describe it as 'Soul Work'. When the middle-aged classical musician Shujaat Husain Khan plays the sitar and sings a ghazal, he is engaged in WA 1 because his musical skill is inborn, he has given it a marketable format by learning music formally. But, his late father Ustad Vilayat Khan is credited with the creation and development of gayaki ang on the sitar (Ref: Google Search Engine). So Vilayat had links with WA 2. WA 1 represents 'Autonomy' as the performer operates independently, whereas WA 2 represents 'Mastery'—the performer no doubt gains an 'Authority' status.

WA 2 is most helpful for brain health. So, it is not that some people are brainier or born creative (that was true in the case of WA 1 where it is an inborn flair), they have better brain health by devoting greater chunk of their time to WA 2 tasks and assignments.

Why better brain health? Let me explain. The long wire-like axons are a 'key' component of a 'neuron' (= brain cell). Each axon conducts electrical signals in the form of an 'action potential' from the cell body of the neuron to its axon terminal where it 'synapses' with another neuron through the latter's 'dendrite'. Every axon is insulated by a 'myelin' sheath throughout its length to increase the velocity of these electrical signals allowing the signals to propagate quickly. Axons which are covered by a myelin sheath, a multilayer of proteins and lipids, are said to be 'myelinated'. If an axon is not surrounded by a myelin sheath, it is unmyelinated. Myelination is the formation of a myelin sheath.

The amount of myelin in the body (in the central as well as peripheral nervous system) increases throughout development, from foetal development up until maturity, with the myelination in the 'Pre-Frontal Cortex (PFC)' being the last to complete in the 2nd or 3rd decade of life. The more myelin and myelination an individual have, the quicker is the response to stimuli because myelin sheaths increase the speed of nerve impulses. Treatment for cancer—chemotherapy and radiotherapy destroy the myelin coats.

Getting engaged in WA 2 is the best way to shut your brain off from all distractions. When I was in my early teens and nearing my school-leaving phase, I used to feel totally out of the world when I would study English or Bengali literature as I used to develop my own perceptions and interpretations which were quite different from what all were taught in the class or in special tutorials. That cognitive strategy helped my brain to get into WA 2 frequently thus helping the myelination activity in my brain circuits.

If you are a Smart leading parent, you will help your teenage kid to get into WA 2 by making him (no gender bias) go through a passage and do 'Lateral Thinking (LT)' [Refer to Edward de Bono's colossal work on LT] by thinking not literally but laterally—meaning thinking differently by bypassing the literal idea. Or, a simpler way would be to read a passage and dig out the 'cream' or the 'essence'—the 'key idea' and then express it with the help of a few 'key words'. For some teenagers, WA 2 experience comes while studying history or geography, while for some others it comes while studying physical, mathematical, life, or social sciences.

I checked up with Arka Ghosh Chaudhury, a 15 year-old, Class X student and he said he gets WA 2 feeling while studying physical and mathematical sciences. He cannot focus his attention while studying any other subject; every 10 minutes, he will lose his concentration—but not so while studying physical and mathematical sciences.

Nobel Prize winning scientist Richard Feynman was almost obsessed to be engaged in what he would call 'real good physics' which was a WA 2 for him. To quote Feynman: "To do real good physics work, you do need absolute solid lengths of time...it needs a lot of concentration...if you have a job administering anything, you don't have the time. So I have invented another myth for myself: that I'm irresponsible. I'm actually irresponsible. I tell everyone I don't do anything. If anyone asks me to be on a committee for admission, 'no', I tell them: I'm irresponsible."

Feynman was adamant in avoiding administrative duties because he knew they would only decrease his ability to do the one thing that mattered most in his professional life: "to do real good physics work". Feynman, I can assume, was probably bad at responding e-mails and would likely switch universities if you had tried to move him into an open office.

For teenage kids, whenever and wherever possible big chunks of time must be allocated for WA 2. But how would you know which WA would qualify as your kid's WA 2?

For your teenage kid, WA 2 is where he (no gender bias) would lose the sense of space, time, self, Ego and everything else and enter into what Mihaly Csikszentmihalyi (the name is too long; I will use MC taking the first two letters) described as 'FLOW'. In MC's own words: "The best moments usually occur when a person's body or mind is stretched to its limits in a *voluntary effort* to accomplish something difficult and worthwhile." [*Flow: The Psychology of Optimal Experience*, New York: Harper Perennial Modern Classics, 2008. 'Flow' is described as 'The key to unlocking meaning, creativity, peak performance and true happiness'].

MC's FLOW theory pushes back conventional wisdom that relaxation makes the brain cool, calm and happy. MC says: "Ironically, jobs ('Work Activities' in my language) are actually easier to enjoy than free time [remember the mental turbulence created by your brain's 'Default Mode Network (DMN)' when you are relaxing with an idle brain], because like FLOW activities they have built-in goals, feedback rules, and challenges, all of which encourage one to become involved in one's work, to concentrate and lose oneself in it. Free time, on the other hand, is unstructured, and requires much greater effort to be shaped into something that can be enjoyed."

In my workshops with teenage schoolchildren—both from privileged and underprivileged backgrounds, to provide the kids with WA 2 experience, I give them two exercises to be completed—individually and in groups: Number One: to find out some totally new and novel application of common bricks (10 × 5 × 2.5 inches)—unheard, unseen, unread, untold; and Number Two: design of a Novelty Omelette—the concept of use of eggs and frying being the baseline, you have to come up with new size, shape, colour, taste, flavour, texture—something which is not listed in any hotel or restaurant in the world. And, you have to see the enthusiasm and excitement of the teenagers—provided by the CREATIVE drives of their brains. Human beings, including kids are at their best when immersed deeply in something challenging.

Now, enough of WA 2 we had. Let us move over.

Work Activity (WA) 3

This constitutes a group which includes jobs that the performer considers 'Valuable' and 'Important' for him, for his family, and also for the organisation that he belongs to—for the present as well as the forthcoming future. Before I miss it, let me mention that those family people and householders (not monks and missionaries) who go for meditation in order to discipline the mind, to develop calmness and concentration, it is a WA 3 for them. For WA 2-strong people, meditation is a luxury as by pursuing such an activity, the mind is not giving any 'creative' output which is the 'Goal' of WA 2.

For a teenage student, his academic or curricular studies would come under this group. When I was young and my children were teenagers, I used to motivate and influence them to pursue their academic studies seriously as that would provide them with the base for their future career. Later on, when I was guiding research scholars for their Ph.D. degree, I guided for Calcutta University 1 scholar in Applied Physics, 2 scholars in Physiology, 1 scholar in Community Health and Preventive Medicine (for his MD—he already had his MB BS and DPH); for Kalyani University—1 scholar in Physiology and Physical Education; for Bhagalpur (Bihar) University—1 scholar in Mechanical Engineering; for Netaji Subhas Open University—1 scholar in Business Management. In retrospection, when I try to apply my 'Theory of Work' on them, I find none of them took their research studies as WA 2—all of them primarily had as their goal—getting the Ph.D. for furtherance of their career.

The medical doctor, after his MD, bagged a full professorship at JIPMER, Puducherry; the mechanical engineer, after his Ph.D. got promotion from Reader's to Professor's post at Bhagalpur University; and the MBA with experience got full professorship at a private university in Punjab on very attractive terms. During my long and short stays abroad, I have observed the same phenomenon in UK, USA, Canada, Europe and Australia. Very few of the faculty members indulge in WA 2; those 10 to 20 percent who do, they 'create' some new concept or technique or write authoritative books on their specialised subjects—the bulk 80 to 90 percent go for doctoral and post-doctoral studies and publish papers in peer-reviewed journals to get tenured positions in the universities where they are employed. In those countries, the norm is 4 to 5 such papers published every year. In the Indian corporate world, you hardly come across examples of WA 2 unlike in USA (Bell Laboratories, General Electric, Intel, IBM, Apple, Google, Microsoft to mention a few), Europe (Philips, Siemens, Novartis, Mercedes Benz, Volvo and so on), in Japan (Sony, National Panasonic etc.). In those advanced countries, many corporations now try to provide environment for WA 2.

WA 3 for personal benefit or adding value to personal or organisational resource involves the 'Ajna Chakra (the Third Eye)' in the Vedic Chakra System as you engage yourself in such work being driven by the logic that it is 'Valuable' and 'Important' for you or your organisation. Ajna is the seat of intelligence and associated with it are the 'Pituitary Glands' which secrete hormones for 'Growth and Development'.

When you do something out of 'concern' (empathetic feeling) for someone or more than one person, such work activities also come under WA 3. For example, what my mother did selflessly for my father after his laryngectomy (removal of cancerous larynx/voice box); or what my wife Utpala and I did for the double below-knee amputee teenage boy Tanmoy Chakrabarti from Tripura; or what I am doing now for my chronically indisposed wife quite willingly—out of feeling for her. This is equivalent to 'volunteering' as I have volunteered to groom up a few boys in my gurukul who deserved my care and mentoring. Here the 'Anahata (Heart) Chakra' is involved and the associated gland is 'Thymus'. This Chakra becomes active when we are 'detached' from the 'Self' which means 'Selfless'. The lower 3 chakras (Root/Muladhar, Sacral/Swadhisthan, and Solar Plexus/Manipura) are designed to fulfil the Biological Imperative of 'Survival and Replication' which are 'selfish' activities. The 12 (twelve) 'vrittis' or divine qualities of heart are: bliss, peace, harmony, love, understanding, empathy, clarity, purity, unity, compassion, kindness and forgiveness. In yogic practices, there are quite a few strategies for awakening and balancing of your Heart Chakra ('Anahata'), but I recommend 'selfless service' and 'volunteering' from teenage itself. Smart parents would motivate their teenage kids to take care of their grandparents and parents by giving them medicine, Volini massage, hot and cold compress as the need may be. I was quite impressed when I heard my 15-year old participant in the 'Teen Mentoring Project (TMP)' would provide such services to his family elders at times of need.

Donation of any kind is a WA 3. To drive this point home, I was commissioned to run a number of motivational workshops for the West Bengal Voluntary Blood Donors' Association (for donation of blood) and The Lions Club of Calcutta (for eye donation).

I presume, you have understood the difference between work activities for your future growth and development and work activities for providing selfless service to others—although both are 'Valuable' and 'Important'.

In my 'Work Activity (WA) 1' where the performer engages in a task for which he has an inborn, natural flair and enjoys 'Autonomy', his 'Muladhar (Root) Chakra' gets involved because he feels confident and thus 'grounded'. In 'Work Activity (WA) 2' the highest chakra 'Sahasrar (Crown)' is involved and it is an 'Anandamaya Kosha (AnK)' experience. Unless the performer has attained 'Mastery', he cannot 'create' or 'pioneer' as he must be at a super-authoritative level in his specific domain. In 'Work Activity (WA) 3', the performer comes in contact with his 'Ajna (Third Eye) Chakra' when he performs a work activity which will benefit him at present or in future (he understands it logically, applying his intelligence). However, when he works selflessly or provides a voluntary service willingly, he is using his 'Anahata (Heart) Chakra'. The prime-mover in WA 3 is 'Value'.

What is the role of the 'Visuddha (Throat) Chakra'? In all work activities the performer is not working alone. That happens only in cases of 'Self-Engagement (SE)' and 'Physical Engagement (PE)'. In all 'People and Social Engagement (PSE) types of work activities, he is working in one to one, one to two, one to a few or one to many combinations. There he has to communicate with others and naturally, therefore, the 'Visuddha (Throat) Chakra' gets involved. In this context, I have already exposed you to the Brain Tool (BT) 12: 'Communication For Influencing (CFI)' which must be observed and followed.

Performance of Work Activities WA 1, 2 and 3 all lead to a positive outcome for the brain (release of happiness chemicals and happiness electricity) as well as for the body (regular cardio-respiratory rhythms, free and relaxed muscular-skeletal system, digestive system at peace). This happens to be the zone of the 'Parasympathetic Nervous System' of our 'Autonomic Nervous System (ANS)'. Now, I come to work activities which produce negative outcomes.

Work Activity (WA) 4

This group includes tasks and assignments which have become 'routine' and thus 'boring'; as well as work activities which others always point out and remind you: "It's your duty." While performing such activities, you get irritated or suffer from anxiety ("...when it will be over..." "I'm just fed up of doing this day in and day out!"etc.) and since you do not have positive motivation, you tend to postpone them falling a prey to the bad habit of procrastination. You have molecules of stress hormones released into your system as the 'Sympathetic Nervous System' component of your 'Autonomic Nervous System (ANS)' is switched on.

Let me elaborate a little on the difference between 'Responsibility' and 'Duty'. [This distinction is based purely on my own deep thoughts. You may disagree here.] 'Responsibility' is where you genuinely feel that the WA is so 'Valuable and Important' that you must do it—it is a positive feeling; whereas 'Duty' is when you feel although it is a part of your job, you are being forced into it as it is against your grains. It is a 'burden' for you. So, while WA 3 is linked with 'Responsibility' WA 4 is correlated with 'Duty' which you feel unwelcome for you.

To reduce WA 4-related 'stress', I will prompt you to ask the following questions:

- Can you bring some of the WA 4 activities into the WA 3 zone to reduce WA 4 percentage?
- Can you not find something interesting in it by looking at it from some other angle?
- Can you not compete with yourself in its performance (improving quality, reducing errors/defects, improving work speed, quantity of output, reducing cost and increasing profitability)?
- Can you carry out such tasks with music being played in the background in your PC or laptop so that music absorbs the boredom; or keep fresh plants or flowers in a vase on your desk or burn some incense sticks which will do respectively visual therapy and aromatherapy for you?

Work Activity (WA) 5

The WA 5 category includes tasks and assignments where your 'attention' is 'stolen' by any or a combination of the following: (i) unwanted interferences by the drone-like boss (by helicopter parents for teenage kids); (ii) workplace politics (joint family/ inter-family politics for teenage kids); (iii) imposition of tough targets and attempts to control by the boss (over-demanding parents for teenage kids); (iv) change of priorities (boss or parents likewise); (v) uncongenial environment full of undesirable distractions; and (v) any other deterrent.

In the present situation overcast with the Covid-19 pandemic and intermittent lockdowns everything is in disarray for a teenage kid. Some of them who are in higher classes are attending on-line coaching sessions for engineering or medical entrance tests at night time for 2 hours (for some, even beyond 12.30 am); 2 to 3 hours of on-line classes from school; and, 2 to 3 hours of on-line tutorials from 2 private tutors; totalling to minimum 6 to maximum 8 hours. For novelty- and challenge-seeking teenage brains, these on-line classes, by and large, can easily and conveniently come more under WA 4 and less under WA 5. If the percentage of WA 4 and WA 5 is more in your daily study schedule, how many hours of effective study one can manage to accomplish?

You may be aware that in order to establish my Smart leadership concepts and techniques in practice, I have undertaken a 'Teen Mentoring Project'. One of the very first things I had to do with the TMP participants was to use my 3-D (DREAM, DRIVE, DOMAIN) approach for career selection. 3 of the participants have chosen their careers firmly. On these chosen fields, they take up what may be described as 'Self-directed projects' where they do everything without taking anyone's help depending entirely on one's own thoughts and plans and on Google and YouTube. These 3 participants are all from Class X. One boy wants to be an 'Automobile Designer', another boy's ambition is to be a 'Comedy Film-maker' and the lone girl has set her eyes on 'Fashion Design' as her career. For all the 3 of them, I have proposed a Work Activity pattern as follows:

- Work Activity 1 (curricular subjects which they follow easily without much effort): 20 percent
- Work Activity 2 ('self-directed projects' related to their own chosen career): 20 percent
- Work Activity 3: (curricular subjects which are considered 'Valuable and Important'): 40 percent
- Work Activity 4: (curricular activities like online classes and tutorials which are found boring): 10 percent
- Work Activity 5: (curricular activities where distractions kill your concentration and motivation): 10 percent

All the 3 teenage participants said that WA 4 and WA 5 percentage could be reduced to only 20 percent due to compulsive inclusion of 'self-directed projects' as WA 2 every day without exception. This 80 +ve—20 –ve has to be taken as a BENCHMARK for Teenage Education.

Brain in Top Gear

Brain may be in 'Top Gear' while performing any of the Work Activities WA 1, WA 2 or WA 3. By 'Top Gear' I mean, your brain is stretched much beyond its ZCC.

[I will remind you about my 'Zone of Comfort and Convenience (ZCC)' concept. For all our sensory receptors, body organs and extremities there are 'Tolerance Zones' (ZT-moving beyond which we break down) and 'Comfort and Convenience Zones' (where we perform or operate with comfort and convenience). In between the ZCC and ZT, there are the 'Zones of Discomfort and Inconvenience (ZDI)' where our capabilities are over-stretched and recurrent over-stretching may lead to 'Stress'. All modern manual and intellectual labour-saving devices are endeavours for reducing the extent of ZCC.]

'Top Gear' means stretching yourself beyond ZCC into ZDI ('Zone of Discomfort and Inconvenience') coming almost close to the 'Zone of Tolerance (ZT)' (= Tolerance Limits).

In practical world, "Great creative minds think like artists but work like accountants" (David Brooks, *The New York Times* columnist). David Brooks talks about 'Practical Creators'. There are 2 (two) types of creative people: 'Theoretical' and 'Practical'. 'Theoretical Creators' do not calculate the 'Return on Investment (ROI)' factor—both qualitative (earning of positive brain chemicals and positive brain electricity) and quantitative (economic return) whereas the 'Practical Creators' do. Therefore, 'Practical Creators' are customer-oriented whereas the 'Theoretical Creators' are not. A creator may start as a 'Theoretical' one because of 'Passion' but may turn into a 'Practical Creator' later on if he finds enough opportunities for earning ROI. Such people have an entrepreneurial streak in their brains. [As highlighted in the Bill Gates's case study below.]

Some people may wonder: for how long can the human brain be in top gear. My perception of our brain's 'Top Gear' state is when it attains 'Total Focus and Uninterrupted Flow of Output'. Charles Darwin was undoubtedly a super-genius. From Darwin's historians we understand that he used to spend 90-minute chunks in 'Top Gear' while perfecting—giving final touch to his classic 'creation'—*On the Origin of Species*. According to some work-watchers, it is a brain process where you spend 90-minutes inside (the mind), take a 90-minute break, and repeat it 2 or 3 times—at which point your brain will have achieved its limit of concentration for the day.

Performance management scholars like me have extensively studied how much such outstretched efforts can be sustained by an individual in a given day. In their seminal paper on 'Deliberate Practice', K. Anders Ericsson and his collaborators at the Florida State University have surveyed these studies to arrive at a general conclusion. They note that for someone new to such practice (citing, in particular, a growing child—from pre-school to high school level—in the early stages of developing an 'Expert Level Skill'), an hour a day is a reasonable limit. Nevertheless, for those familiar with and accustomed to the rigours of such activities, the limit expands to something like 4 hours, but rarely more.

[K. Anders Ericsson (1947–2020) who was popularly known as the 'Expert on Experts' spent his whole life researching on 'Mastery'. His research helped inspire *Outliers*, Malcolm Gladwell's best-selling book on the keys to 'Excelling'.

K. Anders Ericsson and Robert Pool, *PEAK: Secrets from the New Science of Expertise*, New York: Houghton, Miflin Harcourt, 2016.

K. Anders Ericsson and Kyle W. Harwell, "Deliberate Practice and Proposed Limits on the Effects of Practice on the Acquisition of Expert Performance", *Frontiers of Psychology*, 25 October 2019.

Janie Kliver, "Get Better at Anything: 6 Steps of Deliberate Practice", *CROSS/OVER*, May 30 2017.]

A Peep into Bill Gates's Brain

In the winter of 1974, a young Harvard student named Bill Gates sees the ALTAIR, the world's first personal computer, on the cover of the magazine 'Popular Electronics'. It strikes him deeply. Gates realises that there is an opportunity (typical of an entrepreneur's brain) in designing software for the machine, so he drops everything and, with the help of Paul Allen and Monte Davidoff, spends the next 8 (eight) weeks working together to develop a software for the ALTAIR.

As Walter Isaacson explained in a 2013 article on Gates's story for the *Harvard Gazette*, Gates worked with such intensity for such lengths during the 2 (two)-month stretch that he would often collapse into sleep on his keyboard in the middle of writing a line of code. He would then sleep for an hour or two, wake up and pick up right where he left off—an ability that a still-impressed friend and colleague Paul Allen describes as a 'prodigious feat of concentration'.

In his book, *The Innovators,* Isaacson later summarised Gates's unique tendency toward 'Deep Work' as follows: "The one trait that differentiated [Gates from Allen] was FOCUS. Allen's mind would flit between many ideas and passions, but Gates was a SERIAL OBSESSOR."

[Walter Isaacson, *The Innovators: How A Group of Hackers, Geniuses and Geeks Created the Digital Revolution.* New York: Simon and Schuster, 2014. You may also read: Cal Newport: *Deep Work: Rules for Focused Success in a Distracted World,* New York: Grand Central Publishing, 2016.]

Points to be Pondered Upon

Was Bill Gates's brain engaged during that period in my Work Activity WA 2 which represented 'Flow' and 'Mastery'? Was he apparently experiencing 'Bliss' at his 'Anandamaya Kosha (AnK)' and was engaged at the 'Sahasrar (Crown) Chakra' level?

Or,

Was he engaged in my Work Activity WA 3 which his entrepreneurial brain had identified as 'Valuable' and 'Important'?

The ACM Style of Parenting

Please do not start wondering now as to how in a discussion on 'Motivation For Good Performance (MFGP)', the ACM Style of Parenting has found a place, uncalled for. Let me first unfold the ACM abbreviation, then I shall elaborate.

In ACM, 'A' stands for 'Adaptation', 'C' for 'Control' and 'M' for 'Motivation' and it is the normal or standard style of parenting adopted for grooming a child from infancy to adolescence. So, a treatise on 'Brain Tool (BT)' -13 will remain incomplete if I do not talk about ACM.

Every newly born added to the world's human population is a bundle of instinctive behaviours which had been programmed from its animal past. Apart from the physical features, hairy body and an active and agile tail, there is very little difference between a human and a chimpanzee or bonobo infant. The British primatologist Jane Goodall's field research studies in Africa more than confirm this. The human infant, however, has to be made acceptable in its own community and society. That *nurturing* is the basic responsibility of the parents. In that context, I have theorised the ACM style.

The infant's care-givers, especially the mother 'motivates' it to get 'Adapted' to certain types of conduct and behaviour using largely the 'Reward (pleasure)-and-Punishment (pain)' technique because that comes very handy—as it gets spontaneously retrieved from the care-giver's own childhood memory—how her mother used to deal with her. The entire gamut includes: training in proper breast-feeding, toilet training, training to refrain from bed-wetting and signalling the moment the pampers are soiled, training in effective brushing of the teeth, training in taking a complete bath; training in language—written-spoken (including in the nuances of non-verbal and verbal social communication), eating, drinking and sleeping habits, good study habits (including how to use a desk and a chair while studying), manners and etiquette and so on. The parent's endeavour is to have the growing child get 'Adapted' to certain ways of behaviour and if, deviations are found any time with respect to any specific behaviour, to try and 'Control' using the 'Reward and Punishment' 'Motivation' technique (examples: "If you do this...you will get that", "If you fail to do, you'll miss the lunch/pocket money"...etc.).

The blossoming of our neuronal population begins in utero and extends to our pre-teens, to about 11 years of age in girls and 12.5 in boys. Some pruning begins early as we learn and develop skills, but the removal of our overall number of neurons and their connections reaches its peak during the robust remodelling period of teenage. During teenage we prune those excess connections away, leaving the ones we have been using and discarding the ones we do not seem to need any more.

Smart leading parents are those who take timely action on the following habits of their teenage kids: (Some Bad, Unsmart parenting cases are placed within brackets)

- *Good Eating Habit:* Instead of being fed by the mother, eating on one's own (1–16 year-old Class XI boy was found to be fed by his mother still)
- *Good Sleeping Habit:* Instead of sleeping with the mother/parents, sleeping alone (2–16 year-old Class XI and 2–14/15

year old Class X boys were found to sleep with their mothers still)

Sleeping for 8.5 to 9 hours for teenage kids (most teenage kids are found to oversleep by 0.5 to 1 hour)

(*Note:* 1–14 year old Class X boy still sleeps in between his 2 parents. In spite of him having a separate study where he can comfortably sleep on the divan but despite his regular insistence on changing his bad sleeping habit, his mother is reluctant to allow him to sleep alone.)

- *Good Study Habit:* Instead of studying on the bed, using a desk and a chair (1–16 year-old boy continues to study on bed despite him having his own study station and it is being tolerated by his mother even for on-line classes and exams)
- *Good Toilet Habit:* Instead of spending too long a time in toilet, having a reasonable time limit for using the toilet (1–14 year old Class X boy was found to use the toilet for 1 long hour).

The examples within brackets are some of the findings from the 'Teen Mentoring Project (TMP)' that I have been busy with since May 2020. My conclusion is that the kids are not to be blamed. The parents have failed to act 'Smartly' in applying their ACM style. Right at the onset of adolescence, if they would have taken steps to reorient the habits, I would have classified them in the 'Smart Parent' category.

I will conclude this piece with a real-life case. Several years ago, the HR head of one of the largest Indian IT companies having international operations contacted me to solve an embarrassing problem. They had sent 2 (two) batches of brilliant young (21–23 year old, still in teens as per the new standard made by me: 13 to 23 for girls and 13 to 28 for boys) B.Techs, BCAs, MCAs to USA for helping out in their US-based projects, but both the batches had been rejected and returned, lock-stock-and-barrel. The reasons were most embarrassing: these youngsters could not express them in fluent English, could not sip tea without making any sound, would dip the biscuits into their teacups to soften and then eat them, did not know how to use knives-forks-and-spoons, would not put the toilet seats up after using the toilet, would use water spray instead of using toilet paper and would not clean up the wet floor, would cluster in their own country groups avoiding inter-mixing with the American employees, and the like. Obviously, although the kids were academically brilliant—may be more apt than their US counterparts, they were socially and culturally unacceptable. My job was to train and retrain them thoroughly using mock tea and lunch sessions apart from spoken English practice for a period of 4 (four) long months before they were sent off to another country in Europe. *Obvious conclusion:* These kids were not 'Smartly Parented'.

BRAIN TOOL 14 Attention: Focus

'Key' Points: *Attention: A Coordinated Activity; Focus: Razor-sharp Attention; The Focus-Unfocus Cycle; Brain's Energy Costs; A Recommended Work Schedule for Teenage Kids; Negative vs. Positive Attention; SMART Parenting Tips; Indeed, a Novel Focus Strategy; Use of Slow, Soft, Instrumental Background Music; The Focus-Unfocus Harmonious Jugalbandi; Focus on A Long Healthy, Happy Life; The Secret of A Long Healthy, Happy Life; A Point to Ponder.*

Attention: A Coordinated Activity

For survival on this planet, any creature needs the Brain Tool (BT) of 'Attention': for organising own food for eating, water for drinking, shelter for resting and sleeping, and keeping oneself away and apart from dangers including sudden attack by predators. 'Attention' is a coordinated activity of our eyes (visual attention), ears (auditory attention), nose (olfactory attention), taste (gustatory attention), touch (tactile attention), feeling (emotional attention) and thinking (mental/intellectual attention). It could work through one of the channels, like when I look at a lush green parrot biting raw fruit sitting on the branch of a mango tree in my back garden, I am using my visual channel to 'attend' to the stimulus; whereas when I concentrate on the cooing of a cuckoo having its nest in the jackfruit tree in the same garden, I am using the auditory channel. I presume, it is not difficult for you to follow me.

Focus: Razor-Sharp Attention

For excellence in anything you need razor-sharp 'Attention', which I would describe as 'Focus' (you may differ here regarding nomenclature but leave aside any argument in order to proceed with the business). My post-graduation studies at the University of Glasgow in Scotland, UK, at some stage, had total thrust on 'Research'. For 'Searching' something you need 'Attention' and alertness (free from all distractions) and for 'Researching' you need 'Focus'. I had to take courses on 'Research Methodology'. Possibly finding me to be a rare material with some potential, all my three professors: WT Marshall, PD Arthur and RM Kenedi recommended that I should join the University of Glasgow Rifle Club to develop 'Focus'. Membership was free for research students having some special potential. I joined and went for regular rifle shooting practice.

The Focus-Unfocus Cycle

And, some remarkable things that I learnt, I will share with you. A normal, average brain cannot remain in 'Focus' for long. The brain is an oscillating mechanism like the heart and the oscillations are affected (as much as in the case of the heart—slow, moderate, fast according to externally as well as internally generated stimuli). So, most simplistically I can express it as 'Focus-Unfocus'–'Focus-Unfocus'...like this it goes on. When you are 'Unfocussed', since you are not paying attention to anything, your brain's 'Default Mode Network' (DMN) circuitry may become active and all kinds of disturbing thoughts may pop up on your mental screen. So, you have to practice to make the 'Focus' phase of your 'Focus-Unfocus'–'Focus...Unfocus' cycle longer than usual. When you are focussing on the target (bull's eye), your brain becomes engaged in the 'Task Mode Network (TMN)'. You must train yourself to remain in the TMN for long by being away from diversions and distractions.

Brain's Energy Costs

Now, your brain's 'Focus' circuits cost a lot of energy. So, to follow the energy conservation principle, your brain automatically follows the 'Focus-Unfocus'–'Focus-Unfocus' rhythm as when you 'Unfocus', you save on energy expenditure. So, my rifle shooting training was to train my brain to stretch itself regularly to develop energy-saving 'Focus' circuits. But, when 'Unfocused', your DMN takes over and spends 20 percent of the energy available to you if you do not get engaged in some TMN which is least energy costly—that is the energy cost is only 5 per cent. DMN costs so much energy because it has the mind wandering from one pole to another—from your remote to recent past and also your proximal to distant future. Its bright side is that it gives you self-awareness and a sense of personal relevance.

But, then how to identify such TMN activities which will not cost much of your brain's energy? I have already outlined for you in my BRAIN TOOL-12 ('Motivation For Good Performance'), 'Work Activity 1 (WA 1)' which comes naturally and spontaneously to you without any effort and 'Work Activity 2 (WA 2)' which you passionately love and enjoy and, while engaged in it, lose the sense of time, space and self.

Your goal, in rifle shooting, is to hit the bull's eye. It is for your personal achievement—related to your personal growth and development. So, you can put it as 'WA 3' for which the key words are: 'Value' and 'Importance'.

A Recommended Work Schedule for Teenage Kids

Let me spend two minutes now on this WA 3 which is a positive work for you. WA 3 has 2 parts. WA 3 (i) has a clear purpose: your personal or organisational growth; whereas WA 3 (ii) is 'Selfless Service or Volunteering'. When you perform WA 3 (i), your brain costs high energy as you have to put special effort to perform, but WA 3 (ii) does not cost your brain much energy. It is on par with WA 1 and WA 2—the less energy-costly activities. However, amongst WA 1, WA 2 and WA 3 (ii), WA 2 where you get into 'Flow' is the least energy consuming work. So, in order to have a work schedule which keeps your brain active and stimulated but costs the lowest possible brain energy, you must allocate maximum time for WA 2. A golden rule would thus be: WA 1: 20; WA 2: 40; WA 3 (ii) 10; WA 3 (i): 10; and, WA 4 and WA 5 together: 20. Smart parents should follow this golden rule while scheduling the waking hours of their teenage kids.

Negative *vs.* Positive Attention

On 25th January, 2020, I was returning from my local market on foot with both the hands fully engaged in heavily loaded bags. I was 'Focusing' on my balancing act trying to maintain the 'System of Proportions' of my body and its flexible, movable parts. So, I was 'Unfocused' (unmindful) about the pavement on which I was walking. The outcome: I tripped, I 'Fell Forward' (to quote Denzel Washington from one of his motivational videos where he says 'Always try to fall forward, not backward') and injured my right knee plus had bruises on my nose and chin. On the next day, the X-ray revealed that I had a hairline fracture in my right knee joint. On a renowned orthopaedic surgeon's recommendation, I wore a crepe bandage but never consciously gave 'Negative Attention' to my injury. [By 'Negative Attention', I mean, 'feeling the pain'.] Most unexpectedly to others (but as expected by me) I became 'painless' within the next few days and could stop taking the pain-killer pills. 'Negative Attention' would have delayed my natural healing process.

What is this natural healing process? When you have a cut, blood comes out from a cut blood vessel and it heals within the next few days automatically (our biological system possesses that auto-healing power which is very strong in those having a healthy and positively active immune system) and a scar is formed. When there is a bone fracture, a body fluid comes out and a callus is formed to heal the injury. I certainly had pain in my fractured knee joint but if I had given a lot of attention on this pain (which I am calling 'Negative Attention'), the healing process would have been interrupted due to negative hormones secreted. I hope, this simple principle is clear now.

At the present moment, I have excellent opportunities for applying this 'Attention' principle on three ladies. One of them is my own wife who has just completed 77 years recently. She had a critical fall resulting in a broken right shoulder joint with multiple fractures. It was soon managed with an expert orthopaedic surgeon with rush nails. She had to follow the surgeon's post-operative instructions for some time, then went for a full course of physiotherapy. But since she also suffers from a psychotic disorder and depression, physiotherapy was not very effective and she developed a most painful fixed flexion deformity in her right hand taking away all her abilities for daily living and working. She needed help. Not only that, any movement of the right hand led to excruciating pain which called for her 'Negative

Attention' all the time making her more depressed in the mind. With a 2nd corrective surgery, the rush nail was removed but although the wound healed, the pain did not go. I could have taught her to give 'Positive Attention' to the painful hand. What is 'Positive Attention'? It is the 'Belief' that the pain will go; I will get complete relief from the pain. But she being a patient of depression, she does not have the ability to think 'positively'. So, I used another strategy. She has great regard for Swami Vivekananda. So, I taught her to think of and pray to Swamiji for her good health, taking her mind away from pain. Since she is thinking of and praying to Swamiji all the time, her brain's 'Default Mode Network (DMN)' has become disengaged and her 'Focus' is on the Swamiji-related 'Task'. She does not talk about the pain at all now only unless certain specific body movements act as triggers.

The same technique has been used by me on a young lady who is a patient of blood cancer undergoing chemotherapy and another lady in her early forties who has a long history of paranoid schizophrenia. Both are academically brilliant and talented in music, arts, writing and so on. 'Negative Attention' in their cases would have been: in the first case about the painful experiences of bone marrow transplant and chemotherapy; and, in the second case, unhappy painful memories of her being mentally tortured during girlhood and subsequently in her professional career. These would have preoccupied their brain's 'Default Mode Network (DMN)'.

SMART Parenting Tips

What would a SMART parent do if her teenage kid has not scored well in a terminal exam? Not drawing 'Negative Attention' to such shortcomings, instead giving 'Positive Attention' to the kid's past achievements by saying: "Last year, in the final exam, you had scored so well and we became so proud of you; this time, there must have been something that went wrong as a result of which you did badly. Does not matter at all! I have full confidence on you! Tell me if you want any kind of support from us, I am ready to arrange provided it suits our budget. Don't worry (you pat on the back and hug the child to allow a rush of Oxytocin inside his brain), you will certainly do well in the next exam."

Indeed, a Novel 'Focus' Strategy

In 1981, my brain guru Dr. Roger Sperry (1913–1994), neurobiologist and neuropsychologist of the California Institute of Technology (Caltech) got the Nobel Prize for physiology and medicine for his epoch-making split-brain research, and we his followers, were all over-filled with happiness and pride. One of his major findings was that, for a right-handed person, the left cerebral cortex (shall be referred as 'Left Brain' or 'LB' henceforth) is responsible for all linear, reductionist functions like logical-analytical processes, reasoning, arithmetical calculations and measurements (like TIME, for instance), language (grammar and composition), science and technology, systems-procedures and processes. The right cerebral cortex (shall be referred as the 'Right Brain' or 'RB'), on the contrary, is responsible for parallel, networked and holistic thinking, vision and visualisation, higher human emotions and feelings (like compassion, kindness, empathy, respect, faith and trust), motivation and the ability to motivate and influence others. Further studies by Sperry and his followers including me have revealed that although all of us have both LB and RB, one of them is more active, meaning people are either 'Right-brained' or 'Left-brained'. Cross-cultural research has shown that we Indians are generally 'Right-brained'—that is our RB is more active.

I started my workshops through my own organisation 'Learning Club' in 1983. My workshop inputs are science-based and thus meant for the LB whereas the participants happen to be RB-active being from this part of the world. So, I could anticipate that during my lecture sessions, the 'Focus-Unfocus' problem will crop up with the participants. I could visualise the problem clearly. As long as the participants are 'Focused' on my presentation (that is, their LB is engaged as the Receiver Organ), they would be learning. The moment the LB got 'Unfocused' and the RB gets activated, their 'Default Mode Network (DMN)' would be operative giving rise to all kinds of random thoughts totally unrelated to my workshop. So, I did a pilot study and it clicked. I innovated 'Biorhythmic Music' for brain management under such circumstances.

The participants would be seated in a U-format facing the Faculty Area where on one side there will be a 'Biorhythmic Music' corner.

A trained and skilled young boy will sit looking at the participants having the music system placed on a desk in front of him. As I start my presentation, he starts his music at a very slow pace and on a very low volume. Now I start in a psycho-dramatic style so that the participants will get 'Focused' on to me with their LB on. This LB engagement will remain for some time until the LB brain can feel the pressure as 'LB Attention' is about to taper off. The Brain Operating System is now shifting to 'RB Focus'. As this happens, the presence of the musical melody (which the participants were not 'Conscious' about so long although it had been going on in the background) will now enter into their RB. Since the RB will remain engaged with the melodious music, the DMN will fail to distract the mind. 'Attention' will soon come back in the LB which will get back its FOCUS.

The sooner I got the green signal from the pilot project, I started using on a much wider scale and it was a hit.

We were the first in the world to use 'Biorhythmic Music' in developmental workshops. The pioneering news was covered by all printed media—Bengali, English and Hindi in Calcutta. We also gave 'live' demonstrations on FM radio stations. It became a scientific breakthrough.

Use of Slow Soft Instrumental Background Music

If you're a SMART parent, to help your teenage kid's mind to get 'Focused' during home study, you can play slow soft instrumental music in the background at a distance, You can also use such music in your desktop or laptop while working to avoid distractions and allow your mind to be in 'Attention' and fully 'Focused' itself towards the work activity. This strategy can be gainfully tried out on kids suffering from ADD (Attention Deficit Disorder) or ADHD (Attention Deficit Hyperactivity Disorder) which are not uncommon now-a-days because over-stressed pregnancy may lead to the birth of such problematic kids.

The 'Focus-Unfocus' Harmonious Jugalbandi

Controlled studies have revealed that, in this materialistic competitive world, an average person lives around 46.9 per cent of a typical day with his mind wandering here and there—'Unfocused', the mind-filling material being 'I'—his self-awareness. It drains out his neuronal energy.

[Srini Pillay, *Tinker Dabble Doodle Try—Unlock the Power of the Unfocused Mind*, New York: Random House, 2017, p. 75.].

There are a few effective ways of preventing this phenomenon. One strategy (but only those having a burning passion, a clear vision, and an appropriate mission can use this) is to plan the post-40's life in a manner that the individual is engaged the bulk of his waking hours in 'Work Activity (WA) 2'—with a 'Focus-Unfocus Harmonious Rhythm'. Continuous 'Focus' is not advisable. The 'Focus' phase should be stretched to the extent he does not feel strained; then it should be followed by 'Unfocus'.

The moment he 'Unfocuses' from deep down layers of his mind, some 'Creative' ideas may come up to the surface. During the 'Focus' phase, he should be dedicated to tasks and assignments which are closest to his heart where he loses his self-awareness—his 'Ego', so that he can 'Create' something. As long as your 'Ego' is there as a drone hovering over your mind (like a helicopter parent not having trust on her teenage kid), you cannot 'Create' anything as your 'Ego' is change-resistant, closed to 'Novelty'. Such rare people have a long, celebrated life as the 'telomeres' in their chromosomes do not get frayed and depleted due to the stress of a continuous meaningless and purposeless 'Unfocused' life. 'Telomeres' are the caps at the end of each strand of DNA, that protect our chromosomes, like the plastic tips at the end of shoelaces. 'Telomeres' are responsible for an individual's lifespan. One whose telomeres are intact and undisturbed would have a long, happy, fully lived life beyond 80 years whereas another individual who passes through stressful phases in living and working would have frayed telomeres and a physically or mentally unhealthy life span even if he has a chancy life beyond the age of 80 but during that indisposed, ailing phase of life would hardly be productive physically or intellectually.

I shall share a case to which I was exposed a little less than 60 years ago. The location was: 24 Finsbury Park, London NW, where I had just checked in to spend a fortnight with Prodyot and Mina Sen on my way to Glasgow to join the University there for my post-graduate studies. Prodyot Sen was from Allahabad and had training in North Indian classical music. On the 2nd day after my arrival, he said that Pandit Ravishankar would be his guest for a day as the sitar maestro was scheduled to travel to give a recital at the famous Edinburgh Festival. Mr. Sen would play the tanpura while Ustad Alla Rakha (Ustad Zakir Hussain's dad) was expected to be on the tabla. Pandit Ravishankar came and I was introduced to him. I could not resist the temptation of asking Panditji what special he will be performing at Edinburgh. He was cool for a couple of minutes. Then he said: "'East is East and the West is West. The twain shall never meet' is the common saying. But I had a 'Dream' which has now been converted into a 'Vision' that although the Western and Indian classicals are apparently oceans apart, I have been experimenting very 'boldly' whether we can 'Create' a 'Fusion Music'. And in order to translate that 'Vision' into reality, I have taken up the 'Mission' to collaborate with the famous violin maestro Sir Yehudi Menuhin of Britain. We are going to present our first 'Creation' of fusion music in the Edinburgh Festival this weekend. Why don't you join us to see for yourself?"

Panditji invited me to join the group and I readily accepted as in any case I was Scotland-bound. I was mesmerised and overwhelmed when the trio—Panditji, Sir Yehudi and Ustad Allah Rakha made their debut presentation which ended with unending applause and encore. That was as an example of 'Work Activity (WA) 2' and all the three performers were swept away by the 'Flow' of 'Creativity'. When Panditji was playing he was 'Focused', Sir Yehudi was 'Unfocused'; and, when Sir Yehudi was on his violin, he was 'Focused' and Panditji was 'Unfocused'. It was a 'Focused-Unfocused Harmonious Jugalbandi'. The secret of 'Creativity' is you get engaged on WA 2 for some time until you are fully 'Focused'. 'Creativity' does not take place when you are fully focused; no other new or novel ideas will pop up on your mental screen although they are being brewed in the 'Subconscious' or 'Unconscious' part of your mind. So, the moment you're off 'Focus' and thus 'Unfocused', but your 'Ego' has not yet taken over your brain's 'Default Mode Network (DMN)', you may get an 'Insight' or 'Intuition' or 'Inspiration' or come up with a 'Creation' or 'Innovation'.

Such 'Focus-Unfocus' harmonious rhythm comes to some people naturally but one can also develop that skill by practice. Because of their dedication to WA 2 type of 'Focused' activity and regular practice of the 'Focus-Unfocus' harmonious rhythm, all the three lived beyond the age of 80. Pandit Ravishankar (1920–2012 = 92); Sir Yehudi Menuhin (1916–1999 = 83); and Ustad Allah Rakha (1919–2000 = 81). I have not done any statistically valid research on this, but two other names of 'Creators' that readily come to my mind are those of: 'Creative' choreographer-danseuse Amala Shankar (1919–2020 = 101) and Michael DeBakey, MD. (1908–2008 = 100) the Texas-based heart surgeon who had 'Created' an artificial heart. Such WA 2-rich people are very rare though. They are the people with seemingly tireless productivity and razor-sharp clarity.

SMART parents would not hesitate to sow the seed of such 'Focus-Unfocus' harmonious rhythm in their teenage kids. It is a matter of intelligent planning and time management.

'Focus' on A Long, Healthy, Happy Life

Even at the age of 80 today, my gut health is as fit as it used to be 60 years ago when I was 20. Good gut health means a healthy mix of gut microbes. Some of my friendly gut microbes become zombies and come up to my brain to share gut feelings which turn out to be valid. Those feelings are literally out-of-the-box. I shall share one such feeling here. It may raise eyebrows leading to controversy but the feeling is entirely personal.

There is an established fact that solid family bonding and relationships based on loving-kindness lead to a long happy life. The molecule behind it is 'Oxytocin (O)', produced in the 'Hypothalamus'—the 'control centre' located in your mid-brain (that is, 'paleo-mammalian') and released from the 'Pituitary Glands'. Formerly believed to be a gynaecological chemical, now we know that 'O' has a close link with happiness from birth till death. The common belief is thus that people who are not lonely after they retire from their working lives post-60's, live a happy life. However, there is a recent research finding reported by Harvard psychologists Matthew and Daniel T. Gilbert that most common people spend 45.9% of their time thinking about something other than what they are doing (that included in the research project: walking, eating, shopping and watching television) and that makes them significantly unhappy. [news.harvard.edu/gazette/story/2010/11/wandering-mind-not-a-happy-mind]

The research subjects were 2,250 in number in the age group of 18 to 88 years.

What is not common knowledge is that even without being thickly social, you can have a very long happy and healthy life provided your brain is hardwired with the 'Focus-Unfocus Harmonious Jugalbandi' circuit about which I wrote just a little while ago. My parents were highly social, so was everyone on my wife's side including her parents and siblings. Amongst these highly social creatures, I existed like an island, having been branded as an 'unsocial' person. I had a very special personality which common people would consider as 'strange'. I was very friendly and light-hearted outside the family in formal relationships, including with my thousands of workshop participants but I had never been a 'party' animal. In drawing room conversation, I was a big zero. Most contrarily, I won the Golden Peacock award being the country's best trainer and public speaker in 2002. I never avoided people but, at the same time, I was not so much attached that I started missing them if I did not interact for a few days.

From the very day I set up Asia's first hospital-based Bio-engineering Unit in 1968 at the University College of Medicine (Goenka Hospital) (UCMGH), University of Calcutta, my life took a 180-degree turn—24 × 7 days' workweek and 14–15 hours' workday (8 hours as a manager and 6 to 7 hours as a research scholar). And, I enjoyed this schedule (may seem 'hectic' to many) immensely as I had found my 'Brainmate'—Human Engineering, the subject I conceived from the wide spectrum of Bioengineering in which I had been trained abroad. I began delving deep into the 'Body-Brain-Mind-Soul' complex. Now, in hindsight, if I start evaluating what kind of brain molecules I earned, I get goose-bumps all over my body. Why you know? Bonded relationships, social happiness leads to 'Oxytocin (O)' release primarily (the other happiness molecules may or may not follow) whereas the knowledge entrepreneurial career where I have been engaged in 'Focus-Unfocus Harmonious Jugalbandi' all along, has given me, because of my 7 to 8 hours of intermittent WA 2 engagement: 'Dopamine (D)'—the reward brain chemical; 'Oxytocin (O)'—the bonding chemical (because of my capability for bonded team-building and team-management); 'Serotonin (O)'—the 'feel good' and 'mood balancing' chemical; and because of my daily without-fail exercise regime 'Endorphin (E)'—the endogenous stress management chemical; as well as due to my effective sleep management habit—'Melatonin (M)'—brain's sleep inducing chemical.

I am 80 now, but neither retired nor tired at all. I maintain the same daily schedule totally dedicated to Neuro-management (NM). If I look at my Gurus, I might have followed their footsteps unknowingly.

My Body Guru, Prof. John Paul of the University of Strathclyde, Glasgow, who died at the age of 86 was in perfect health till the end. He took great risks on his own body as at the age of 51, when he was ready with the design of the first artificial hip joint, he got the surgeon to remove his healthy hip joint to be replaced by the one of his own design to see how it works in reality. When he came to visit my research unit in Calcutta and became my house guest for a few days, both his hip joints were artificial by his own choice. My Brain Guru, Dr. Roger Sperry of Caltech, USA although being a bio-psychologist took great risk to perform split brain surgery with his own hands on epileptic patients and gave them relief from frequent painful seizures to bag the Nobel in medicine in 1981. He died at the age of 81 in good health but a happy man basking in the glory of his post-pioneering achievement. My Management Guru, Prof. Peter Drucker of Claremont College, California changed the face of old-fashioned management by introducing 'Management by Objectives (MbO)' and being an Austrian in origin used to dictate notes on a Dictaphone and his English-American wife would transcribe them turning out several best-selling management classics. He died a healthy but happy man at the age of 86. Lastly, Prof. Amartya Sen was not my Guru but he taught us Economics at Jadavpur University and from him only I came to know of Sir Adam Smith, the founding father of Economics at the University of Glasgow, took risks in propounding new economic theories leading to an Economics Nobel. He is still happy and in good health at the age of 87 (born in 1933). These stalwarts in their respective fields never 'Retired'. They continued to seek the truth in their respective realms much beyond the retirement age of the commonplace populace.

The Secret of A Long Healthy, Happy Life

I can share with you the secret of a long healthy, happy life. I never allow my brain's 'Default Mode Network (DMN)' to switch on its mind-wandering circuit the moment I end my brain's 'Focused' phase to transit into the 'Unfocused' one. Whatever new ideas emerge at that transitory phase I note down on a copy or on my smartphone's note pad. I teach the same technique to the participants of my 'Teen Mentoring Project (TMP)'. Just an example to share. Arka Ghosh Choudhury (15 years), a participant of my TMP, was coming back from his cricket coaching centre on 14 August 2020 at around 9.15 am. He was in an AC bus with his dad. He had left his smartphone at home. All the other passengers, including his Dad were 'Attending' to something or the other on their smartphones thus keeping their DMNs engaged. Arka remembered my mentoring tips that whenever your mind tends to start wandering, being 'Unfocused', 'Focus' it on your 'Dream', 'Vision' and 'Mission' and you may get some new idea the moment it gets 'Unfocused'. That's exactly what he did and he came back home happy as he had got some new intuitive flashes.

A Point to Ponder

Have you now got the secret to a long happy, healthy span striking the 80th year of your life? If you are already down and out with some health problem—even a trivial one like lack of appetite or lack of sound sleep, please do not try to catch up with me (because even at 80, I do not even consume a single pill or capsule every day); instead, share my tips with a teenage member of your family who may benefit like, I am sure, my mentee Arka Ghosh Chaudhury will.

Brain Tool 15 Positive Visualisation (PV)

'Key' Points: *Journey as A 'Knowledge Entrepreneur'; Selection of My Workshop Venue; Reconnaissance Survey of the Banquet Room; Practice of Positive Visualisation (PV); My Positive Visualisation (PV) Worked; My First Exposure to Schooling; The Headmaster, JMB Sir; A Novel Grooming Technique; Positive Visualisation (PV) Training; At the Examination Centre; JMB: A Real Genius; 'Success': A (2) Two-dimensional Model; What Is 'Success'; The Positive Visualisation (PV) Training at School; A Practical Example; Positive Visualisation (PV) for Career Success; A Live Case Study; Discover the Passion in Your Teenage Kid; Examples; Further on Aryaman's Case Study; Holistic Success: Self-Actualisation; Self-actualisation and Customer Satisfaction.*

Journey as A 'Knowledge Entrepreneur'

In 1983, I took a big risk. I left the MD and CEO's suite in an Indo-German company to start my own journey on a new highway as a 'Knowledge Entrepreneur'. I chose the name and style: *Learning Club.* In a few years' time my team members worked smart to develop it into a 'brand' in its own right.

However, the risk was a calculated one—not on a 'gross' black-and-white but on a 'subtle' plane. I could feel that the way I was planning to design my workshops—the learning inputs, the methodology of conducting them, the way I would do the advance preparation—all would lead to a hilarious outcome. I was nurturing this DREAM from the core of my heart.

Selection of My Workshop Venue

As regards the selection of the venue for my first few workshops I had made a deal with the Hotel Oberoi Grand on Chowringhee,

Calcutta. In those days, Grand was the king of hotels in the City of Joy, The Park and the Hotel Hindustan International being on the toes. Great Eastern had turned into a collector's item. Taj Bengal, ITC Sonar and other national and international brands were still on the architect-planners' drawing boards. Hotel Airport Ashok was there but not centrally located. And, Hotel Peerless Inn, a neighbour of Grand did not represent a high status.

Reconnaissance Survey of the Banquet Room

I had sent printed brochures in advance to hundreds of companies in the whole of Eastern India inviting participants (my target was not to have more than 25 in a batch) and just a day before the workshop's commencement, I had prepared the final list of who were joining in. In the forenoon, I made a visit to The Grand, went to the Banquet Room that I had booked, supervised the Hotel staff to arrange the furniture as I wanted—in a horse-shoe pattern with the faculty area in front. In the faculty zone, there would be a 4 ft by 3 ft table on which we were going to place all my models and displays as well as the music system and a special flower arrangement. Behind the table, facing the participants, was a chair for my team member who was going to operate and control the 'Biorhythmic Music'. There was a white marker board and a set of marker pens and a duster, a pointer and also an armless chair for me placed in front. Inside the horse-shoe was a table on which we were going to place the Carousel 35 mm slide projector (ever since the introduction of a video/power point slide projector, we have been using one of Epson or Sony make).

I observed with great 'focus' the entire banquet hall with all the arrangements in minute detail and came back home.

Practice of Positive Visualisation (PV)

After lunch, I walked to my local park, Maddox Square, and took a seat on a bench facing the North. I placed my hands on the lap, kept my spine straight, and practiced deep breathing a few times. Thereafter, with my eyes shut, I started my 'Positive Visualisation (PV)' exercise. I began running a video film on my mind's screen what I wished to happen in my next day's workshop at Oberoi Grand.

I could visualise vividly that after a brief introductory session at 9.30 am, I started my deliberations in a psycho-dramatic style. The biorhythmic music was being played in the background. The participants' eyes were fixed on me and my movements; nothing could be heard except for my sonorous voice and the slow, soft instrumental music. I could imagine that within just 15 minutes' time, the participants got spellbound and mesmerised. During the tea break at 10.45 am, instead of moving to the tea and coffee corner, the participants started coming to the faculty area to express their appreciation and delight to say that they had never had any occasion to attend such an interesting event. From their entire body language (eye expressions, postures and gestures) and voice was oozing happiness and excitement. I could see high degree of motivation surfacing from all the 25 participants. There was not a single one who showed signs of boredom. I could hear some of their exclamatory remarks: Fabulous! Awesome! Unforgettable! Stupendous! Spectacular! I practiced PV for half an hour. Again, in the evening, sitting at my work station, I did it for the second time.

Next morning, when I got up, I cut short the duration and practiced PV for 15 minutes.

My Positive Visualisation (PV) Worked

The workshop that day was a glorious success. And, thereafter, there was no looking back. Workshops after workshops were success after success. From Calcutta we moved to the whole of Eastern India, then to the whole of India and subsequently, we did cover Bangladesh, Nepal and Bhutan.

'Positive Visualisation (PV)' is a power hidden inside our brain but very few utilise it. 'Negative Visualisation (NV)' is more common with most of us. PV can make an ordinary person extraordinary, a poor dad's son a billionaire. How I got the seed of PV during my boyhood, I shall tell you now.

My First Exposure to Schooling

I must have been chubby as a kid; otherwise why would the red-faced British and American soldiers loitering outside the

Ballygunge Army Camp offer me French, Swiss and Belgian candies and chocolates. This would happen almost every morning on my way to school.

I had just joined the then reputed Ballygunge Govt. High School (BGHS) in Class III; the year was 1947—the World War II armed forces were just about to wind up—these were the pre-partition days in undivided India.

BGHS was a class by itself as its grounds, classrooms, assembly hall and corridors had daily footfalls of creative people like the famous portrait artist Atul Bose, Satyajit Ray, and Sambhu Mitra who used to be students from their boyhood to adolescence. Since the BGHS premises and its adjoining Sir David Hare Basic Training (BT) College were occupied by the military, we had to attend our classes in a makeshift building almost opposite to the Ballygunge Army Camp and Barracks which had a sprawling campus. This area of Calcutta, in those days, was one of the prettiest, having lots of flowering trees like Krishnachura and Kanakchura.

The Headmaster, JMB Sir

Our new headmaster Jatindra Mohan Banerjee (JMB Sir) was fresh from Oxford, England. He had completed his BA (Tripos) and MA in English with flying colours. He could have continued to live in England as he already had an offer for a doctoral scholarship but due to patriotic reason, he returned to serve his motherland. He spoke with an immaculate Oxonian accent, but because of his 'swadeshi' temperament, he would always wear a dhoti and a kurta. Scientist Satyen Bose and ICS litterateur Annanda Shankar Ray both were his close friends and they had put their sons in BGHS under his tutelage.

A Novel Grooming Technique

JMB had introduced a new and novel grooming technique for selected boys of Class IX and X. I do not know whether it was his brainchild or he had imported it from Oxford which was well-known for its tutorials system.

In 1951, Partha Sarathi Gupta and Sukhamay Chakrabarti of Class lX were selected for this grooming. In 1952, these two boys stood 1st and 2nd in the School Final exam of the West Bengal Board of Secondary Education. In 1952, Ashok Chatterjee and Dibyendu Sengupta of Class lX were selected. In 1953 School Final, Ashok stood 1st and Dibyendu 4th. In 1953, Sabyasachi Bhattacharya and Subol Das Gupta were selected from Class lX. In 1954, Sabyasachi stood 1st and Subol 4th in School Final. When our turn came, from our class three of us were selected. Ashoke Chatterjee for History, Geography, Maths and Science, Tapan Bhattacharjee for Biology and myself for English and Bengali. In the 1955 School Final, Ashoke got the 4th place overall, Tapan stood 1st in Biology and I stood 1st in both English and Bengali amongst all the West Bengal Board candidates.

All the grooming sessions were exclusively one-to-one and held in total confidence. I have no idea in what ways Ashoke and Tapan of my batch were groomed. I can only share with you how I was mentored. For English, JMB himself grilled me thoroughly whereas for Bengali I had two of our best teachers—Probodh Ram Chakrabarti and Basanti Kumar Bhattacharya to grill me both in Bengali grammar and literature. But the best part was the POSITIVE VISUALISATION (PV) training.

Positive Visualisation (PV) Training

I had to sit with my spine erect on a wooden school chair without armrests, keep both my hands with inter-locked fingers on my lap, shut my eyes, start deep 'full breathing' (making sure that right from my throat to the lower abdomen—the entire breathing region did participate) and concentrate on that—to follow 9 to 10 breathing cycles (in-hold-out), then imagine that I am in the exam hall, question paper has been distributed, I am glancing through it and finding that answers to all of them are known to me. I start answering them one after another, without any hassle, without any cutting and rewriting, completing within the right time and submitting. I had to visualise what marks I would get for each answer and also the total score.

At the Examination Centre

Our batch had St. Lawrence School on Ballygunge Circular Road as our examination centre. On the 1st day, while the English Paper 1 exam was going on, JMB suddenly appeared on the scene—came straight to me, cheered me up with a pat on the back and left. On the day of Bengali Paper 1, both Probodh Ram Sir and Basanti Kumar Sir came straight to me and cheered me up. That year, 1955, I scored the highest (and with almost 95% accuracy as visualised by me) in both English and Bengali in the West Bengal Board and earned several laurels.

So, the secret is: Hard work to develop a thorough grasp over the subject (total study—not selective), appearing in frequent mock tests; and, 'Positive Visualisation (PV)' with a 'Can Do' Brain Tool which has already been covered earlier.

JMB: A Real Genius

Finally, let me tell you that JMB was a real genius otherwise, one generation after, how can his own grandson Abhijit Binayak Banerjee snatch the Nobel Prize for Economics in 2019!!! Yes, Abhijit is JMB's grandson—son of his son Dipak and daughter-in-law Nirmala, both of whom had their own respective career accomplishments! Did JMB teach Abhijit 'Positive Visualisation (PV)'? I feel proud and honoured to have been mentored in PV by JMB's team.

'Success': A 2 (Two)-dimensional Model

The last five (5) years, being immersed in a Neuro-management (NM) reverie most of the time, have brought about changes in some of my brain circuits. Anything that I come across, I always think in terms of brain and its functions without any exception. Let me come to the context of the 'Positive Visualisation (PV)' technique introduced to a few teenage minds by our immemorable headmaster Late Jatindra Mohan Banerjee (JMB Sir) and his team. I have no idea what they had perceived as 'Success', but if you ask my opinion today, I shall be tempted to describe it as a two (2)-dimensional model involving the neo-mammalian and the paleo-mammalian portions of our brain.

What is 'Success'

Let me elucidate. What is 'Success'? 'Success' is the end-result or outcome of the performance of some 'Work Activities (WA)' with some motive to fulfil some need or desire. To fulfil some need or desire, we set a 'Goal' and move towards it by performing some WA with a motivational force or 'Drive'. Motivation, converts the 'potential energy' stored in our tissues into 'kinetic energy' or action. When we reach the 'Goal', we earn 'Success'; and, if we do not reach it, we face 'Failure'.

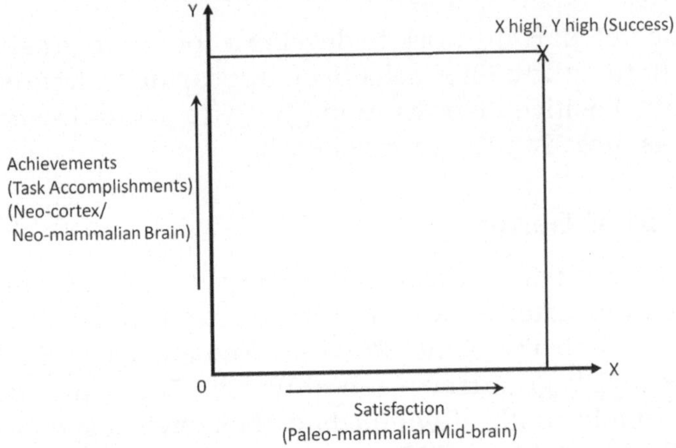

Fig. 10: The 2-dimensional 'Success' Model

'Success', therefore, can be looked at as a 2 (two)-dimensional phenomenon. One dimension represents your 'Achievements' (or 'Task Accomplishments')—which are tangible: can be seen, calculated, quantified, evaluated in concrete terms. If we put it as the Y-axis, it corresponds to the Left portion of your Neo-cortex or neo-mammalian Forebrain, which covers all quantifiable, calculable and measurable brain functions. The other dimension represents your 'Satisfaction'—the X-axis which corresponds to the Paleo-mammalian Mid-brain, that is responsible for all your basic emotions and feelings including the 'Joy' that comes as a 'Reward' due to the 'Achievement' (or 'Task Accomplishments').

The Positive Visualisation (PV) Training at School

In my 'Positive Visualisation (PV)' training session at school, I had to visualise very clearly the 'Score'—the marks that I was expecting to get in a particular paper—in figures, like 90, 95 or 100 (a more fool-proof PV exercise would be visualising the score, question-wise, when you get the question paper at the exam hall; I will cite a practical example within a minute or two).

I also had to evoke in my mind the feeling of 'Joy' (that is the 'Satisfaction' part—X-axis) that I would have if I had earned that 'Score'. [Now I know, that 'Feeling' is a combined effect of Dopamine (D) – the 'reward' chemical, Serotonin (S) – the 'feel good' or the 'good mood' chemical; Endorphin (E) – the brain chemical that makes you free from tension/stress; Oxytocin (O) – the 'love' molecule (as you would visualise the love and affection that would be showered on you on your earning that 'Score'); and, finally, Melatonin (M) – the 'sleep well' chemical that will be released from your brain's pineal gland.]

A Practical Example

I will keep my promise by citing a practical example. In my School Final Bengali Paper I, there was an essay to be written carrying 25 marks. I could choose any one of the three topics given. I had chosen 'Monsoon in Bengal'. When I started writing the essay in the exam hall, I visualised earning nothing less than full marks which was 25. This 'Nothing less than 25' PV led to a very interesting outcome.

After the exams were all over, the day of announcement of results was approaching. 3 days were left and I was playing street cricket with my local friends in the afternoon. A peon type man came with a sealed envelope and asked: "Who is Siddhartha Ganguli? There is a letter for him." When I approached him, he gave the envelope to me. It was from the famous Bengali poet of those days—Kalidas Roy. I opened the letter which said in Bengali: "Dear Siddhartha! I do not stay far away from where you stay. Take permission from your guardian and accompany the courier to meet me at my place. It is urgent."

Kalidas Roy Sir was the Head of Bengali Dept. in a reputed private school in South Calcutta and he was also the Head Examiner of Bengali in West Bengal Board of Secondary Education in those days. My dad was away to work, so I took my mother's permission, accompanied the courier and walked to Roy Sir's house. When we rang the bell, Roy Sir himself opened the door. As I was about to touch his feet, he hugged me to his chest and exclaimed: "What have you done? In Bengali Essay, the examiner had given you more than the full marks 25; he had given you 26 as he told me that what you had written was beyond his imagination and expectation—it was so good. As per the Board Rules, it was re-examined, and the 2nd examiner shared the same opinion and gave you 26. Finally, your answer script came to me as I am the Head Examiner. I was spellbound to read what you had written and thought you really deserved more than the full marks. But since the Rules do not permit, I struck out 26 and gave you 25 much against my heart-felt wish."

You have got a concrete example of the power of 'Positive Visualisation (PV)'. Isn't it?

Now that I have very lucidly explained PV and what should be the methodology adopted, would you not be able to guide your teenage kid most Smartly?

Positive Visualisation for Career Success

One can make good use of 'Positive Visualisation (PV)' for career success. A live case study is always helpful for relating than just the statement of a theory. So, let me take a live case again.

A Live Case Study

Aryaman Chaudhary of 21 years age in 2020 was born and settled in Jaipur, Rajasthan. From a very early age, he was extremely fond of cakes, pastries, cookies and chocolates. He would always save his pocket money to buy and enjoy such stuff. You can conclude straight that his DRIVE (= source of motivational force prompting him to ACT) originated from the 'Annamaya Kosha (AK)' in the 'Pancha Kosha Model that was proposed in the Taittiriya Upanishad a few thousand years ago. AK is the materialistic sheath part of our personality representing 'Dietary Energy (E-D)'. As a young kid, Aryaman used to DREAM of being a 'Bakery Chef' so that he could make such confectioneries himself and come up with designs novel in shape, size, colour, texture, flavour and taste.

While in high school, Aryaman chose his DOMAIN where his DRIVE will find expression and DREAM will lead to fruition. And, that was nothing else than 'Hotel Management'. His father Shiva Choudhary, a well-to-do farmer—now working in Saudi Arabia, did not mind and mother Durga—a typical rural homemaker 'bohu', preoccupied with thoughts of how she could manage the household better, had no 'say' in the matter.

Aryaman sat for the selection test for admission in the Institute of Hotel Management in Jaipur. Since he was obsessed with a 'Positive Vision' (he used to vividly visualise himself in the Baking Chef's role frequently), he did very well in the written test followed by orals and got selected. He completed his course with flying colours and got campus placement in a 5-star hotel in Jaipur as an intern. Highly motivated Aryaman enjoyed his internship, got confirmed as Asst. Bakery Chef and, in 2 years' time, got promoted as 'Chef-in-charge' of a section in the hotel bakery. In early 2020, he moved to Bhopal as Chief Baker in an exclusive patisserie—the best brand in the town. Now, if you take my 2 (two)-dimensional 'Success' model introduced to you a little while ago, and apply it in Aryaman Choudhary's case, you get on the 'Achievements' side: much higher remuneration, furnished accommodation, free food, attractive leave and paid travel facilities, a 2-wheeler with free fuel up to a limit; and, on the 'Satisfaction' side: happiness and increase in self-esteem (as he felt his 'Worth' and 'Value' have been properly recognised).

He confirmed all this during our WhatsApp chat. I also talked to his father, who is a friend of mine located in Riyadh, the capital of Saudi Arabia; and could figure out his feeling of pride in his son's success. Both Aryaman and his father Shiva have started nurturing the DREAM of opening up a cake shop in Jaipur in 5 years' time and, without any exaggeration, both are practicing 'Positive Visualisation (PV)'. So, there is no reason why their DREAM would remain a mere 'Daydream'. My 'DRIVE-DREAM-DOMAIN'—the 3-D approach used for career selection, if it could be wisely combined with PV, will certainly lead to the desired outcome.

Discover the 'Passion' in Your Teenage Kid

'To visualise' is a 'verb' representing action or work; and, the result is a noun—'Vision'. In order to visualise positively, you ought to have a burning desire—a 'Passion'. Aryaman had developed a strong 'Passion' from his teenage. If you are a SMART parent, you must think out ways and means of identifying the 'Passion Material' in your teenage kid, like I do in my 'Teen Mentoring Project (TMP)'. I am sharing some examples below.

Examples

Arka's (15) passion has been automobiles. As a young kid of 6 or 7 years, he used to play with his toy cars, open them up, dismantle and again reassemble. His DREAM is to be an Automobile Designer. The DRIVE is from his 'Pranamaya Kosha (PK)'—'Breath Energy (EB)' representing life force and movement.

Sanchayan (15) has been making comedy videos using his grandma's smartphone from the age of 10. He has already posted several well-produced comedy videos in YouTube and has earned an audience. His DRIVE is from the 'Monomaya Kosha (MK)' representing 'Emotional Energy—(EE)'.

Prarthana's (15) passion has been 'Designer Wear' and she DREAMS to be a 'Fashion Designer'. Her DRIVE is again from the 'Monomaya Kosha (MK)' representing 'Emotional Energy (EE)'. in her leisure time, instead of getting digitally addicted, she used old clothes and discarded cut pieces to make some designer clothes and display those on specially made cardboard mannequins.

These teenage boys and girls are regular positive visualisers laying the roads for their 'Career Success'.

Further on Aryaman's Case Study

Let 'Success' be defined as 'Achievements-High' and 'Satisfaction-High' [according to my Two (2)-dimensional model] and we have the example of Aryaman Choudhary ready at hand. Now, if we examine this case of 'Success' from the 'Kosha Engagement (KE)' point of view, then his KE PIE will be 'Annamaya Kosha (AK)'—60% (as his DREAM-DRIVE-DOMAIN are all related to AK); 'Pranamaya Kosha (PK)'—20% (as he never misses his 'Keep Fit' regime any day whether by freehand exercises or yogic asanas, jogging, skipping, or brisk walking); and, 'Monomaya Kosha (MK)'—20% (as he bonds extremely well with his seniors, juniors and colleagues in the patisserie where he is employed.

His other 2 Koshas—'Vijnanamaya Kosha (VK)' and 'Anandamaya Kosha (AnK)' are not engaged at the moment. If such circumstances continue then these two Koshas will ATROPHY (meaning, the tissues will waste away) due to lack of use as per the bio-spiritual law: "USE ME, or LOSE ME". 'VK' represents thirst for deep knowledge, going to the root of a problem seeking the right solution and making the most appropriate decisions. It is responsible for our 'Intellectual Energy (EI)'. 'AnK' represents original creativity, discovery, innovation, invention, intuition and insight—any of these brings us close to the 'Cosmos'—the 'Universal Self' leading to a 'Blissful' state of mind. It stands for 'Creative Energy (EC)'.

Holistic Success: Self-Actualisation

A young boy or girl who has just embarked upon a successful career journey must be trained to reach the level of 'Holistic Success' that includes the engagement of VK and AnK. Possibly, this is what the Russian-American psychologist Abraham Maslow described as 'Self-actualisation' and showed it as the highest step of his famous 'Hierarchy of Human Needs' which followed the sequence: Physiological and Survival Needs > Safety and Security Needs > Social Needs > Need for Prestige, Power, Status and Authority and finally > the Need for 'Self-actualisation'.

Now that Aryaman has been engaged in the AK, PK and MK, he should find time and opportunity to study books and technical journals and browse the internet to keep abreast of the latest concepts and techniques in Bakery Science. He should make suggestions to his higher management with workable schemes along with the financial feasibility tips for upgrading the patisserie for providing better products and services to its customers.

Customer Satisfaction

Now, we come to the point of 'Customer Satisfaction'. His bakery products must provide customer delight in looks (shape, size and colour), sound (product names), flavour, taste and texture. However, all of these are related to sensory pleasure. Such sensory experience would make the customers smile, express satisfaction, order for more, visit again and again and talk about the place, the products and services to people with whom they are close and connected.

Such happenings would serve as a source of 'Happiness' for Aryaman and his 'Anandamaya Kosha (AnK)' would get stimulated to get 'self-actualised' by throwing up new and novel ideas for bakery products which can be made in lesser time, at higher speed and lower cost, and will be better for health and fitness (low fat, gluten-free etc.).

Self-Actualisation and Customer Satisfaction

When you are self-actualised—you are your 'Pure Self'—detached from your 'Ego' (AK, PK, MK an VK are all 'Ego-attached'—you have that strong 'I'-feeling), you can give 'Happiness' to your 'Customers'.

Who is your 'Customer'? Everyone that you are interacting with happens to be your 'Customer'—your spouse, your parents, your kids, your friends, your acquaintances, your business associates. In Marketing Management, the challenge is to turn a Prospect into a Customer, a Customer into a Client (a regular buyer), a Client into an Advocate (who vouches for you) and an Advocate into an Evangelist (who promotes you everywhere).

You are not Aryaman Choudhary. You may not be involved in making any product. But you are definitely providing service to people in the manner I have explained above. Your family members are your 'Customers'—your 'Internal Customers'. A Smart Parent will teach a teenage kid to promote 'Total Satisfaction' or 'Happiness' to his grandparents, parents, other elders in the family, his siblings and so on. And, to get into this habit quickly, 'Positive Visualisation (PV)' will certainly be of great help.

Point to Ponder: Did you ever think that even though you are not in Sales or Marketing, providing 'Satisfaction' to your 'Internal Customers' is an essential part of life's ball game?

Brain Tools for Smart Parenting

I have already exposed you to 15 (fifteen) specially chosen Brain Tools (BTs) for application both by a parent as well as by a teenage kid. Now I shall be presenting a few essential BTs to be used for SMART Parenting.

BRAIN TOOL X

Teenage Nature Study

'Key' Points: *Teenage Nature Study; Reading the Kid's Nature from His Body; A SMART Parent Would Utilise Such Data; Avoid Nature-Nurture Conflict.*

Teenage Nature Study

The purpose of this 'Brain Tool (BT)' is to help a parent to study the nature of the teenage kid and deal with him effectively to get a positive outcome.

As the kid crosses the threshold of pre-teens and steps into his (no gender bias) thirteenth year, we would have noticed that there are some visible changes in his body—baby fat is shed, body hair appears (in girls, in addition, breasts), there are distinct changes in the organs for reproduction, the voice also undergoes a change. Along with all these perceptible transformations are there any changes in the kid's nature, his attitude, temperament, conduct and behaviour? Yes, several changes are expected. However, without getting lost in the forest of these changes, let me provide you with some general guidelines for reading and judging teenage kids.

Reading the Kid's Nature from His Body

First of all, notice the shapes predominant in the kid's body. If the face, nose, eyes and nails are roundish and there is predominance of fatty tissue (protruding paunch, the bony prominence at wrist joint is covered under a layer of fat making it invisible, heavy buttocks etc.) plus height is relatively short for the age, then the kid is very friendly and sociable, although need not be extroverted but a good mixer; would tend to spend a lot of time chatting with friends, watching videos, movies, TV programmes and listening to music. Would love to entertain and also to be entertained. This teenager is physically lazy and tries to keep away from outdoor work activities including sports and games.

If the facial features, as mentioned, are squarish, rectangular, or, in rare cases, may be trapezoidal; and fat is present only between layers of muscles (and not underneath the skin as in the case of a plump kid) and the bony prominence at the wrist joint is perceptible, the kid would be physically very active; interested in physical pursuits, sports, games and outdoor work. He is friendly and extroverted but does not enter into very close, intimate relationship as the fatty one. Wrong side is: tends to be straightforward in communication which stands as a relationship barrier. Sometimes, he may behave in a rude and aggressive manner. Would possess good leadership quality but not of that shrewd, too much diplomatic, political type. Stature is well-proportioned and height medium.

If the facial features are longish (long eyes, sharp pointed nose, oval or inverted triangular face, longish nails with tapering fingers), then the kid is creative and artistically talented. Nature is, however, introverted, secretive and non-expressive. Could be extremely sentimental and, should there be a trigger, can fall a victim of depression. Refined by nature, this kid is very selective in relationship. Would love to spend time indoors and get digitally addicted to watch movies, listen to music and browsing the net to collect information.

A SMART Parent Would Utilise Such Data

To be a SMART parent, you will have to use such 'Nature Study' data in a way that you deal with the kid according to his nature so that you get good result. For example, do not 'push' a fat, plump kid to go for fitness activities in a gym or participate in outdoor games like football, cricket or hockey. Do not dissuade him too much from mixing and chatting with friends. In the same note, if the kid having a balanced, well-proportioned body wants to join others for outdoor activities, do not discourage. Do not pressurize him to have a lot to eat because, by nature, he is controlled. If a lean introverted kid wants to paint, write poems or lyrics and spend time alone, do not nudge him to mix with people and make friends.

Avoid Nature-Nurture Conflict

Have you not understood that your 'Nurture' (parenting style) should be according to the kid's inherent 'Nature' to avoid any conflict leading to 'Stress; where you are the 'Irresponsible Stressor'?

BRAIN TOOL Y

A Teenager's Mood Assessment

'Key' Points: *A Teenage Kid: Unpredictable; Teenager's Mood Assessment; Two Kinds of Responses: 'Toward' and 'Away'; The Negative Response of 'Aggression' with 'Anger'. What Is the Solution; Anger and Anxiety.*

A Teenage Kid: Unpredictable

A teenage kid tends to be quite unpredictable, temperamental. He is neither a toddler, nor a pre-schooler, a pre-teen or an adult. He has a typical teenage brain. Nevertheless, a motivated parent with a little patience can assess his teenage kid's mood from his (no gender bias) body language, especially facial expressions.

Teenager's Mood Assessment

A happy kid having a positive disposition will establish and maintain positive eye contact while talking or listening. Gaze avoidance by keeping the gaze downward, looking away, looking sideways or shutting the eyes are all signs of lack of interest or anxiety. The kid is expressing his disinterest through his eye expression. In extreme cases, it may take the form of not responding when called by name, reluctance to show up when sent for, or leaving the location for going elsewhere.

I know of a teenager from Diamond Harbour who, in order to avoid his highly authoritarian father having a roaring hardware business, used to go to a local old man's (with whom he had an excellent rapport) house straight after school without visiting his own home. Obviously, the hardware merchant was not a Smart parent. He had made tons of money but had failed to build a bridge with his teenage son.

Two Kinds of Responses: 'Toward' and 'Away'

There are two kinds of responses that we get from teenage kids. The positive one is a 'Toward' response—meaning moving towards, going or coming close to the parent, indicating 'liking' ('I like you, I love you, I want to be close to you'); the negative one is an 'Away' response, indicating 'disliking' ('I dislike you, I do not want to be close to you')—physically moving away from the object of dislike.

Such responses come from the teenage kid's brain's 1st floor—the mid-level-placed 'Paleomammalian' brain. You find the same behaviour in dogs. I had dogs as pets right from my boyhood and the last one that I had was named 'Joy'. After the whole day's work, whenever I would be back home and ring the doorbell, Joy will start barking and the moment the door was opened, he would jump on me in joyful excitement. But with strangers he did not like and would feel a little scared to go near, he will maintain a safe distance and will start barking.

The Negative Response of 'Aggression' with 'Anger'

The other negative response would be 'Aggression' accompanied with 'anger'. It has a graded developmental sequence. Mild anger has to be assessed in your kid from his 'irritability'. It may, with provocation, turn into annoyance, culminating—with further provocation, into violence—throwing things, breaking things, tearing things. To be a SMART parent, you have to develop the sensitivity about the 'trigger'—what kind of handling, what kind of dealing with, what kind of provocation leads to such outbursts.

In my 'Teen Mentoring Group (TMG)', there is a young lady (just 13 year-old) who, with slightest provocation, throws up temper tantrums and, if handled wrongly, becomes violent and starts physically assaulting her mom for reasons unknown to the family members. The real factor, which I could readily make out, when she joined the TMG, is that she was not very happy about sleeping in the middle of both the parents. She longs for the sole ownership of the father and with little indication of not getting adequate attention (both physical and emotional) from her dad, she loses her balance and starts hitting, beating and biting the mother. Nobody can control this off-mood girl. At that moment, she is full of hatred for her mother; it becomes too obvious from her conduct and expressions.

What Is the Solution

But, is there no solution? Yes, there is; which is to divert her attention to something which is more attractive and important for her. Soon after she joined the Teen Mentoring Group, I persuaded her to crystallize her thoughts about a suitable career choice and she chose 'Fashion Design'. It suits her squarely as she can sketch, draw and paint exceptionally well.

The moment some appreciative inputs are provided regarding her sketches and paintings, the adrenalin in her neurons are washed away by a sudden rush of Dopamine—the reward neurochemical.

Anger and Anxiety

Anger and anxiety are two off-beat moods that become constant companions of many teenagers owing to wrong dealing by their unsmart parents. Occurrence of such negative temperament has increased under the current Covid 19-produced pandemic circumstances. Most teenagers are suffering from a deep-rooted feeling of insecurity and uncertainty which have made them extra-sensitive. On the one hand, there is the boredom of home confinement and uninteresting on-line classes by teachers and private tutors, on-line tests and exams; on the other, there is the fear of invasion by the Corona virus.

Under the present circumstances, don't you think that the need for intelligent handling by Smart leading techniques have become most imminent now?

BRAIN TOOL **Z**

A Special Night Resolution

'Key' Points: *The Story of A Parent and A Child; Does Sleep Really Provide Peace; The Sleep Cycle; Negative Sleep Health; A Similar Story from Spain.*

The Story of A Parent and A Child

I got the 'key' idea from a beautiful story that I had read long ago. The story had two characters—a parent and a child. I have since made some amendments. The child is a teenager and his (no gender bias) profile is typical of his age—full of turbulence. He is disobedient, rebellious, naughty, unruly. The kid has fallen asleep but the parent is still widely awake watching him in deep slumber. In sleep, all the turbulence of the kid has disappeared. He looks sober and at peace with himself. But is he really stress-free and at peace? The parent ponders in his mind and observes the kid minutely.

Does Sleep Really Provide Peace

For anyone, sleep provides solace from all external stressors which fill the environment during our wakefulness. A typical teenager gets bombarded with critical remarks arising out of the frustration of his parents whose real child's profile does not tally with the picture nurtured in their minds of a dream adolescent who is serious in studies, intelligent and smart, well-behaved and polite, physically healthy and fit, friendly and sociable. The teenager gets relief from such shell bursts during sleeping hours. But, does he really get relief? The parent in my story still ponders and observes.

The Sleep Cycle

He had read somewhere that a disturbed sleeper changes his posture more than 10 to 15 times during one night's sleep (I may not be correct in this information). But on one thing I am sure, if the sleeping arena is spacious—left all to himself, and he is not under a heavy blanket but wrapped up with a light linen, the sleeper rotates from minimum 180 to maximum 360 degrees. The 1st Stage of sleep is NREM (Non-Rapid Eye Movements)—deep, sound, dreamless, undisturbed slot, lasting only 5 to 10 minutes. Then comes NREM Stage 2 for 20 odd minutes followed by NREM Stage 3 for another 20 minutes. Thereafter, NREM Stage 2 is repeated for 20 minutes, followed by the REM (Rapid Eye Movements) phase—the disturbed, light, dream-filled sleep for 20 minutes. The whole cycle is thus for 90 minutes. This represents a normal, healthy sleep cycle.

Negative Sleep Health

But if the teenage kid has a disturbed mind due to continuous adverse criticism from parents, teachers and tutors during his waking hours, his sleep cycle will be disproportionate representing negative sleep health. The sleep cycle of 90 minutes is repeated minimum 5 times (totalling 450 minutes, that is a little less than 8 hours) to maximum 6 times (totalling 540 minutes—that is, 9 hours) during a total 24-hour long day. But, if this sleep operational cycle is not effectively completed—if there are any disturbances in any of the phases, then the kid either suffers from 'Sleep Debt' (that is, he will feel sleepy from time to time and may doze off when he is supposed to be wide awake attending to his curricular work) or becomes irritable by nature—suffers from lack of poise and concentration. Cannot FOCUS on anything even for a short while—a problem which gets aggravated with over-use of digital gadgets to compensate for the 'Dopamine (D)' and 'Oxytocin (O)' deficiency which is the outcome of a home environment full of stressors, lacking a peaceful ambience.

The Parent's Affirmative Self-message

The parent in my story finds a lot of disturbances in his kid's sleeping behaviour as he continues to watch. And, he feels guilty as the child is not free from internally generated bombardments coming from his memory. During sleep, when the conscious mind is switched off, the subconscious mind that contains our memory becomes active. The parent now realises his mistakes and feels he should not have been so rough, intolerant and inconsiderate with his lovely teenage son who is the product of he himself and his beloved spouse. Tears roll down his cheeks. He takes a resolution which I call an 'Affirmative Self-message': "Dear my son, you're a gem. I'm fortunate to have you as my child. You have so many qualities and strengths which have become overshadowed by my constant rebukes and criticism. From tomorrow, I promise, I must not look at your simple shortcomings and stop making snap criticisms; instead, I must appreciate whenever I find you're doing something good however trivial it may be."

A Similar Story from Spain

My story has some similarity with a story from Spain documented in "Is This the Exact Moment a Bullfighter Became an Anti-BullfightingActivist?"[https://www.snopes.com/fact-check/the-last-bullfight/]. This story goes like this: A bullfight was going on. In the middle of the fight, the matador Alvaro Munero, suddenly, in remorse, sat down at the edge of the arena. He saw not the horns that provoke a veteran matador like him, instead he saw the eyes of the bull he was fighting.

The bull looked at Alvaro and watched, standing still, making no attempt to attack. His innocent eyes were filled with a plea for help. Alvaro suddenly felt as if the animal was addressing him the way we address God in prayer: "I don't want to fight you, please spare me, because I did you nothing wrong. Kill me if you want, if you will but I cannot tolerate any more pain. What wrong have I done to you that you started fighting with me? Please have mercy on me."

The bull's unspoken language touched Alvaro's heart and he felt himself to be the worst creature on earth to be a professional bullfighter. From that very moment and day, he became a vegetarian and stopped participating in the bullfighting sport. In my story, the parent had a similar feeling watching his teenage kid in sleep. He felt like a most cruel, heartless person to have been intimidating the innocent kid for trivial lapses. From that day, he stopped behaving like a dictatorial autocratic parent and became SPIRITUAL.

Don't you realise that for Smart parenting you ought to have a spiritual streak?

APPENDIX I Gut Brain Facts

'Key' Points: *Gut Feelings Are Not the Same in All; Speculation No. 1: Brainpower Vis-à-vis Gut Feelings; Speculation No. 2: The Role of the Head Brain-Gut Brain Axis; Speculation No. 3: The Role of Gut Microbes; 'Gut Brain (GB)' Health Management; 'Gut Brain (GB)' Health Rules; 'Gut Brain (GB)' Happiness; The 'Gut Brain (GB)' Stage – 3 (Three) Main Chemical Actors;' Gut Brain (GB)' Biotics; Building Up of the Gut Microbe Population; The 'Gut' Under Stress; The 3 (Three) Types of 'Biotics'; More Facts About Gut Brain Health.*

Gut Feelings Are Not the Same in All

Some people report that they never had or have any 'Gut Feelings (GF)' as such, whereas a few have frequent GF, while some others experience it when they are creating something—may be a painting, a craftwork, a piece of sculpture, an architectural perspective drawing, a story, a poem or a film. Based on the GF, the creator makes amendments. Why is it so? Do different 'Gut Brains (GB)' have different sensitivities? Let me do some speculation regarding the probable answers.

Speculation No. 1: Brainpower Vis-à-vis Gut Feelings

When our ancestors used to live as hunter-gatherers, they would live more on 'gathered' food, namely, fruits, plants, herbs, nuts, and raw vegetables. In many forests where they inhabited—preys to be hunted were scarce so the hunters played more the role of 'scavengers'—eating the flesh of freshly dead small and fragile animals—killed by ferocious predators who had to leave the carcasses uneaten, because of their other priorities. Raw food required longer time for processing so it necessitated somewhat larger and stronger digestive system with tough Guts.

Primatologist Richard Wrangham of Harvard University thinks that fire played an extremely important role by allowing us to collect more nutrients from our food. EATING COOKED FOOD LED TO THE SHRINKING OF OUR GUTs, he suggests. Since Gut tissue is expensive to grow and maintain, this loss would have freed up precious resources, favouring further brain growth. Will that mean that those who are 'More Brainy' would have 'Less Gut Feelings' than those who have a weak digestive system (symptoms: lack of appetite, irregular bowel movement, constipation or loose motion, flatulence, indigestion, acidity)?

Speculation No. 2: The Role of the Head Brain-Gut Brain Axis

The 'Gut Brain' [alias 'Enteric Nervous System (ENS)'] is only technically a component of the 'Peripheral Nervous System (PNS)' [Our nervous system is divided into: 'Central (CNS)' and 'Peripheral (PNS)'—the CNS is made up of the brain and the spinal cord] as it does not follow any command from the CNS, nor does it send any information to the CNS. It is not a slave of the Head Brain if I compare the latter to the 'King'. There are over 100 million 'neurons' (= nerve cells) in your small intestine alone the length of which is, in an adult, on an average 22 feet (7 metres) -three and a half times the length of your body. It is called 'small' as its diameter is only about 1 in (2.5 cm). The adult large intestine is about 5 ft (1.5 m) long having a diameter of about 3 in (7.6 cm). The small and the big together are about 27 ft (8.5m) or more. The total surface area of your intestines is about half the size of a badminton court. There is, however, an exception to this 'Gut Brain Independence' rule with respect to one vital function. Your dietary input passes from the mouth into the food pipe or oesophagus and moves into the stomach. Once the food has been sufficiently pulverized, sterilized, and partly digested in the stomach with the help of internally-generated enzymes, it is dribbled out into the small intestine in quantities that are not hard for that organ to handle. The stomach feeds the duodenum (the intestinal region adjoining the stomach) through the 'Pyloric Sphincter (PS)'—a gateway which can close and open. This specific operation is conducted by your 'Head Brain (HB)' in collaboration with the 'Gut Bain (GB)'. The HB's connection to the GB is through the 'Vagus Nerve (VN)'. As long as the process is followed satisfactorily in all respects, there is no issue. If there is any deviation from the norm (such as, the presence of too much of corrosive acid in the stomach etc.), the message is transmitted to the HB through the VN. And, this may be a 'Gut Feeling (GF)'.

Speculation No. 3: The Role of Gut Microbes

Your Gut is full of trillions of microbes which include a variety of bacteria. The microbe population is a mixture of friends and foes. If the desirable balance is maintained with the help of a well-planned balanced diet, there is no problem. If there is imbalance due to any reason including unplanned, unbalanced diet, it may lead to some 'Gut feeling (GF)'.

'Gut Brain (GB)' Health Management

You must be aware, by now, how much vitally important your 'Second Brain'—the 'Gut Brain (GB)' is for your health and fitness—both physical and mental. The 'Gut Brain' health, therefore, has to be properly managed to meet 5 (five) primary objectives: (i) your weight and waist management (consult the standard height-weight and waistline charts and try to remain within +/− 10–15% variability from the norm); (ii) strengthening the immune system for keeping illnesses away; (iii) adequate physical and mental energy availability; (iv) earning efficiency in body functions; and (v) meeting the nutritional need.

For GB health management, you have to always ensure a 'Balanced Diet (BD)'. BD is a diet that contains different kinds of food in certain quantities and proportions so that the requirement for calories is met. [An average adult having a sedentary habit does not require more than 2,000 to 2,200 Kcal (Calories) per day—any extra energy gain can lead to fat deposit or can explode into a disease if not controlled timely.]. The nutrients in the BD must be: carbohydrates [obtainable from cereals like rice and wheat and root vegetables like potato—all these contain sugar, so must be controlled]; proteins (veg. protein from dal or lentil, chana, matar, rajma, dry beans, soybean)—lacto- or milk protein (dairy milk, paneer, 'chhana', cheese, yogurt)—non-veg. protein (egg, fish, chicken, meat); vitamins and minerals (fresh fruits and vegetables); fats and oils (cooking medium used in limited quantity is good enough—all white fat from animal protein must be discarded—fish oil is good for the brain—bony and sea fish varieties containing Omega-3 fatty acid is very good for the brain—vegetarians can get Omega-3 from flaxseed and flaxseed oil); salt and sugar—restrict quantities; spices—just for taste; herbs: dhania, pudina, tulsi, curry leaves are good for health; plenty of water.

'Gut Brain (GB)' Health Rules

Do not skip any of the 3 (three) major meals of the day, especially breakfast; Eat more raw food such as fresh fruits, vegetable salads, home-made fresh juices of tomato, pineapple, mango, water melon etc; Never eat to the brim—stop eating when you feel that you are almost approaching the full capacity of your stomach; Drink lots of plain water every day—minimum 3 to 4 litres—do not get habituated to mineral water or chilled water from the fridge; Keep a supply of healthy snacks (like nuts) handy; Take dal with every meal and its ratio to cereal should be—cereal 4: dal 1; Give up coffee, limit tea (have it with a touch of milk and refined sugar); Organise packed lunch for working men and women and packed tiffin for children in the family; Enjoy the food—do not eat anything forcibly because of its nutritive or medicinal value; Avoid processed meat (ham, bacon, salami, sausages), packaged snacks (like chips and bhujiyas), Indian snacks-sweets and western confectioneries because the preservatives and colouring agents used are harmful—for dessert, make fruit salad, rice pudding, fruit custard, or souffle at home and serve; Avoid refined flour or 'maida' which is only blank calorie, has no nutritive value—use whole wheat flour or 'atta' instead; Ensure having low-fat plain (and not flavoured) yogurt regularly as it is of probiotic value—good for the gut microorganisms; Fat in your food should be kept to the minimum as it does not get dissolved in your bloodstream (blood is watery) and gets deposited on the inner wall surface of your blood vessels forming 'plaques' causing obstruction to the normal flow of blood; Blot your fried food to take away the extra oil; Good to take a fistful of germinated red grams or whole moong dal early in the morning before physical exercise, morning walk or jogging—have dal at lunch and dinner—egg or fish at lunch—veg. protein (and not animal protein) at dinner; for sandwiches to be made to be eaten as snacks or taken as packed midday refreshment, use peanut butter or low-fat cheese as spreads—add plenty of raw vegetables: tomato, cucumber, onion, radish, lettuce, dhania leaves and, at times, egg for a change; Try to follow the same meal timings and do not talk, watch the TV, listen to the radio or making or attending to phone calls while eating—instead concentrate on effective chewing and mastication—at the most you can play slow, soft instrumental music in the background.

Triguna Diet: (a) Sattvic: (pure vegetarian—no onion, no garlic)—whole grains, pulses, sprouts, plenty of fresh vegetables, seasonal fresh fruit, fresh herbs, dried nuts, honey, milk and dairy products (including plain yogurt); (b) Rajasic (non-vegetarian): millet, corn, potato, cauliflower, broccoli, spinach, squash, apples, banana, guava, red lentils, fish, shrimp, chicken; (c) Tamasic (non-vegetarian): wheat, brown rice, mushrooms, garlic, onion, pumpkin, urad dal, rajma, cheese, watermelon, plums, apricots, beef, lamb, pork.

'Gut Brain (GB)' Happiness

It took me a couple of weeks to settle down at the University of Glasgow (known as the Mecca of Engineering in those days, while Edinburgh was famous as the Mecca of Medicine) in Scotland, UK. During this period, I was in a 'Paying Guest (PG)' accommodation (known as 'Digs' in Britain). Once settled in the fourth oldest British University (set up in 1451), I started looking for hostel accommodation and finally shifted to the Great Western Hotel (GWH) which was the recently taken over Annexe of the Glasgow YMCA. Having been accustomed to Bengali cuisine for 21 (twenty one) years ever since my birth, my entry and exposure to the typical British diet was full of curiosity since I had always possessed a scientist's mind. In GWH, for lunch and dinner, we were served soup as a starter, and thereafter, potato, turnip, broccoli, cabbage—all in boiled and mashed form along with chicken or lamb or fish fillet—boiled to make it soft and tender. Serving of boiled carrots, beans and capsicum cut into small pieces were also available on the dining table for you to help yourself. (Salt, pepper and 2–3 varieties of sauce and vinegar would be there for you to add if you liked). Occasionally, for a change, Italian dishes such as pasta, ravioli and moussaka would be served.

I had two questions about the typically British main meal: one, why boiled and mashed; two, why the boiled vegetables were cut into small pieces. When I became friendly with our hostel super Mrs Kelly, an octogenarian of my grandma's age, I asked her but her answers could not satisfy me. Now, after 58 years, I am getting those questions answered by Prof. Richard Wrangham of Harvard University.

Prof. Wrangham talks about an incident that took place on June 6, 1822. One 28-year-old Alex Martin was accidentally shot from a very short distance inside a store in a town in Michigan, USA. A large portion of one side of his body was blown off, the ribs fractured, the cavities of the chest and the abdomen got exposed and protruded portions of the lacerated and burnt lungs and stomach along with the 'Gut' became visible. The stomach had a big hole through which food was leaking. Dr. Bill Beaumont, MD, a young war-returned surgeon happened to drop in soon after the accident. He took Alex in his car to his own home to treat him under personal care. Although the fist-sized wound mostly filled in, it never completely closed. For the rest of Alec's life, the inner workings of his stomach were visible from the outside. Dr. Beaumont took this opportunity to study 'Gut Behaviour' from close proximity much before technology was invented to do it by indirect means. He continued his observations and experiments for 8 (eight) long years and drew the following conclusions:

- the softer and more tender the food is (boiled and mashed?) the more rapidly and completely it gets digested;
- the same effect was noted for food finely cut and divided (boiled vegetables cut into small pieces; Russian salad with raw tomato, cucumber, capsicum etc. cut into small pieces and mixed with mayonnaise);
- boiled mashed potatoes were more easily digested than French fries which remained long undissolved in the stomach and yielded slowly to the action of the gastric juice;
- the same principles held with respect to fish, chicken, and meat; if tender and finely divided, they are disposed of readily; if in large and solid masses, digestion is proportionately retarded;
- minuteness of division and tenderness of fibre are the two ground essentials for speedy and easy digestion.

Dr. Beaumont's discovery that soft and finely divided food are more easily digested conforms to our preference for such items. The main goal of cooking should be to soften the food. The second goal is to facilitate and hasten digestion. That these are more than justified is evident from both the smaller mouth and teeth in the case of modern humans compared to the Neanderthal, Peking men and other prehistoric ancestors of ours who had bigger jaws, bigger mouth and stronger and larger teeth before cooking came in vogue and we had to survive on raw vegetarian and non-vegetarian food items.

Is it not adequately clear to you that the type of oily, spicy food—both veg and non-veg that we have in India is not ideally designed for 'Gut Brain Happiness'?

The 'Gut Brain (GB)' Stage: 3 (Three) Main Chemical Actors

Mother Nature ensures that all living things are made of the same basic ingredients: sugar molecules, fats, and amino acids (which are the building blocks of 'proteins'). Everything we eat comes from living things and their destination is the 'Gut Brain (GB)' in our 'Enteric Nervous System (ENS)'. Hence those 3 (three) are the main chemical actors on the 'GB' Stage.

SUGAR molecules, that we obtain from carbohydrates ('carb' in short) like plain white bread, rice, pasta, or roti made from flour (maida) are simple actors or role players on the 'GB' stage. There is no complication with them as they contain simple sugar chains. A piece of toast eaten for breakfast once acted upon by the appropriate enzymes leads to the same number of sugar molecules as a couple of spoonful of refined household sugar. Our 'Gut' is hungry for household sugar and Indian sweets specially those immersed in sugary syrup like 'rosogollas' as these do not require so much work from our enzymes. Those food items are already broken down into small pieces when they arrive in the small intestine to be absorbed directly into the bloodstream. The sugar contained in white toast or plain white rice is digested relatively quickly by the enzymes available in our gut leading to a sudden sugar explosion in the blood stream. In contrast, toast made from brown bread, brown rice and roti made from wheat—everything moves at a much leisurely pace as they contain complex sugar chains, which have to be broken bit by bit.

So, the 'carb' input recommended is, a cup-size bowl of puffed rice or 2 to 3 toasted plain white bread (and not any more in quantity) for breakfast between 8 and 9.30 am to maintain a healthy level of sugar in the bloodstream, followed by just a bowl of plain white rice for lunch between 1 and 2 pm to bring up the blood sugar level after the drop due to the energy expended by you between breakfast and lunch. In late afternoon or early evening, instead of snacks, a serving of fresh fruits is advisable to maintain the blood sugar balance as fruits are a source of natural sugar. For dinner between 8.30 and 9.30 pm, half a bowl of rice and 1 roti made from ground wheat is recommended as the carb input. One or two soft tender potatoes mixed with dal or vegetables or in boiled and mashed form is permissible for each meal. This dietary pattern will facilitate quick entry of sugar in the blood stream. Sugar is an important raw material for our bodies and brains as it is used as fuel for our cells but too much of it is harmful. Therefore, the quantity of carb input must be controlled and intake of household sugar must be restricted in beverages. When you would go for a sweet dish like custard or rice pudding at dinner time, eliminate the bowl of rice and stick to one roti only.

FAT is the most valuable and efficient of all food articles. It coats our nerves, meant for transmission of signals from one brain cell to another, called 'axons' which are hair-like members coming out of a 'neuron' (= nerve cell). The 'axons' are thus myelinated—just like the plastic sheath on an electric cable. This coating makes us fast thinkers. Our 'Gut Brain Stage' knows the special character that FAT represents. It, unlike the other nutrients, cannot be absorbed straight into the blood from the 'Gut' as it is not soluble in water. Shortly after we eat a fatty meal (fried or oily stuff or oily fish, fatty chicken or red meat), the fatty, oily droplets enter into the 'Ductus Thoracicus' which is where all the Gut's lymph vessels converge into to allow the fats to gather without the risk of clogging. The lymph fluid loses its transparency and turns milky white. Fats are divided into 'Good Fats' and 'Bad Fats' and detoxification of the latter is a complicated process which we need not get into. Nutritional physiologists recommend we get between 25 to 30 percent of our body's daily energy requirement from FAT. This works out an average 55 to 66 grams of FAT a day (athletic types need a little more and sedentary types a little less). If we are going for boiled food in the European style, we can get it from the fish, meat or egg that we consume. If we are going for items cooked in oil in the Indian style, we get some fat from the cooked dishes and also from the veg or non-veg protein items. You have to be careful about your sugar intake as excess sugar gets converted into fat and stored in the fatty tissue. SUGAR is the only substance our body can turn into FAT with little effect.

There is just one more nutritional building block—or 'Gut Brain Stage' actor group to consider: the ***AMINO ACIDS***. Amino acids are the makers of 'protein'. Digestive enzymes break down the amino acid chains in the small intestine and then the Gut wall nabs or gets hold of the valuable components. There are twenty of these AMINO ACIDS and an infinite variety of ways they can be linked to form 'protein'.

Nevertheless, which one of these three chemicals will play in what role following which script and for how long would possibly be dictated and directed by the gut microbes which are present—100 trillion in number in our 'Gut Brain (GB)'.

'Gut Brain (GB)' Biotics

Our body is the habitat of trillions of microscopic organisms, living components of a community which is described as 'Biotics.' Of our entire 'microbiome'—that is, the 100 trillion microorganisms of a thousand different species that teem on the inside and outside of our bodies—90 percent are found in the 'Gut' (that is, the entire gastro-intestinal or digestive system). Most sit in our mucous membrane of the different parts of the 'Gut', diligently training our immune system, soothing our villi (tiny finger-like projections on the surface of the small intestine), eating what we do not need, and producing vitamins for us. Others keep close to the cells of the 'Gut', needling them or producing toxins. If the good and bad microbes are in equilibrium, the bad ones can make us stronger (capable of coping with them without getting adversely affected) and the good ones can take care of us and keep us healthy.

If the microbiome's weight is measured, it will come up to almost 2 kg. The bulk of this bacterial population lives inside the large intestine or 'colon'. 80 percent of our immune system is located in our 'Gut'. Even harmful bacteria can be useful for us when the immune system uses them for 'Familiarisation Training' (about the characteristic features of the bacteria) of the Gut's Defender Cells.

Building Up of the Gut Microbe Population

The newly born is endowed with the first serve of such bacteria from the mother's vaginal passage during normal delivery (which does not happen in the case of Caesarean sections). More supply comes from the mother's body during breast-feeding. Bacteria live on the milky nipples. (Such bacteria are particularly common in the guts of breastfed babies: Bifidobacteria and Lactobacilli). More bacteria may enter the child's body from the hospital environment, the attending nurse's, the gynaecologist's and the father's bodies if the father has touched and taken the newly born into his lap. Following weaning, the typical bacteria that first colonise the infant gut are those possessing genes needed to break simple carbohydrates ('carb' in short) such as those in rice. The child's baby gut flora will not be able to deal with plant-based foods. For such dietary inputs, he is going to need new kinds of digestive bacteria. For small children, the 'Gut Brain' develops in parallel with their 'Head Brain (HB)'.

The 'Gut' under Stress

The large intestine or the colon is the tranquil home of our gut flora, which deal with anything that gets swept into the large intestine undigested. The question now is: if our dietary pattern is so well-designed and balanced, then most of the food gets digested before it reaches the colon, then would the gut bacteria remain starved and may start a rebellion? The point is, nobody's diet and digestive process, in today's fast-pace world, are so perfect that nothing is left to move into the colon undigested, because everybody in the digital era is affected by stress—small, moderate or acute. Stress of any kind and dimension activates nerves that inhibit the digestive process, which means we not only extract less energy from our food, but also take longer to digest it, putting the 'Gut' under unnecessary extra strain.

When the 'Head Brain (HB)' senses a major problem under 'stress', it naturally wants to solve it. To do so, it needs energy which it borrows mainly from the 'Gut'. The 'Gut' is kind enough to save energy on digestion, producing less mucous and reducing the blood supply for the digestive process. The altered circumstances that stress creates in the 'Gut' affect those different types of bacteria which can survive there only in periods of low stress. So, a large portion of our faeces is made up of such bacteria which die under such circumstances. Stress changes the weather of the 'Gut'.

Bacteria can produce particles that are small enough to make it through the coating of the blood vessels into the brain. Examples include: 'Tyrosine' and 'Tryptophan'. These two amino acids are converted into 'Dopamine (D)' and 'Serotonin (S)' in the cells of the brain. 'D' is associated with the brain's 'Reward System' and 'S' can make us feel contented and happy.

So, the theory is that our bacteria can reward us when we send them a decent serving of food. It feels pleasant and whets our appetite for the next meal.

The 3 (Three) Types of 'Biotics'

The 3 (three) types pf 'Biotics' are: 'Antibiotics', 'Probiotics' and 'Prebiotics'.

Antibiotics: 'Anti bios' means against life. 'Antibiotics' thus kill bacteria and rid us of acute pathogens. Antibiotics work in three different ways: by filling bacteria with holes, by poisoning them, or by destroying their ability to reproduce. They have no effect on 'viruses' at all. Antibiotics can alter our gut flora significantly. However, there is no reason not to take antibiotics when it is medically appropriate to do so. Antibiotics is used in large-scale animal farming. In India, there is almost no regulation of the amount of antibiotics given to animals and birds. This turns the creature's guts into giant breeding zoos for resistant bacteria. Antibiotics is used in animal feed as 'performance enhancers'—to enhance the ability of an animal not to die from infections in a crowded and dirty pen. So, we have to be careful when going for poultry birds and red meat.

Probiotics: 'Pro bios' means 'for life'. 'Probiotics' are edible living bacteria that make us healthier. We swallow many millions of living bacteria every day, without knowing whether they are good or bad for us. We must make it a point to take probiotics every day to maintain good gut health. Probiotics are most readily available from yoghurt which can be home-made or purchased from dairies. You can have it as it is or in the form of 'lassi'. In Europe probiotics are popular in the form of sauerkraut, pickled gherkins, preserved olives, holey cheese for vegetarians and salami for meat-eaters. For making probiotics, the fermentation process, which is used, results in the production of acid which makes the yoghurt or vegetables taste sour. Fermented rice which is a common diet for many Indian farmers is also a probiotic item. Ilya Metchnikoff (1845–1916), the Russian zoologist, who got the 1908 Nobel Prize for physiology and medicine was a pioneer in the field of immunology research. He was one of the early twentieth century scientists who believed that good bacteria were of great benefit to us as he studied the dietary habits of Bulgarian mountain peasants who regularly consumed milk which became sour as it transformed into yoghurt in the bags before they reached home after walking long distances. He became convinced that the secret of their long lives (often crossed a century) was their regular consumption of this bacterial product (Ref: His book *The Prolongation of Life*; New York: Springer Publishing Co., 2004.)

Prebiotics: 'Pre bios' means 'before life'. 'Prebiotics' are foodstuff that pass undigested into the large intestine where they feed our beneficial bacteria and ensure that good bacteria must always be present in the gut. Therefore, prebiotics are much more suitable for daily use than probiotics as they give more power to the good bacteria over any bad bacteria that may also be present. Food that we cannot digest in the small intestine is called 'dietary fibre' or 'roughage' The bacteria in the large intestine simply love them. Some love undigested lettuce, spinach, celery, leek, pui saag; some may love undigested cabbage, cauliflower or broccoli or even carrot, onion or garlic; and, amongst non-veg items undigested meat or chicken fibres. In fruits, there are fibres in pineapple, mango, orange, musambi, guava, and banana. If your gut microbes get enough to eat, they can produce vitamins and healthy fatty acids, or put the immune system through a good training season. Bad bacteria cannot process prebiotics at all or hardly any.

More Facts about Gut Brain Health

Our different emotions, arising from the 'Limbic System (LS)' in the mid- or 'Paleo-mammalian Brain', involve different dance forms of our facial muscles. The emotions get reflected on our facial expressions because our 'Head Brain (HB)' sends out a distinct pattern of signals to the face's many small muscles. There are 43 muscles altogether most of which are controlled by the 7th cranial nerve which comes out from the forebrain's 'Cerebral Cortex' and emerges from the skull bone just in front of your ears. Every emotion thus has a corresponding facial expression. Similar expressions of our emotions occur in the different regions of our 'Gut Brain (GB)'.

'Anger' sets your stomach to go into vigorous contractions, which increases its production of acid and slows the digestion, thus emptying, from the stomach, the foodstuff you had in your last meal. Meanwhile, your intestines get twisted and spit mucous and other digestive juices. A similar yet distinct pattern happens when you get upset and suffer from 'Anxiety'. Your 'Enteric Nervous System (ENS)' makes you feel uneasy due to a disruption of the regular digestive process. When overcome by 'Sadness' or 'Depression', your intestines hardly move at all. Your 'Gut' mirrors every emotion that arises in your brain.

Besides, 'Anger' prompts your adrenal glands to release the aggressive hormone known as 'Adrenalin (A)'. 'Anxiety' and 'Sadness' leads to the release of the stress hormone 'Cortisol (C)'. Your such emotional hang-ups also affect your gut microbiota. So, there is a harmonious orchestration all along the 'Gut Brain (GB)- Head Brain (HB)' Axis. Let us call it the 'Emotional Response (ER)' principle.

Now, let us look at our dietary inputs from this 'Emotional Response (ER)' principle. The chicken that you had brought home for cooking, did you notice what emotion the bird had when it was killed and throttled to death? Was it 'Anger', 'Fear' or 'Sadness' (for which the bird will have the spontaneous release of the same stress hormones)? The butcher could hear the bird scream but he hardly paid any attention. If you're present there, you could also hear the bird's emotional outbursts but you were relishing the presence of your anticipatory reward chemical 'Dopamine (D)' being released as you had been imagining the delicious taste of the chicken curry. You were living at that time in the world of your own gastric emotions. My question is: the endogenous chemical secretions and electrical reactions in the bird, will they not be carried over in the cooked chicken—irrespective of whether it is curried, roasted, or grilled and thereafter enter into your 'Gut Brain (GB)' in the same profile thus affecting the sobriety of your gut bacteria, ultimately affecting your own emotional profile?

The same story is repeated when you go for the meat of a goat or a lamb. The only difference is that when you buy the meat in the meat shop, it has been slaughtered already either in a municipal slaughterhouse or in a slaughter-room or yard in the back. Such questions bother me when I deal with a subject—as important as 'Diet'. I am not looking from any religious point of view; I am looking at it as a hardcore scientist. This is where Science and Religion perhaps has a meeting point.

Among non-vegetarian items, 'fish' is perhaps the best bet as even if you choose a few fresh, live fishes from a drum full of such creatures, you get hold of them (and not throttle to kill them) in a way that they do not escape, put them in the vendor's pot for weighment. By the time the weighment is complete and the vendor has put them in a plastic bag and hands it over to you, life has left them due to lack of oxygen. They, I hope and imagine, did not die with 'Anger', 'Anxiety' or 'Sadness'—they faced an almost natural death. Neither you nor the fish vendor did kill them. And, at the time of cutting, they were already lifeless.

I will postpone the discussion on 'egg' for another time as the more important fruits and vegetables are still left over. Fruits and vegetables are living as long as they are attached to their mother plants or trees. Once they have fallen having attained maturity or picked or plucked in full ripe form, they are ready to be eaten or cooked. The same 'Emotional Response (ER)' principle will apply if those have not matured and collected by the heartless farmer to be put up for sale.

Can we leave out the emotional profile of the cook? Certainly not! Her 'Anger' will transmit 'Anger' into the cooked dish, her 'Anxiety' will infect the cooked item with 'Anxiety' waves, and her 'Depression' will make the dish 'Depressive'. This is why it is always desirable to have your food cooked by a happy member of the family. Nevertheless, even if you have a paid cook who cooks your meals, you can keep her in good humour or allow her to listen to songs in the FM radio while cooking. But what happens when you eat out in a restaurant or even in a multi-star hotel? Do you have any idea whether your ordered items have been cooked by an 'Angry', 'Anxious' or 'Depressed' chef? When me and my team members used to address hotel and hospitality course students in their institutes (we had at one time ran several such workshops) one thing we used to teach them was 'Mood Management' so that their mood did not travel to their guests through their cooked food or service.

I am making the issue unnecessarily complicated. Some of us, hardcore scientists, suffer from that bad habit. We can simplify the issue also. Offer your diet to 'God' if you believe in God. If you do not, offer them to your 'Gut Bacteria' as they have full control over your 'Gut Health'.

If you don't believe that you can transmit your emotions to others through the product you make or the service you render, please read about Japanese scientist Dr. Masuru Emoto's (1943–2014) work on 'Transmission of Human Consciousness' and watch his most interesting videos how your different attitudes and thoughts can affect even simple, plain drinking water differently.

Healthful Diet for the 'Gut Brain (GB)'

Let me expose you to what it would mean when you plan your and your family's daily 'Diet' for keeping your 'Gut Brain (GB)' active and your 'Gut Bacteria' happy.

Bikash, my regular vegetable vendor at the local Lansdowne Market, stopped me as I had concluded my business with him. "Doctor Saab!"—his voice was full of emotion while he was holding a 'desi' papaya in his hand. "I've brought this for you! I know you love fruits and have a lot of fruits to eat every day. I had planted this papaya tree and used to take very good care with the dream that one day it will bear fruit so sweet that the taste will be unforgettable. This is the first fruit from the tree and instead of us eating it, I've brought it for you!" I was not very happy from the looks of the fruit but I knew he did not mean business—his urge to make me happy in my 'Gut' was so strong that I simply could not refuse him. "How much should I pay?" I asked him. "Nothing", came the prompt answer. "You take it, cut it, taste it, enjoy it—it is a gift from Bikash".

Believe me or not—not only me and my wife Utpala, I served to some of the scholars who visited me that day; and, everybody said that the taste was superb—simply unparalleled and unforgettable. Living things—plants, vegetables, fruits, flowers, fish, birds, animals—we, humans die but 'We Die by Pieces'. Cared for living beings take a longer time to get degenerated because of the high level of 'Love Hormone' present in their tissues and cells. Many of the cells continue to metabolize and produce proteins even after death has been declared. These proteins are attempting to stave off pathogens—harmful killer bacteria, trying to fire up immunity and inflammation. They can continue to fight for up to 4 (four) days in normal cases but longer in exceptional cases. So fondly grown plants, vegetables and fruits—fresh from the garden should be your target for which you should be friendly with your vendors to win their trust and your 'Gut Bacteria' will remain happy.

Rita and her husband Tarun are a DINKs ('Double Income No Kids') couple who are in regular touch with me for getting guidance. Tarun runs his own small business from home and Rita holds a responsible post in a digital electronics showroom. Rita has a spacious terrace garden where she has grown a number of flowering and fruit-bearing (lemon and lime) plants. For her earlier job, she could leave home at 10.30 am as it was close by; therefore, she could take good care of her garden which was 'Flourishing'. For her new showroom duty, she has to leave early at 8.00 am so the garden is getting neglected and the plants are losing their lushness. She approached me for prompt guidance. I recommended that her mother or husband whoever is at home during daytime should water the plants and clear the dry leaves and twigs. When she came back, she should switch on the music system and play Pt. Hariprasad Chaurasia's slow and soft flute recital so that the plants and their products get good rest. On Sundays and holidays, Rita should spend some time with them, talk in 'motherese' (baby language), touch them, kiss them, fondle them so that their cells can feel her genuine loving vibrations. Believe me or not, in a fortnight's time 'Rita reported to me about a miracle. The plants have not only regained their lush green looks, they have grown much bigger than expected and started bearing beautiful flowers and fruits (lemons and green-red chillies). So much is the power of vibrations!!

How much strong is the scientific basis of 'Nurturing' fruits, plants and vegetables have been proven by the healthfulness of the Mediterranean diet, acclaimed as the best for the 'Gut' by the famous doctor of the world-reputed Mayo Clinic of USA. Dr. Emeran Mayer, MD, author of the book *The Mind-Gut Connection* (New York: Harper Wave, 2016) and his wife had been invited by their friends Marco and Antonella to spend a vacation in the small town of Fermo located on the Adriatic coast in Italy.

Dr. Mayer describes vividly that Marco went on explaining some of the unique aspects of how people there grew, harvested, and consumed their food and wine. Fermo is a spiritual place not just because it had produced four popes. Its history of agriculture dated back to A.D. 890 when Benedictine monks came to the area and established a monastery. For 400 years, the monks contributed to the great prosperity of the region, largely through their farming and their teaching of farming. Following their belief in the concept of 'Ora et labora' (= pray and work), they worked the land, studied, and wrote down their 'Insights'. [Many of these handwritten volumes can still be viewed in the old town library.]

Marco pointed out how the logo of his winery depicted a monk picking a bunch of grapes so tenderly that it is almost a 'Caress'. He emphasized that this same passion, attention and respect for nature and its products still lives on in his vineyard which is named after the Benedictine monks: "Le Corti Dei Farfensi."

The western world is aware of the health benefits of the Mediterranean diet that the people of Fermo are habituated to which leads to a long healthy and fit life, many of them being in their late eighties and nineties.

Now, just a line or two about my daily morning fruit-cutting and dressing habit. I assemble a whole collections of fruits on the table, put those with thin skin (like apples, pears, guava, grapes and berries—not bananas, papayas, mangoes or oranges) in bowls of lukewarm water which the bacteria on the surface enjoy; switch on soft, slow instrumental music (especially strings like sitar, sarod and santoor) in the background and then concentrate on my cutting and dressing assignment with full positive focus on the task and never ever me and those who consume those fruits had any 'gut problem'!

Have you ever stretched your mind's arm so much into this vital topic of 'Balanced Diet' and how to keep the 'Gut Brains (GB)' of you and your family members happy? If not, make a beginning now.

APPENDIX II

Teenage Diet Chart and 7-Point Programme

Morning

On School Days

Late School: Early Morning: (after brushing/washing)

A fistful of germinated red grams (chana) or whole moong dal or a bowl of puffed rice (muri) with some sliced cucumber, sliced tomato, sliced green chillies, germinated red grams

A cup of dairy milk without/or mixed with a health drink like Horlicks
(same diet on Sundays/holidays)

Early School: Pre-school

If hungry after wake-up, can have 2–3 plain branded biscuits after brushing.

At 7.30/7.45 am

Two pieces of plain white bread toast; one half/full-boiled/poached egg; one banana/sliced mango (in season); one cup of dairy milk with a health drink or One cup of rice; one cup of dal; sabji (any green veg.—lightly cooked—not fried); fish (2 small pieces) or egg (1 egg) curry with 2–3 slices of potato/beans.

Late School

Same as above—quantity may be reduced.

Afternoon

Tiffin: 2 pieces or roti; dry vegetables/aloo (potato) with black pepper; chura-pilao; 1 apple or 1 guava or 1 orange.

Post-school (at 4/4.30 pm)

Fruits [seasonal-mango/pineapple/water melon/chiku/orange/grapes/dates/blackberries/jamrul/futi (kharm-uja)]

No packaged snacks/bottled or canned fruit juices/no Indian or western snacks or sweets unless occasionally for a change—only when you have a party at home or go to a party; no Maggie or other noodle prepn.

Evening/Night

Optional (6/6.30 pm)

One cup of dairy milk; or one cup of masala tea with lot of milk, ginger paste, elachi, dal chini in paste form in small quantity added.
(If hungry, then 2–3 plain branded biscuits—not cream or chocolate; or can have the smallest bar of Cadbury chocolate/or any other chocolate snack bar)

Dinner (between 8.30 and 9.30 pm)

One cup of plain boiled rice or 2 plain atta roti; dal; fresh salad; veg. protein curry (chana/matar/soybean/rajma/kidney beans); egg (1 egg) curry for a change with sliced lightly cooked veg.; occasionally a sweet dish—may be rice pudding/bread pudding/custard/fruit salad/or ice cream.

On Sundays and Holidays: For Lunch

Same mid-day meal as on a School Day. Instead of fish or egg curry, once in a fortnight can have country chicken curry (not poultry chicken as they are injected with antibiotics for disease prevention) and once in a month red meat—not more than 2 pieces—40 to 45 gm/piece.

Dietary Rules for Teens

1. Don't force yourself into any food item.
2. Avoid junk food (all items of savouries and sweets that are available in an Indian or Western style confectionary shop

are simply JUNKS.) If they are your favourites. You can have them only once in a while. Junk food includes Burgers, Pizza, French Fries, Fried Chicken etc. which are mouth-watering. Chinese noodles are junks but because of the light style of cooking in China shops, you can have them once in a while when you eat out.

3. Avoid red meat of any type as our 'Digestive/Enteric Nervous System (ENS)' follows the chimpanzee design. Chimpanzees are basically vegetarians and insect eaters (please see films on chimpanzees on YouTube) and, therefore, the digestive process takes us a very long time to break the red meat into small granules—then convert them into pulverised form. Same is the problem with poultry chicken. The flesh that you consume must be soft and tender. So the best choice is fish. Of course, egg is also there to nourish you.
4. Do not fill your stomach to the brim during a meal. Some space should be left as although stomach is flexible regular too much eating spoils its natural design characteristics.
5. Maintain regular meal timings.
6. Those who get up late and go to bed late—much though you may make them eat healthy, they can never have HEALTHY LOOKS. Either they will be thin and small or fat and big. They can never have a well-proportioned athletic body.
7. Do not allow your mother, grandmother or elder sister to serve. You are now a teenager, you serve yourself only that much which you can consume comfortably. Do not waste food.